PHP Beyond the Web

DATE DUE

			PRINTED IN U.S.A.

Rob Aley

Apress®

PHP Beyond the Web

Rob Aley
Oxford, United Kingdom

ISBN-13 (pbk): 978-1-4842-2480-9   ISBN-13 (electronic): 978-1-4842-2481-6
DOI 10.1007/978-1-4842-2481-6

Library of Congress Control Number: 2016961229

Managing Director: Welmoed Spahr
Lead Editor: Steve Anglin
Technical Reviewer: Jamie Rumbelow
Editorial Board: Steve Anglin, Pramila Balan, Laura Berendson, Aaron Black, Louise Corrigan,
    Jonathan Gennick, Robert Hutchinson, Celestin Suresh John, Nikhil Karkal, James Markham,
    Susan McDermott, Matthew Moodie, Natalie Pao, Gwenan Spearing
Coordinating Editor: Mark Powers
Copy Editor: Sharon Wilkey
Compositor: SPi Global
Indexer: SPi Global
Artist: SPi Global

Distributed to the book trade worldwide by Springer Science+Business Media New York, 233 Spring Street, 6th Floor, New York, NY 10013. Phone 1-800-SPRINGER, fax (201) 348-4505, e-mail orders-ny@springer-sbm.com, or visit www.springeronline.com. Apress Media, LLC is a California LLC and the sole member (owner) is Springer Science + Business Media Finance Inc (SSBM Finance Inc). SSBM Finance Inc is a Delaware corporation.

For information on translations, please e-mail rights@apress.com, or visit www.apress.com.

Apress and friends of ED books may be purchased in bulk for academic, corporate, or promotional use. eBook versions and licenses are also available for most titles. For more information, reference our Special Bulk Sales–eBook Licensing web page at www.apress.com/bulk-sales.

Any source code or other supplementary materials referenced by the author in this text are available to readers at www.apress.com. For detailed information about how to locate your book's source code, go to www.apress.com/source-code/. Readers can also access source code at SpringerLink in the Supplementary Material section for each chapter.

Printed on acid-free paper

Contents at a Glance

About the Author xv

About the Technical Reviewer xvii

Acknowledgments xix

▓Chapter 1: Introduction 1

▓Chapter 2: Getting Away from the Web—the Basics 7

▓Chapter 3: Understanding the CLI SAPI, and Why You Need To 13

▓Chapter 4: Development Tools 29

▓Chapter 5: User-Facing Software... 49

▓Chapter 6: System Software 75

▓Chapter 7: Interacting with Other Software 93

▓Chapter 8: Talking to the System 109

▓Chapter 9: Performance and Stability—Profiling and Improving....................... 133

▓Chapter 10: Distribution and Deployment Issues 157

▓Appendix A: Compiling and Installing PHP, Extensions, and Libs 167

▓Appendix B: File and Data Format Libraries for PHP 175

▓Appendix C: Sources of Help.. 183

▓Appendix D: Interesting Libraries, Tools, Articles, and Projects........................ 187

▓Appendix E: Integrated Development Environments for PHP 197

▓Afterword: Where Now? 201

Index.. 203

Contents

About the Author xv

About the Technical Reviewer xvii

Acknowledgments xix

■Chapter 1: Introduction 1

"Use PHP? We're Not Building a Web Site, You Know!" 1

    Further Reading 2

Are You New to PHP? 2

    Further Reading 2

Reader Prerequisites 3

An Important Note About Operating Systems 3

PHP on WSL: Windows Subsystem for Linux 3

    Further Reading 4

About the Sample Code 4

External Resources 4

    Further Reading 4

PHP 7 5

■Chapter 2: Getting Away from the Web—the Basics 7

PHP Without a Web Server 7

PHP Versions: What's Yours? 8

A Few Good Reasons Not to Do It in PHP 9

    High-Performance Requirements 9

    Don't (Necessarily) Reinvent the Wheel 9

    Keeping the Source Closed 9

Thinking About Security 10

    Further Reading 11

CLI-Specific Code Frameworks 11

    Further Reading 11

■Chapter 3: Understanding the CLI SAPI, and Why You Need To 13

What's Different About the CLI SAPI? 13

    Further Reading 14

CLI SAPI Installation 14

PHP Command-Line Options 14

    Further Reading 18

Command-Line Arguments for Your Script 18

The Many Ways to Call PHP Scripts 20

    From a File 20

    From a String 20

    From STDIN 21

    As a Self-Executing Script: Unix/Linux 21

    Further Reading 22

    As a Self-Executing Script: Windows 23

    Windows php-win.exe 23

"Click to Run" Your PHP 23

    Clickable Icons: Linux 24

    Further Reading 24

    Clickable Icons: Windows 24

    Clickable Icons: Ubuntu Unity 25

    Further Reading 26

Quitting Your Script 26

    Further Reading 27

■Chapter 4: Development Tools 29

PHP REPLs 29

Build Systems 33

Continuous Integration 34

    Further Reading 34

Debuggers 36

Testing and Unit Testing 37

    Further Reading 38

Static Code Analysis 39

    Further Reading 40

Virtual Development and Testing Environments 42

    Further Reading 44

Source/Version-Control Systems and Code Repositories 44

    Further Reading 45

IDEs and Editors 45

Documentation Generators 45

Profilers 46

Other Tools 46

▓Chapter 5: User-Facing Software 49

Command-Line Interfaces 49

    Command-Line Interface Basics 50

Advanced Command-Line Input 53

    Further Reading 56

Working with STDIN, STOUT, and STDERR 56

CLI Helper Libraries 58

Partial GUI Elements—Dialog Boxes 59

    Dialogs Invoked from the Shell 59

    Windows Dialog Boxes 61

Static HTML Output 61

    Further Reading 63

Complete Graphical Interfaces 63

    Further Reading 63

    Understanding GUI and Event-Based Programming 63

Further Reading 64

wxPHP 64

Further Reading 65

PHP-GTK 68

Local Web Server and Browser 70

Further Reading 70

PHP's Built-in (Testing) Web Server 70

WebSocket and Browser 71

SiteFusion 72

WinBinder 73

Adobe AIR 73

NW.js 73

Electron 74

PHP-Qt 74

PHP/TK 74

▓ **Chapter 6: System Software** **75**

Daemons in PHP **75**

Creating a Daemon **76**

Further Reading 80

Network Daemons Using libevent **80**

Further Reading 85

File Monitoring Daemons Using inotify **85**

Using the inotify PECL Extension 86

Further Reading 88

Further Reading 88

Using the inotifywait Command 89

Inotify Limits 90

Task Dispatch and Management Systems **90**

Gearman and PHP **90**

Further Reading 92

Other Task Dispatch Systems 92

Further Reading 92

▓Chapter 7: Interacting with Other Software 93

Starting External Processes from PHP, or Shelling Out 93

Further Reading 94

Further Reading 94

Talking to Other Processes 94

Semaphores..94

Further Reading 96

Further Reading 96

Shared Memory 96

Further Reading 100

PHP Message Queues..100

Further Reading 104

Third-Party Message Queues 104

Further Reading 106

APC Cached Variables 106

Further Reading 106

Virtual Files—tmpfs 106

Virtual Files—Windows RAM Disks.. 107

Further Reading 107

Standard Streams 107

Linux Signals 108

Task Dispatch and Management Systems 108

▓Chapter 8: Talking to the System 109

File-System Interactions 109

Data Files and Formats 109

Dealing with Large Files... 110

Further Reading 111

Understanding File System Functions 112

    Further Reading 112

The PHP File Status and realpath Caches 112

Working with Cross-Platform and Remote File Systems 113

Accessing the Windows Registry 114

    Further Reading 115

Linux Signals 116

    Further Reading 117

    Sending Signals 119

    Linux Timed-Event Signals 119

Printing (to Paper) 121

    Further Reading 121

Audio 123

    Further Reading 124

Databases—No Change Here 124

Other Hardware and System Interactions 124

PHP and the Raspberry Pi 125

    Raspberry Pi: The Basics of Tri-State Logic 125

    Raspberry Pi: Accessing the GPIO Ports from PHP 128

    Raspberry Pi: Using the Rest of the Hardware 131

    Raspberry Pi: Further Resources 131

    Further Reading 131

▓Chapter 9: Performance and Stability—Profiling and Improving 133

The Background on Performance 133

    Further Reading 134

Specific Issues for General-Purpose Programming 134

Profile, Profile, Profile! 135

    Manual Profiling 135

    Profiling Tools 137

Further Reading...137

Low-Level Profiling...139

Further Reading...139

Profiling—The Likely Results...139

Further Reading...140

Silver Bullets **140**

Silver Bullet 1—Better Hardware...140

Silver Bullet 2—Newer PHP Versions...140

Silver Bullet 3—Opcode Caching...141

Further Reading...141

Silver Bullet 4—Compiling...141

Further Reading...143

Silver Bullet 5—JIT Compilers and Alternative Virtual Machines.......................................143

Further Reading...144

Further Reading...145

Further Reading...146

The Standard PHP Library **146**

Further Reading...146

Garbage Collection **147**

Further Reading...147

Multithreading and Concurrent Programming in PHP **148**

Further Reading...148

Big Data and PHP—MapReduce **149**

Further Reading...149

Data Caching **150**

Further Reading...150

Know Thy Functions **151**

Further Reading...151

Outsourcing Code to Other Languages...**151**

Further Reading...152

Other Performance Tips and Tricks 152

    Further Reading 152

Stability and Performance of Long-Running Processes 153

Avoid Micro and Premature Optimizations 154

■**Chapter 10: Distribution and Deployment Issues** **157**

Error Handling and Logging 157

    Further Reading 159

Installers and Bundling Files 159

    Embedded Data Files at the End of a PHP Script 159

    Phar Executable Bundles 160

    Further Reading 161

    Generic Installers 161

Controlling the (PHP) Environment 162

Extending Your Application with Plug-ins 163

    Further Reading 163

Documentation 163

    Further Reading 163

Licensing and Legal Issues 164

    Further Reading 165

Deploying Frameworks 165

■**Appendix A: Compiling and Installing PHP, Extensions, and Libs** **167**

Compiling and Installing PHP 167

    Windows 168

    macOS 168

    Linux/Unix 168

Compiling and Installing (Extra) Core Extensions 170

Installing Multiple Versions of PHP 171

    Further Reading 172

Using PEAR and PECL...172

Using Composer 172

Using Symfony2 Bundles..173

▓ **Appendix B: File and Data Format Libraries for PHP** **175**

Office Documents..175

Compression, Archiving, and Encryption 178

Graphics 179

Audio 180

Multimedia and Video..181

Programming, Technical, and Data Interchange..181

Miscellaneous 182

▓ **Appendix C: Sources of Help**.. **183**

The PHP Manual 183

Official Mailing Lists...183

Stack Overflow 183

Other Books...184

Newsgroups 184

PHP Subreddit 184

PHP on GitHub 184

PHP News Sites..185

▓ **Appendix D: Interesting Libraries, Tools, Articles, and Projects**...................... **187**

Alternative Programming Styles..187

Machine Learning, Artificial Intelligence, and Data Analysis 188

Databases 190

Natural Language 190

Graphics and Imaging 191

Unicode 192

Audio 192

Event-Driven PHP 192

PHP Internals... 193

Web Site/Service APIs 193

Security Related 194

JavaScript 194

Servers 194

Programming... 195

Financial.. 195

Hardware 195

■Appendix E: Integrated Development Environments for PHP 197

Open Source Options.. 197

Commercial Options 198

■Afterword: Where Now? 201

Giving Feedback and Getting Help and Support... 201

Index... 203

About the Author

Rob Aley I've been programming in PHP since late 2000. Initially, it wasn't by choice because my preferred languages at the time were Perl and Delphi (also known as Object Pascal). Things began to change after I graduated from the University of Leeds with a degree in computer science in 1999 and started out in a career as a freelance web developer. After only a couple of months, I was offered the opportunity to take over a (relatively speaking) substantial government web-site contract from a friend who was exiting the freelance world for the safer and saner world of full-time employment. The only catch was that several thousand lines of code had already been written, and they were written in a relatively new language called PHP. Oh, and the only other catch was that I had about a week to learn it before taking over the site. So, as was the way at the time, I popped down to the local Waterstones bookshop. (For the younger among you, that's where we used to get books. And we had to go out and get them. Or order online and wait many days for them to be delivered.) With my paper copy of *The Generic Beginner's Complete Guide to PHP and MySQL for Dummies Compendium* in hand (I may not recall the title completely correctly), I settled down with a pint of ale (I'm in Yorkshire at this point, remember) and set about reading it. A few days later, I was coding like a pro (well, stuff was working); and 16 years later, I haven't looked back. Over those 16 years, PHP has changed vastly (the source code for the government web site I mentioned was littered with comments like "`# Would have used a foreach here, if PHP had one...`") and so have I. I like to think that both I and PHP have only improved and matured over the years.

After a varied career as a freelancer and starting up a couple of, er, startups (IT related and not) with varying (usually dismal) success, I spent the past ten years as a programmer at the University of Oxford. My day job involved performing medium-scale data acquisition and management, doing statistical analysis, and providing user interfaces for researchers and the public. The majority of my development work was done in PHP, either developing new projects or gluing together other people's software, systems, and databases. I recently left the university to concentrate on writing books like this and providing consulting and training (in PHP, information governance, and related areas). But I'm still programming in PHP!

Throughout my career, I've always used PHP for web development; but for desktop GUI work, I initially used Delphi (and then Free-Pascal/Lazarus), complemented with Bash shell scripting for other tasks. This was mainly because I learned them while at University. However, as PHP has matured, I've increasingly used it beyond the Web, and now I rarely use anything else for any programming or scripting task I encounter. Having been immersed in other languages such as C++, JavaScript, Fortran, and Lisp (and probably others that my brain has chosen deliberately not to remember) by necessity during University and in some of my freelance jobs, I can honestly say that PHP is now my language of choice, rather than of necessity.

When I'm not tied to a computer, I would like to say I have lots of varied and interesting hobbies. I used to. I could write a whole book (which wouldn't sell well) about where I've been and what I've done, and I'd like to think it's made me a well-rounded person. But these days, I don't have any hobbies. In large part this is because of the demands of my three gorgeous young daughters, Ellie, Izzy, and Indy; my gorgeous wife, Parv; and my even more gorgeous cat, Mia. And I wouldn't have it any other way. That's what I tell myself, anyway...

About the Technical Reviewer

Jamie Rumbelow is a freelance web developer and an aspiring academic. He's the author of three books on CodeIgniter and is a keen public speaker. He has worked on dozens of web applications during his eight years freelancing. Jamie lives in London, England.

Acknowledgments

Isaac Newton said, "If I have seen further, it is by standing on the shoulders of giants." This book builds on, and I hope adds to, the work of many others, the most notable of whom I would like to acknowledge here:

- *The authors of, and contributors to, the official PHP manual*: An invaluable reference for PHP functions and syntax, to which I referred frequently during writing this book, both for fact checking and as an aide-memoire. Thanks!

- *The collective PHP wisdom of the Internet*: For more than 16 years, I've used you for learning, research, play, and profit. Too many sites and too many people to list here; if you've written about PHP on the Web, then you may well be one of them. Thanks!

- *My family*: For allowing me a modicum of time to write this book and supporting me unconditionally in everything I do. Usually. If I ask first. And there's not something more important going on. And usually with conditions. Thanks!

CHAPTER 1

▨ ▨ ▨

Introduction

"Use PHP? We're Not Building a Web Site, You Know!"

Both its current recursive moniker (PHP: PHP Hypertext Preprocessor) and the name originally bestowed upon it by its creator Rasmus Lerdorf (PHP: Personal Home Page) reinforce the widely held view that PHP is a scripting language for the Web. And that was true back in 1995 when PHP was first created and for a number of years afterward. In the web arena, PHP excels. It's easy to use, quick to develop in, widely deployed, and tightly integrated into web stacks (it's usually the P in LAMP, WAMP, MAMP, and so on), and of course it is free and open source.

But many people don't realize (or haven't noticed or choose not to notice) that PHP has evolved. It now closely resembles a modern, general-purpose programming language. This lack of recognition is partly PHP's own fault because it took a long time to get some of the fundamentals in place, such as object-oriented programming (OOP) language constructs and even the ability to run at all without a web server being involved. Further, the programming community hasn't helped; many programmers had a hard time seeing the potential for PHP to bring its rapid dynamic development model out of the Web and into the wider computing environment, and many simply stuck with the "web scripting for beginners" dogma that was only really true of its early years.

Recent releases in particular have brought mainstream language features (for example, closures, traits, better language support, namespaces, and late static binding, among many others) to the table. Performance has jumped up and up and up, memory usage (a bugbear of older versions) has dropped considerably, and PHP is now one of the leaner popular scripting languages. For even higher-performance needs, PHP 7 has dramatically rewritten the Zend Engine (giving up to twice the performance of 5.6), and Facebook (the biggest user of PHP around) is one of several companies releasing alternative interpreters/virtual machines (VMs), leading to performance increases of up to six times that achievable with the old Zend Engine. The recent release of PHP 7 and the upswing in community involvement are indicative that reports of PHP's demise are quite premature!

If you're a PHP web developer looking to work beyond the Web, there has never been a better time to leverage your existing skill set and try your hand at desktop and system coding in PHP. If you're a new programmer pondering which language to learn, PHP will let you pick up skills to use in a wider range of scenarios than many other similar languages.

But why, why, oh, why create command-line scripts, graphical user interface (GUI), and other software in PHP? Why not whip up a Bash shell script? Why not learn C++ or another language typically used for software projects? The truth is these are valid options, and life may well work out just fine for you. But why turn down the opportunity to use your existing skills? Why not use PHP's integrated database access, reuse existing code and data from your web projects, take advantage of PHP's easy-to-use network libraries and functions, wallow in flexible text and data handling, and mix shell commands and other languages into PHP as needed to get best of both worlds? In short, why the heck not?

Electronic supplementary material The online version of this chapter (doi:10.1007/978-1-4842-2481-6_1) contains supplementary material, which is available to authorized users.

The aim of this book is to give you, the PHP coder, insight into using PHP beyond the Web. You'll look at building desktop apps, command-line tools, system daemons, network servers, and other native applications. More importantly, I'll show you how to do all of this without leaving the comfortable world of PHP and its friends.

Ideally, I've sold you on the story that PHP is a cross-platform, rapid-development, focused, versatile language that is ideal for many types of software. But if you still doubt the power of PHP to deliver real, non-web, software and don't want to read the whole book to find out what is achievable, then skip to Appendix D at the back of the book to find examples of projects such as web servers, database engines, machine-learning tools, and many other projects all written in PHP. I'll show you the essential ingredients needed to transform your existing web-based PHP skills into the skills needed to create all of these types of software. This will enable you to get up and running as quickly as possible with the tools you already know.

Further Reading

"PHP Is Much Better Than You Think": An article by Fabien Pontencier outlining the positives of PHP development and talking about the changes in the PHP ecosystem

- `http://fabien.potencier.org/article/64/php-is-muchbetter-than-you-think`

Are You New to PHP?

This book shows PHP developers how they can use their existing skills to write software instead of web pages. However, I appreciate that some readers may be new to PHP itself and are reading this book to get a feel for what PHP is capable of. If you're already a programmer, albeit not well versed in PHP, the comprehensive official PHP manual may be the best place to begin to get a feel for the differences between PHP and the languages you are used to using.

If you're not already a programmer, numerous beginning PHP books are available from your favorite (e-)book retailer. In either case, the wider Web also provides its usual breadth of in-depth knowledge and tutorials, just a judicious Google search away.

Finally, whether you're a newcomer or experienced programmer, if you're thinking of getting serious about PHP, taking a look at some PHP best-practice web sites may be worthwhile before diving headlong into coding. It may save you a lot of trouble in the long run.

Further Reading

- The official PHP manual
  - `www.php.net/manual`
- A free online PHP course for beginners
  - `www.codecademy.com/learn/php`
- "PHP: The Right Way": A quick reference for PHP best practices, accepted coding standards, and links to authoritative tutorials
  - `www.phptherightway.com`
- A counterpoint to the preceding site that makes some valuable points
  - `www.phpthewrongway.com`

- "PHP Best Practices": A short, practical guide for common and confusing PHP tasks

  - `http://phpbestpractices.org/`

- "PHP Study Guide": A PHP study guide aimed at those wanting to pass the Zend Certified Engineer (ZCE) exam

  - `http://php-guide.evercodelab.com/`

- "Zend Certification Preparation Pack": Sample questions and answers plus a guide to preparing and taking the ZCE exam

  - `https://leanpub.com/zce`

- "PSR-What?": A guide to the PHP Standards Recommendations (PSRs)

  - `www.lornajane.net/posts/2013/psr-what`

Reader Prerequisites

To make the most of this book, as discussed in the preceding section, you should have basic experience of programming in PHP (most likely for the Web), a general programming or IT background, and a willingness to learn and be taken outside your comfort zone.

This book isn't an introduction to PHP or programming in general. Although you don't need a computing degree or knowledge of advanced programming concepts, the book is aimed at the level of an average PHP programmer (one who has explored more than the very basics of PHP) and tries to explain any necessary concepts as we go along. It is also useful for advanced programmers who may choose to use it as a quick reference for exploring PHP's full capabilities.

An Important Note About Operating Systems

PHP runs on many operating systems, including Linux, Microsoft Windows, and macOS, and code often runs in an identical manner. There are, of course, differences because of the file system, operating system (OS), available libraries, and so on, but covering these all in this book would not be practical. In addition, some features such as those reliant on Portable Operating System Interface (POSIX) standards aren't (easily) available on some systems such as Windows. As macOS was derived from a POSIX-compliant operating system, you will likely find more of the code compatible than with Windows, but your experience may still vary. A good source of information for OS-specific issues is the official PHP online manual and, in particular, the user comments at the bottom of each page. Where possible, areas specific to a particular OS will be covered; for instance, we will look at how to access the Windows Registry.

PHP on WSL: Windows Subsystem for Linux

At the time of writing, Microsoft has just released the beta version of a technology called *Windows Subsystem for Linux* (*WSL*) also known as *Ubuntu on Windows 10*. It allows Ubuntu user-mode binaries provided by Canonical to run over a compatibility layer directly on Windows. Think of it as Wine in reverse. This allows you to run your Bash shell in Windows, accessing drives and other facets of your machine as if they were natively part of Linux. And yes, it allows you to run PHP (and most other command-line utilities), although GUI interfaces are not properly supported at the moment. The current release is only in beta, and all facets of PHP haven't been fully tested yet. However, it's part of Microsoft's new commitment to cross-platform interoperability, and so it's likely to keep being developed and supported. As noted in the previous section, the availability of PHP libraries and extensions for Windows can be patchy, so if there are projects in this book that you want to explore on your Windows machine, it may be worth investigating WSL further.

Further Reading

- Bash on Ubuntu on Windows: Microsoft's guide to getting up and running with WSL

  - `https://msdn.microsoft.com/en-gb/commandline/wsl/about`

- PHP/Symfony Development with Windows Subsystem for Linux (WSL)

  - `www.symfony.fi/entry/php-development-with-windows-subsystem-for-linux-wsl`

About the Sample Code

As you'll see throughout the book, I mainly use "traditional" imperative/procedural PHP in my coding examples to keep things as simple as possible for coders of all abilities. This book isn't designed to be a lesson in coding best practices or style, a guide to OOP, or an endorsement of any kind of programming model or dogma. I also avoid the use of any code frameworks. Many frameworks are based around the web model and don't always perform as intended in the kind of applications I'll be covering, although some do now have "console" or "cli" modules. MVC (Model-View-Controller) style frameworks can be useful when building GUI applications (indeed, the MVC paradigm predates the Web considerably!), but because of the many different implementation details and styles, I'll stick to framework-less code here.

It should be clear from the plain, straightforward PHP code presented how it can be used or adapted to suit your own programming style, framework, or model. I focus mainly on the task-specific implementation details, leaving the hot topic of programming itself to the many other books available.

All the sample PHP source code in this book is available for you to use and do with as you please, without limit or license. Use or abuse it as you see fit!

If you have trouble running or understanding the sample code, see this book's afterword, "Where Now?" for details on how to contact me for help.

External Resources

Throughout the book, I will point you in the direction of external tools, resources, and information via toolboxes and "Further Reading" lists as follows:

Toolbox	The Tool Name Here
Toolboxes like this contain details of useful online tools and installable software	
Main web site	`www.a-useful.tool`
Main documentation and installation information	`http://docs.a-useful.tool`

Further Reading

- Useful articles, tutorials, and reference information are presented in "Further Reading" sections like this

  - `www.very-useful-info.book`

PHP 7

The next generation of PHP, PHP 7, was recently released. (Don't ask what happened to 6; it's a long story.). All the code and the techniques I talk about in this book should run and operate in the same way, whether you are using PHP 5 or PHP 7. When I talk about, for example, installing PHP, I'll refer to PHP 5 (for example, `sudo apt-get install php5-cli`) because that is what most people are still using at the moment. However, if your platform supports 7, go ahead and use that instead (for example, on the latest Ubuntu version at the time of writing, 16.04, the package `php7.0-cli` is now in the standard repositories); it should all work in the same way.

If you are lucky enough to have the choice of which version to use and are planning on writing command-line interface (CLI) scripts, here are some points to consider:

- *Speed*: The number-one thing you'll notice with 7 is the increase in speed. While successive releases of 5.*x* versions have consistently pushed speed higher (and resource usage lower), version 7 takes quite a leap, even outperforming Facebook's HHVM PHP in some benchmarks. While this is, of course, welcome on a heavily loaded web server, it is really noticeable on longer-running programs such as typical CLI scripts.

- *Security*: Version 7 has a few minor security enhancements, such as the filtering option added to the `unserialize()` function. Overall, the security picture looks broadly the same in terms of the design and implementation of the language, though. One security-related concern to bear in mind is the availability of security patches going forward. Currently, patches are available for the 7.0, 5.6, and 5.5 versions. But as newer versions are released (7.1 is in the Release Candidate stage at the time of writing), the older versions will cease to receive security updates, so if you are sticking with 5.*x* for now, you may want to have a migration plan in mind for the inevitable upgrade (assuming you want to continue to use a supported version).

- *Features and compatibility*: Version 7 introduced new features and deprecated older ones (you can find full details on the PHP web site). None of the CLI-specific features (on which the types of software in this book are based) have changed, but of course most of the new general features are available to use within CLI scripts. The current adoption rate of version 7 appears to be much higher than that of version 5 when it first came out. However, the version 5 series will still be the most commonly installed for some time, so you may want to consider the needs of your audience before using version 7–specific constructs.

If you are careful, both versions can be installed alongside each other. See Appendix A for full details of compiling and installing PHP on various platforms.

CHAPTER 2

░ ░ ░

Getting Away from the Web—the Basics

This chapter presents a look at the basic steps involved in breaking PHP free from the Web. You'll learn the technical steps as well as the differences in programming practices and focus.

PHP Without a Web Server

Most PHP programmers have used PHP strictly in a web server environment. In such an environment, PHP is a CGI/FastCGI or server module called and controlled by the HTTP server (usually Apache, IIS, Nginx, or a similar option). The HTTP server receives a request for a PHP-based web page and calls the PHP process to execute it, which usually returns output to the HTTP server to be sent on to the end user.

Some attempts to create local applications (scripting systems, desktop apps, and so forth) with PHP by using a locally installed web server have had some success. However, the downsides of using this web-type model for local apps are as follows:

- For the value they provide in these scenarios, web servers such as Apache are often overspecified and resource-hungry.

- Unless properly locked down, a web server running locally introduces a point of access to your machine for malicious visitors from the outside world.

- HTTP is a verbose protocol and (arguably) ideally suited for the Web. However, it's often overkill for local interprocess communication and adds another resource and complexity overhead to your application.

- Your application interface typically runs in a web browser and therefore looks anything but local (and comes with additional support/upgrade headaches unless you install a browser specifically for your app).

PHP, as of version 5.4, includes a built-in web server, which removes some of the problems described earlier. However, it was designed for local testing of PHP scripts destined to be deployed on a fully fledged HTTP server such as Apache in a live environment. It is a route that can be explored for some local apps, particularly where you want to run a private instance of a PHP web app that already exists. However, its stability, reliability, and suitability for production-ready local apps are yet to be proven, and it still comes with the baggage of HTTP and web browsers.

© Rob Aley 2016
R. Aley, *PHP Beyond the Web*, DOI 10.1007/978-1-4842-2481-6_2

Since version 4.3, PHP has had an ace hidden up its sleeve that solves all of these problems: the PHP CLI Server Application Programming Interface (SAPI), which is essentially a long way of saying *stand-alone PHP*. It cuts out the need for a web server and provides a stand-alone PHP binary for you to interact with. For instance, typing the following at a shell prompt

```
~$ php /home/myfiles/myprogram.php
```

will simply execute your `myprogram.php` file (which you write mostly like any other PHP script) and return any output to the terminal (unless you tell it otherwise) instead of being sent to the web server (which doesn't exist!).

In general, PHP scripts called directly using the PHP CLI SAPI will behave in the same way as when called through a web server, although some differences exist. For instance, you won't find any $_GET or $_POST arrays containing user-supplied data, and PHP won't output any HTTP headers by default; these concepts don't mean much beyond the Web. Default settings such as `max_execution_time` are set to sensible values for local use (in this case, to 0 so your scripts won't time out), output buffering is turned off, and error messages are displayed in plain text rather than HTML.

The PHP CLI SAPI is what we will be using for most of the examples in this book as it is designed with exactly the same motivations as this book: taking PHP beyond the Web. The next chapter gives full details of how to install (if necessary) and use the CLI SAPI.

PHP Versions: What's Yours?

PHP has supported the CLI SAPI since version 4.3.0, so many of the examples in this book will run on any PHP version since then. At the time of writing, the current stable version of PHP is 7.0.11, and the code in this book has been tested against this version. If you find that a particular function doesn't appear to exist or work as expected, check the online PHP manual for that function. The manual shows which versions support which functions and describes any breaking changes created by newer versions.

If you are using an older version, there are some good reasons to upgrade:

- Performance has increased markedly (and, correspondingly, the resources used have decreased) in recent versions.

- Although security is not always as critical with nonweb applications (see the discussion in "Thinking About Security" later in this chapter for caveats), the security enhancements and security-related bug fixes in recent versions are essential if you're handling data from external sources and if you're using the same version for web work as well.

- Modern language features are available, which can help your coding productivity as well as help others take your code more seriously.

As with the web versions of PHP, you can compile your own version of the CLI SAPI if you find the need. If you want to include extensions not prepackaged by your OS software repositories, remove nonessential code for performance reasons, or use any of the other compile-time options that PHP supports, then learning to "roll your own" version may be worthwhile. You can find a starter guide to compiling and installing PHP and related extensions in Appendix A.

A Few Good Reasons Not to Do It in PHP

Tell someone you're going to be writing CLI scripts in PHP and often they'll rail about how PHP is a web language and that you should choose a language "more suited" to the task. This book is focused on doing everything in PHP, and for 90 percent of tasks, PHP will do all that is asked of it. PHP is now a general-purpose language, it's Turing complete, and while it's still used in the main to run "web sites," more and more that includes back-end services as well. But before you commit to rewrite your world in PHP, you may want to carefully consider a few pertinent issues before jumping in.

High-Performance Requirements

If you need very high performance, particularly on limited hardware, PHP may not be for you. Performance has improved in leaps and bounds in recent versions of PHP and regularly trounces languages such as Python and frameworks such as Ruby on Rails in benchmarks. However, at its heart PHP is an abstracted scripting language that is never going to get the same performance for some tasks as lower-level languages like C, which are closer to the bare metal. Don't write it off for all high-performance tasks, though; if you're looking at performance with an eye to costs, you may find that the cost savings on developer time (through speed of development in PHP) outweighs the cost of the extra hardware you need to throw at it to get the performance. And given that many PHP functions are just wrappers around native C functions and libraries, in some cases (depending on the data structures you are using) performance for parts of your scripts can approach that of C.

Don't (Necessarily) Reinvent the Wheel

You *can* write a web server in PHP, but won't existing servers like Apache do what you need? For many or most infrastructure "itches," software exists (written in many different languages) to give you the "scratch" you need. Unless you really need other features, the time spent writing your own is usually going to be greater than the time spent learning and implementing an existing piece of software. Of course, for some people the converse is true. "Because I can" can be a valid reason, and writing software is always a valuable learning experience.

Keeping the Source Closed

PHP is a scripting language, which means if you are writing software to sell or deploy elsewhere, you will be revealing your source code to the recipients. Many (including me) will argue that being open source, even commercially, is a good thing. But if that's not your bag, you will need to go to greater lengths to protect your code. Source code obfuscators are available online that use various tricks to make your code hard (but not impossible) to read, and PHP compilers are available to produce binary programs (albeit with limitations in terms of syntax and extension coverage). But the main PHP project hasn't expressed any intention to support code hiding or compiling, so the viability of such methods long term is not certain. The business case for closed-source software is also not a done deal in the medium to long term.

Thinking About Security

Every good programmer is at least aware of the security implications of building web sites and online apps. You deliberately expose your code to the public, to the world, and to anyone and everyone who will come (good people and bad). One of the early failings of PHP was to prioritize ease of use over security of code (the horror stories from relics like `register_globals` are only a quick Google search away). With newer, more secure defaults, and functions and directives such as `register_globals` being deprecated, PHP is safer than ever online. And although most security problems are caused by the programmer rather than the language, even the newest web coders seem to have an appreciation of security issues from day one these days.

Step into the world of offline software, however, and things are markedly different. Typically, we see software for trusted users only, deployed locally on trusted machines and under the full control of the benevolent user. Users aren't going to deliberately attack the software or machine; they're working with their own data. Functionality absolutely can't be compromised. Security is rarely considered at all when developing command-line programs and desktop apps, let alone being features specified at design time, because it's not "necessary."

Except the world doesn't work like that. Take a look at the list of software with the most CVE-ID (Common Vulnerabilities and Exposures ID) vulnerabilities, and you'll find a plethora of "offline" apps such as Adobe Reader, Microsoft Office, and even open source stalwarts like MySQL. The fact is, security is important even in local apps, for two main reasons. The first is the perennial problem of "typical user" behavior. This is not a problem for an intelligent tech-literate user who never makes mistakes (like you, dear reader), but for any software used by the rest of us, disaster is only an accidental-click-on-a-dodgy-email away. The second reason security is important is that for most machines, many nonweb applications aren't really offline. Even when a desktop app or a system daemon doesn't interact with the Web, local network, or other external services itself, the machine it is connected to will invariably have an Ethernet cable plugged into it or a Wi-Fi/3G/4G connection active. Your software will not run in its own cozy little realm, insulated from the world outside (perfectly sandboxed virtual machines notwithstanding, of course, if such a thing exists...).

Software security is the topic of a whole other book (of which others have written plenty; see the "Further Reading" section), and many of the same principles apply to systems software as to web software, so you will be able to use your existing knowledge of web-based PHP security practices to guide you. The following list of typical vulnerability types and attack vectors in both user-facing and systems software should be considered when planning your script security measures and monitoring:

- *Compromised files from external sources (loaded deliberately or accidentally by users)*: These are usually data files, and particularly at risk is software registered as a default viewer for a particular file type because accidental and malicious file activation is much easier.

- *Malware looking for innocent software to exploit to gain privilege escalation*: Scripted software such as PHP code can be easier for malware to rewrite or alter, and the availability of the source code in an uncompiled form can be of help to the malware authors.

- *Legitimate users misbehaving*: John Smith is looking for a way to view the files or surfing history of his boss, Jane Doe, on their shared business system, for instance.

- *Privilege escalation*: Similar to legitimate users misbehaving, this is legitimate software misbehaving, either accidentally or deliberately trying to gain and use access permissions it does not have.

- *PHP vulnerabilities and vulnerabilities in other dependencies and related software*: Your software will be completely free of security issues, of course, but it invariably depends on other libraries, software, and PHP extensions, and of course let's not forget the PHP interpreter. Any of these can contain security bugs and attack vectors.

These are common sources of security issues in all types of software, not just in PHP. Minimize your risks by planning for these in the design stage and testing for them before deployment. Then cross your fingers.

Further Reading

- *Securing PHP: Core Concepts* and *Securing PHP: The Usual Suspects* by Chris Cornutt

  - https://leanpub.com/securingphp-coreconcepts
  - https://leanpub.com/securingphp-usualsuspects

- An online course in penetration testing with free exercises; focuses on web-based penetration but relevant also to offline software

  - www.pentesterlab.com

- *Survive the Deep End: PHP Security* by Padraic Brady: Free online book covering PHP security

  - http://phpsecurity.readthedocs.org/en/latest/index.html

- *Building Secure PHP Apps* by Ben Edmunds

  - https://leanpub.com/buildingsecurephpapps

CLI-Specific Code Frameworks

There are many coding frameworks for PHP, and many of them can be used with CLI applications, although only one is specifically created for nonweb programming. Code in general-purpose or web-based frameworks may assume that it will be called in an HTTP-related context, so you may need to do extra work to code around this when using it offline.

When deciding whether to use a framework, or which one to use, you should bear in mind its applicability (in terms of its focus on the Web) and whether your application's performance will suffer from the overhead it may bring. You will usually also need to look at the framework's license because it will normally have components that need to be distributed alongside your scripts. That's not to say that frameworks can't be useful in general-purpose programming; however, there are none that I can at this time recommend specifically for nonweb projects. If you're currently comfortable using a particular framework on your web projects, it may be worth seeing whether it has a CLI or console module or recommended code path for CLI-type scripts.

Further Reading

- The CLImax CLI-oriented PHP framework

  - https://github.com/apinstein/climax/

- The PHP Framework Interop Group, standardizing interoperability between frameworks

  - www.php-fig.org

- The Symfony Console Component (also used to build the Laravel Artisan Console software)

    - `http://symfony.com/doc/current/components/console/introduction.html`

    - `https://laravel.com/docs/5.1/artisan`

- Zend/Console: Console routes and routing in Zend Framework 2

    - `http://framework.zend.com/manual/current/en/modules/zend.console.routes.html`

- Example of using Zend Framework with a CLI script

    - `http://stackoverflow.com/questions/2325338/runninga-zend-framework-action-from-command-line`

- Framework comparison matrix

    - `http://matrix.include-once.org/framework/`

CHAPTER 3

■ ■ ■

Understanding the CLI SAPI, and Why You Need To

As I mentioned in Chapter 2, most off-web programming you do will involve using the PHP CLI SAPI. It's therefore important to have a good grasp of how to use it, know the options for configuring and running it, and understand how it differs from the web-based SAPIs you are used to using. Luckily, the differences are minimal, and many are intuitive, although it's still worth having a thorough read of this chapter as the CLI SAPI forms the basis upon which most of your code will run.

What's Different About the CLI SAPI?

The following are the main differences between the PHP CLI SAPI and the standard PHP web implementations:

- No HTTP headers are written to the output by default. This makes sense because they hold no meaning in the command line and so would be just extraneous text printed before your genuine output. If your output will later be funneled out to a web browser, you will need to manually add any necessary headers (for instance, by using the echo() PHP function to manually output the header text).

- PHP does not change the working directory to that of the PHP script being executed. To do this manually, use getcwd() and chdir() to get and set the current directory, respectively. Otherwise, the current working directory will be that from which you invoked the script. For instance, if you are currently in /home/rob and you type php /home/peter/some_script.php, the working directory used in PHP will be /home/rob, not /home/peter.

- Any error or warning messages are output in plain text, rather than HTML-formatted text. If you want HTMLified errors if, for instance, you are producing static HTML files, you can override this by setting the html_errors runtime configuration directive to true in your script by using ini_set('html_errors', 1);.

- PHP implicitly "flushes" all output immediately and doesn't buffer by default. Online performance can often be harmed by sending output straight to a browser, so instead output is buffered and sent in optimal-sized chunks when each chunk is full. Offline, this is not likely to be an issue, so blocks of HTML and other output from constructs such as print and echo are sent to the shell straightaway. There is no need to use flush() to clear a buffer when you are waiting for further output. You can still use PHP's output buffering functions to capture and control output if you want; see the "Output Control Functions" section in the PHP manual for more information.

© Rob Aley 2016
R. Aley, *PHP Beyond the Web*, DOI 10.1007/978-1-4842-2481-6_3

- There is no execution time limit set. Your script will run continuously until it exits of its own volition; PHP will not terminate it even if it hangs. If you want to set a time limit to rein in misbehaving scripts, you can do so from within the script by using the set_time_limit() function.

- The variables $argc and $argv, which describe any command-line arguments passed to your script, are automatically set. These are discussed fully later in this chapter.

- PHP defines the constants STDIN, STDOUT, and STDERR, relating to the standard streams of the same name, and automatically opens input/output (I/O) streams for them. These give your application instant access to standard input (STDIN), standard output (STDOUT), and standard error (STDERR) streams.

Further Reading

- "Output Control Functions" section in the PHP manual

  - www.php.net/manual/en/ref.outcontrol.php

- "Standard streams" (STDIN, STDOUT, STDERR) on Wikipedia

  - http://en.wikipedia.org/wiki/Standard_streams

CLI SAPI Installation

To use the PHP CLI SAPI, you may need to install it first. Appendix A gives details on installing (and compiling, where necessary) PHP in all its forms. However, you may find that the CLI SAPI is already installed if you have PHP installed (often in a folder called sapi/cli in the PHP program folders), and if not, it is usually available in modern OS software repositories. (For example, in Ubuntu, a package called php5-cli exists and can be installed from any package manager or via the command line with sudo apt-get install php5-cli.) If it is installed in the command-line search path, typing php -v on the command line will print the version details, confirming it is indeed installed. The same installation procedures apply to PHP 7; the package on most Linux distributions is called php7.0-cli instead of php5-cli. On other Debian-based distributions, you can type apt search php at the command line to search for the package if it is named differently. On Windows, it comes automatically in the zip file with the precompiled version of PHP, and on macOS it is available through MacPorts (see Appendix A for details) as well as (a sometimes out-of-date version) being installed by default.

PHP Command-Line Options

The PHP binary will accept numerous command-line options/switches/arguments that affect its operation. You can see a full list in your installed version by typing php -h at the command line. Although some apply only to the CGI SAPI (used by web servers when there is no module, such as the PHP Apache module), the following are some of the more interesting and common ones used when interacting with the CLI SAPI:

- `-f` *or* `--file`: This allows you to specify the file name of the script to be run and is optional. The `-f` option exists to allow compatibility with software and scripts such as automation software, which can programmatically call command-line programs but require file-name arguments to be formed in this way. It also allows default file-type handlers to be easily set on Windows for PHP scripts. In most cases, the two following lines are mostly equivalent:

```
~$ php -f myscript.php
~$ php myscript.php
```

- The only real difference in usage between the two versions of command come when interpreting command-line arguments passed to the script, which you'll look at in the "Command-Line Arguments for Your Script" section.

- `-a` *or* `--interactive`: This runs PHP interactively, which allows you to type in PHP code, line by line, rather than executing a saved PHP script. This mode of operation is often called a *REPL* (read-eval-print loop). In addition to providing an interactive interface for testing and developing code, it can act as an enhanced PHP-enabled shell or command line, and Chapter 4 covers this more closely.

- `-c` *or* `--php-ini`: This specifies the `php.ini` file that PHP will use for this application. This is particularly useful if you are also running web services using PHP on the same machine. If it is not specified, PHP will look in various default locations for `php.ini` and may end up using the same one as your web service. By providing one specifically for your CLI applications, you can "open up" various restrictions that make more sense for offline applications. Note that by using the CLI SAPI, PHP will automatically override several `php.ini` settings regardless of whether you specify a custom `.ini` file using this option. These overridden settings are those that affect the behavior outlined previously in the "What's Different About the CLI SAPI?" section, and while the `php.ini` file is ignored in these cases, you can revert or change these settings directly in your code by using the `ini_set()` function (or by similar methods). You can also use the `-d` *or* `--define` option to set options (for example, `php -d max_execution_time=2000 myscript.php`). If you are deploying software onto machines that you do not control (for example, if you are selling software for users to install on their own machines), it makes sense to use one of these mechanisms to ensure that PHP will be running with the settings you expect, not the settings the user may happen to have. See `-n` next as well.

- `-n` *or* `--no-php-ini`: This tells PHP not to load a `php.ini` file at all. This can be useful if you do not want to ship one with your application and instead set all of the settings directly within your code by using `ini_set()` (or something similar). PHP will use its default settings if no `.ini` file is provided, and it is worth remembering that these default settings may change from version to version of PHP (and indeed have done so in the past). You shouldn't rely on the current defaults being suitable for your application. You can use `php --ini` to show the default path that PHP will use to look for `.ini` files when the `-n` option isn't used and `-c` isn't used to specify a file.

- `-e` *or* `--profile-info`: This puts PHP into Extended Information Mode (EIM). EIM generates extra information for use by profilers and debuggers. If you're not using a profiler or debugger that requires this mode, you should not enable it because it can degrade performance. You can find more information on profilers and debuggers in Chapter 4.

- -i *or* --info: This calls the phpinfo() function and prints the output. This outputs a large range of information about the PHP installation, in plain-text format rather than the usual HTML (it detects that you are calling it from the CLI SAPI). This can be useful in tracking down issues with the installation, as well as giving you version information, lists of extensions installed, relevant file paths, and so on. As with any other shell command, the output can be piped to other commands, such as grep. So if you wanted to check whether IPv6 was enabled in your PHP binary, for instance, on Linux or macOS, you could try the following:

  ```
  ~$ php -i | grep -i "ipv6"
  ```

- On Windows, you could try the following:

  ```
  > php -i | findstr /I ipv6
  ```

- -l *or* --syntax-check: This option parses the file, checking for syntax errors. This is a basic lint-type checker; more-advanced static code analysis tools are discussed in Chapter 4. Be aware that this option checks only for basic syntax errors—the sort that cause the PHP engine to fail. Subtler bugs, problems in your program logic, and errors that are created at runtime will not be detected. Your code is not executed, so this option can help pick up basic errors before you run code that may alter data and cause problems if it fails. Even when you run such code in a testing environment, resetting data and setting up for another test can take time, so a quick check for basic syntax errors first can be a time-saver. Some integrated development environments (IDEs) and text editors run php -l in the background to highlight syntax errors as you type. For instance, the linter-php package in GitHub's Atom editor uses this method for live linting of PHP code.

- -m *or* --modules: This lists all the loaded PHP and Zend modules/extensions. These are modules that PHP has been compiled with and may include things such as core, mysql, PDO, json, and more. This is useful for checking that the PHP installation has the functionality that your application requires. You can also check from within your scripts by using the extension_loaded() function or by calling the phpinfo() function. -m provides a subset of the information given with the -i flag described earlier, and -i (or the phpinfo() function) will return more information about the configuration, version, and so on, of the modules.

- -r *or* --run: This runs a line of PHP code supplied as the argument, rather than executing it from a file. The line of code should be enclosed by single quotes when using shells such as Bash, as they will try to interpolate PHP variables as if they were shell variables if you use double quotes. However, on Windows you should use double quotes to avoid errors due to single quotes on the command line. The -r option performs a similar role to the -a interactive mode, except that PHP's "state" is cleared after each line is executed. This means that the line of code supplied is treated as the whole script to be executed, and execution is terminated after it has been run. Here's an example that prints out *4* followed by a newline character:

  ```
  ~$ php -r "echo (2+2).\"\n\";"
  ```

- Note that the line must be well-formed, syntactically correct PHP, so don't miss the semicolon at the end! I return to `-r` later in this chapter, in the section "The Many Ways to Call PHP Scripts."

- `-B` *or* `--process-begin`

   `-R` *or* `--process-code`

   `-F` *or* `--process-file`

   `-E` *or* `--process-end`: These four arguments allow you to specify PHP code to be executed before, during, and after input from STDIN is processed by PHP. `-B` specifies a line of code to execute before the input is processed, `-R` specifies a line of code to execute for every line of input, and `-F` specifies a PHP file to execute for each line. Finally, `-E` executes a line of code at the end of the input process. In `-R` and `-F`, two special variables are available: `$argn` contains the text of the line being processed, and `$argi` contains the number of the line being processed. This is mainly useful when using PHP directly in shell scripts. For instance, to print a text file with line numbers, you can do something like this:

   ```
   ~$ more my_text_file.txt | php\
   -B "echo \"Let's add line numbers...\n\";"\
   -R "echo \"$argi: $argn\n\";"\
   -E "echo \"That's the end folks\n\";"
   ```

   This code will output something like this:

   ```
   Let's add line numbers...
   1: Lorem ipsum dolor sit amet, consectetur adipisicing elit, sed do
   2: eiusmod tempor incididunt ut labore et dolore magna aliqua. Ut enim ad
   3: minim veniam, quis nostrud exercitation ullamco laboris nisi ut aliquip
   4: ex ea commodo consequat. Duis aute irure dolor in reprehenderit in
      That's the end folks
   ```

- `-s` *or* `--syntax-highlight`: This outputs an HTML version of the PHP script, with colored syntax highlighting. The PHP script is not executed or validated; it's simply made "pretty." The pretty HTML is printed to STDOUT and can be useful when pouring over code looking for errors, issues, and optimizations. This works only with PHP in files, not with code provided by the `-r` option. Most modern IDEs and code editors provide syntax highlighting by default; however, this can be useful if your only access to a machine is on the command line and the editor you are using doesn't do syntax highlighting. In this case, use `-s` to create a colored version of your script and either download it or view it through your web browser if the machine has a web server installed.

- `-v` *or* `--version`: This outputs the PHP version information. This can also be found in the output of the `-i` option described earlier. Be careful when assuming a particular format; some package repositories (Ubuntu, for instance) include their name and their own build numbers in the version string, so don't just filter it for any numerics.

- -w *or* --strip: This outputs the contents of the source code with any unnecessary white space and any comments removed. This can be used only with code files (not with lines of code supplied by -r) and does not work with the syntax highlighting option shown earlier. This is used to *minify* a file—in other words, reduce the file size. Contrary to popular opinion, this will not speed up most scripts; the overhead of parsing comments and white space is extremely negligible. You should also be wary of support and debugging issues, even if a copy of the "full" code is kept, as line numbers in error reports will no longer match between the original and stripped versions. It also does not minify identifiers such as variable names and so cannot be used to obfuscate your code. There are few reasons to use this option these days. To make a file smaller for distribution, using proper compression (for example, adding it to a zip file) is usually a better method.

- -z *or* --zend-extension: This specifies the file name/path for a Zend extension to be loaded before your script is run. This allows dynamic loading of extensions, which can alternatively be specified in the php.ini file if they are always to be loaded.

- --rf *or* --rfunction

  --rc *or* --rclass

  --re *or* --rextension

  --rz *or* --rzendextension

  --ri *or* --rextinfo: These options allow you to explore PHP structures by using reflection. *Reflection* is the process by which PHP can perform runtime introspection, which is a way to allow you to look into elements and structures of your code at runtime. The first three options print reflection information about a named function, class, or extension. The last two print basic information about a Zend extension or a standard extension, as returned by the phpinfo() function. This reflection information, which is very detailed, is available only if PHP is compiled with reflection support. These options can be used as a quick but precise reference guide to the entities listed earlier and are particularly useful in interrogating unknown code written by others.

Further Reading

- Reflection information in the PHP manual

  - www.php.net/manual/en/book.reflection.php

- "Introspection and Reflection in PHP" by Octavia Anghel

  - www.sitepoint.com/introspection-and-reflection-in-php/

Command-Line Arguments for Your Script

As you've seen, passing arguments to PHP is straightforward and done in the standard way. However, passing arguments for use by your PHP script is a little more complicated, as PHP needs to know where its own arguments stop and where your script's start. The best way to examine how PHP deals with this is through some examples. Consider the following PHP script:

```php
<?php

echo "Number of arguments given : ".$argc."\n";

echo "List of arguments given :\n";

print_r($argv);
```

There are two special variables in this script:

- $argc: This records the number of command-line arguments passed to the script.

- $argv: This is an array of the actual arguments passed.

Let's save the script as arguments.php. Now let's call it as follows:

```
~$ php -e arguments.php -i -b=big -l red white "and blue"
```

You will get the following output:

```
Number of arguments given : 7
List of arguments given :
Array
(
[0] => arguments.php
[1] => -i
[2] => -b=big
[3] => -l
[4] => red
[5] => white
[6] => and blue
)
```

As you can see, all the arguments given from the file name onward in the command are passed to the script. The first, -e, which is used by PHP itself, is not passed through. So, as a general rule, everything after the file name is treated as an argument to the script, and anything before the file name is treated as an argument for PHP itself, and the file name is shared between the two.

There is, of course, an exception. As you learned earlier, in addition to specifying the file name of your script on its own, you can also pass it as part of the -f flag. So if you execute the following command

```
~$ php -e -f arguments.php -i -b=big -l red white "and blue"
```

you get the following unexpected output:

```
phpinfo()
PHP Version => 7.0.8-0ubuntu0.16.04.2

System => Linux desktop 4.4.0-38-generic #57-Ubuntu SMP Tue Sep 6 15:42:33 UTC 2016 x86_64
Server API => Command Line Interface
Virtual Directory Support => disabled
Configuration File (php.ini) Path => /etc/php/7.0/cli
<rest of output removed for brevity>
```

You may recognize this as the output of calling php -i. Rather than treating arguments after the file name as belonging to the script, PHP has treated the -i argument (and those afterward) as one of its own. Because -i is a valid PHP argument, PHP decides that you wanted to pass -i to PHP directly, and invokes its information mode. If you need to pass the file name as part of the -f flag rather than as an argument on its own, you need to separate your script arguments by using two dashes (--). So, for the previous command to work as expected, you need to alter it to read as follows:

```
~$ php -e -f arguments.php -- -i -b=big -l red white "and blue"
```

Everything after the -- , plus the script file name, is passed as arguments to the script, and you get the expected output.

This can make your scripts a little messy, particularly if you are passing lots of arguments, so you may want to look at the following sections on self-executing scripts, which show you how to embed PHP arguments within the script, allowing the script to claim any and all arguments passed as its own.

The Many Ways to Call PHP Scripts

As you can probably tell from the command-line options in the previous section, there are several ways to execute PHP code when using the CLI SAPI. Although I've covered a couple of these already, I discuss them here again for completeness.

From a File

You can tell PHP to execute a particular PHP source code file. Here's an example:

```
~$ php myscript.php
~$ php -f myscript.php
```

Note that -f is optional; the previous two lines are functionally equivalent. The PHP command-line options detailed earlier, where appropriate, work in this method. This example

```
~$ php -e myscript.php
```

will execute the file myscript.php in Extended Information Mode.

As with the web version of PHP, source files can be interpolated (mixed) with HTML (or, more usefully on the command line, with plain text). So, you still need your opening <? or <?php tags; otherwise, your source code will be printed straight out without being executed.

From a String

You can execute a single line of code with the -r flag, as shown here:

```
 ~$ php -r "echo(\"Hello World!\n\");"
```

Many of the other command-line options are not available with the -r method, such as syntax highlighting. Watch out for shell variable substitution (use single quotes rather than double quotes around your code in Bash shells) and other mangling of your code by the shell. Unless it really is a quick one-off, it is likely safer and easier to pop the relevant line into a file and execute that instead. One common use of the -r option is for executing PHP generated by other (possibly non-PHP) shell commands, where the whole shell script needs to execute in memory without touching the disk (for instance, where permissions prohibit disk write access).

From STDIN

If you do not specify a file or use the -r option, PHP will treat the contents of STDIN as the PHP code to be executed, as shown here (note that echo works like this only on Linux or macOS):

```
~$ echo '<?php echo "hello\n";?>' | php
```

You can also use this method with -B, -R, -F, and -E to make PHP a first-class citizen in shell scripting, giving you the ability to pipe data in and out of PHP. For instance, to reverse every line of a file (or any data source that you pipe into it), on Linux or macOS use the following:

```
~$ cat file.txt | php -R 'echo strrev($argn)."\n";' | grep olleh
```

On Windows, use the following:

```
> more file.txt | php -R "echo strrev($argn).\"\n\";" | findstr olleh
```

In this line of code, you pipe the contents of a text file into PHP. The -R option tells PHP to execute the following PHP code on each line of input, where the line is stored in the special variable $argn. In this case, you reverse $argn by using the string-reversing function strrev() and then echo the reversed string out again. Any echoed output goes to STDOUT, which either is printed to the shell or, as in this case, can be piped to another shell command. In this case, you then use grep to display only the lines containing the string olleh, which is *hello* backward. You can find more details on -R and its siblings in the previous section. If you want to use options such as -R but have too much PHP code to fit comfortably on the command line, you can put the code in a normal PHP source code file and include it with include(). Here's an example:

```
~$ cat something.txt > php -R 'include("complicated.php");'
```

If you have a nontrivial PHP script, it may be more efficient to package it into functions and include it once with -B (-B means it's executed before the main code) and then execute the function each time with -R. The following example loads the content of my_functions.php once at the start, and then the function complicated() from that file is called on each line (each $argn) from the data file (data.txt):

```
~$ php -B 'include("my_functions.php");' -R 'complicated($argn);' -f 'data.txt'
```

Although these commands look relatively simple, there is no arbitrary limit to the PHP code you can put behind them. You can use classes and objects, multiple files, and most of the code and techniques explored in this book—exposing only functions or methods at the shell level as an interface for the user. You can also open the standard streams as PHP streams within PHP and access their file pointers to read data in from, negating the need to use -R, as discussed in the next chapter.

As a Self-Executing Script: Unix/Linux

On Unix/Linux systems, you can turn a PHP script file into a directly executable shell command. Simply make the first line of the script file a #! line (usually pronounced *shebang line* or *hashbang line*) with a path to the PHP binary, as in this example:

```
#!/usr/bin/php

<?php

echo('Hello World!');
```

21

Then set the executable bit by using chmod or similar. Here's an example:

```
~$ chmod a+x myscript.php
```

Simply typing ./myscript.php at the command line will execute it. You can also rename the file to remove the .php extension (assuming you had one in the first place), so you would just type the following at the shell prompt to run it:

```
~$ ./myscript
```

You can further simplify this command by moving the script to a directory somewhere in your shell's search path and removing the initial ./. Note that when running a script in this manner, any command-line options are passed directly to the script and not to PHP. In fact, you cannot pass extra command-line parameters to PHP at runtime by using this method; you must include them in the shebang line when constructing your script. For instance, in the previous example, if you wanted to use Extended Information Mode, you would alter the first line of the script to read as follows:

```
#!/usr/bin/php -e
```

If you were to instead call the script as follows

```
~$ myscript -e
```

then the -e flag would be passed as an argument to your main script, not to PHP directly, and so PHP would not enter EIM. This is useful for scripts that have lots of user-supplied arguments. However, it also makes options such as -B and -R (discussed in the previous method) cumbersome to use for processing STDIN data because you have to include all the PHP on the shebang line, where it is harder to change. You can simply use include() to include the necessary files and use standard file streams to process the STDIN stream (created and opened by the CLI SAPI automatically for you) line by line instead.

If your script may be used on other systems, please bear in mind that the PHP binary will quite often be located in a different directory than the one on your system. In this scenario, you need to change the shebang line for each system if you hard-code the location in it. Fortunately, if installed correctly, PHP sets an environment variable (called php) with its location, available via the /usr/bin/env shell command. So if you change the shebang line as follows, your script should be executable wherever PHP is located:

```
#!/usr/bin/env php
```

On Windows, the shebang line can be left in because PHP will recognize it as a comment and ignore it. However, it will not execute the file as it does on *nix.

Further Reading

- Standard I/O streams information in the PHP manual
  - http://php.net/manual/en/features.commandline.iostreams.php

As a Self-Executing Script: Windows

In a similar manner, scripts can be executed by calling them directly under Windows. However, the process for setting up Windows to do this is slightly more involved. First, you need to add your PHP directory (the directory containing php.exe, phpwin.exe, or php-cli.exe) to the Windows search path (specified in the environment variable PATH) so that you can call PHP without having to specify the full directory path. To do this, follow these steps:

1. (pre-Windows 10) From the Start menu, go to the Control Panel and select the System icon from the System and Security group.

    (Windows 10) From the Start menu, click Settings and search for *Environment*. Then select Edit the System Environment Variables from the drop-down list.

2. On the Advanced tab, click the Environment Variables button.

3. In the System Variables pane, find the Path entry (you may need to scroll to find it).

4. Double-click the Path entry to edit it and add your PHP directory at the end, including a semicolon (;) before it (for example, ;C:\php). Make sure that you do not overwrite or remove any of the text already in the path box. In Windows 10, simply add a new line in the editor.

You also need to amend (or add) the PATHEXT environment variable in the same way, so find the PATHEXT entry in the same window and add .PHP, again using a semicolon to separate it from the rest of the entries while taking care not to alter them.

Next you need to associate the .php file extension with a file type and then tell Windows which program to run for files of that type. To do this, run the following two commands at the Windows command prompt, which you should run as Administrator. Make sure to change the path/file name in the second command to match your installation.

```
assoc .php=phpfile
ftype phpfile="C:\PHP5\php.exe" -f "%1" -- %~2
```

These changes allow you to run myscript rather than C:\php\php.exe myscript.php. Note that under Windows 10, you will not be able to run scripts in this way at an elevated (Administrator) command prompt because the PHP executable is not run as administrator by default. To fix this, right-click the php.exe executable, select Properties and Compatibility, and select Run This Program as an Administrator in Settings. Apply the change to all users. Scripts should now execute as expected in all command prompts.

Windows php-win.exe

PHP for Windows also ships with php-win.exe, which is similar to the CLI build of PHP, except that it does not open a command-line window. This is useful for running system software in the background or running scripts that create their own graphical interface.

"Click to Run" Your PHP

The previous section presented the different ways that PHP commands can be formatted, and showed them in the context of the command line (typing them in). But let's make things easier on ourselves and give them clickable icons so that we can run them directly from the desktop. How we achieve this depends on the operating system.

Clickable Icons: Linux

On most Linux systems, specifically those that support the freedesktop.org Desktop Entry Specification standard, you can create a clickable launcher icon by simply creating a text file. Most mainstream Linux distributions and their window managers follow at least the basics of this standard. To create a launcher for your app, create a text file in the folder where you want it to appear (for example, in /home/rob/Desktop) called, for instance, myscript.desktop. It is important that it has the .desktop extension. In the file, add the following lines:

```
[Desktop Entry]
Type=Application
Name=My Funky App
Terminal=true
Exec=/usr/bin/php /home/rob/scripts/myscript.php
Icon=/usr/share/icons/Humanity/emblems/32/emblem-OK.png
```

The first two lines tell the system what you are creating here. The Name= line gives your launcher a name, which will be shown below the icon. The Terminal= line determines whether a terminal window is opened for this program. Set this to true if you are creating a shell script that takes input from, or sends output to, the terminal. If your script interacts with the user via GUI elements, you should likely set it to false. Exec= specifies the command to execute when the user clicks the icon. This is the command to call your PHP script, as we discussed in the previous sections. Finally, the Icon= line points to the location of a pretty icon for your app. You can supply your own icon file or use one of the system-provided ones. This example uses the Ubuntu smiley-face OK emblem icon, to show the look on your face when you get your first PHP desktop app working. You will usually need to also give the .desktop file execute permission by using chmod u+x myscript.desktop (or a similar method).

You can set many other options in this file; see the following standards site for more info. Support for some options varies from distribution to distribution.

Further Reading

- Freedesktop.org Desktop Entry Specification standard

  - http://standards.freedesktop.org/desktop-entry-spec/latest/

Clickable Icons: Windows

As mentioned previously, PHP has two executables for Windows: the standard php.exe and the newer php-win.exe, which allows windowless running of scripts. There are likewise two ways to make clickable scripts.

First is the simple Windows batch file. This is a text file with a list of commands to execute. Batch files have the .bat extension in their name and are executable by default. So if you have a PHP script called display_stats.php that displays a list of numbers and then exits, and you want to run it in Extended Information Mode, you can make it a clickable script by creating a file called, say, our_stats.bat with the contents:

```
"C:\Program Files (x86)\PHP\php.exe" -e "C:\users\Rob\PHP
Scripts\display_stats.php"

Pause
```

If you click our_stats.bat, it will open a command prompt window, execute your PHP script and display your statistics, and finally wait for the user to press a key before closing the command prompt window. The last step, achieved here with the pause command, is important, because the command prompt window will close again as soon as the batch file finishes executing, and if you have output for the user to view, you will want to keep it open. This can, of course, be achieved directly in your PHP script by pausing execution or waiting for user input, but the preceding script shows how you can mix PHP and other commands/programs in the same batch file. Don't forget to change the paths to php.exe and your script as appropriate. You can use relative filenames or rely on default search paths, but it is often best to use the full path name to ensure that the correct instance of php.exe is used and avoid problems if moving your PHP script relative to the batch file.

The second way of making a clickable PHP script is by calling it from within a Windows VBScript. The preceding example using a batch file will always open a command prompt window, even if you use php-win.exe rather than php.exe, as it does it by default to execute the commands in the file. A VBScript, on the other hand, needs no command prompt or other visual form by default. So if you want to use php-win.exe to run a script that either provides its own GUI interface or runs hidden in the background, you should create a script with a .vbs extension. Let's say you have a PHP-GTK script (more on that in Chapter 5) called text_editor. php that provides a visual text editor such as Notepad. You can make it clickable by creating a file called, say, our_text_ed.vbs with the following contents:

```
Set WinScriptHost = CreateObject("WScript.Shell")

WinScriptHost.Run Chr(34) & "c:\Program Files (x86)\PHP\php-win.exe" &
Chr(34) & " -e c:\Users\me\text_editor.php", 0

Set WinScriptHost = Nothing
```

Click the .vbs file, and your PHP script should spring into life, sans command-line prompt. The WinScriptHost.Run line does the heavy lifting of running a command that you provide. You format that command in the same way you would if you were typing it by hand at the command prompt, and pass it as a string. Note that in VBScript, & is the string concatenation operator (the same as . in PHP), and that Chr(34) is the" double-quote character (needed because the directory path to php-win.exe contains a space). Don't forget to change the paths to the php-win.exe and your script as appropriate.

The final piece of the puzzle, whichever of the two methods you use, is to give your clickable file a better icon. The files will have the default icon for batch files or VBScripts, and it is not possible to change this directly without changing it for all files of the same type. There are, however, two workarounds. Windows allows you to change the icon of a shortcut (via Right-Click ä Properties), so the first workaround is to hide your script file somewhere out of sight, and create a shortcut icon where you want to be able to click it. Then change the icon of the shortcut. The other workaround is to change the file extension to one that Windows does not recognize (for example, .phpsc) and create a new file extension with the same actions as .vbs or .bat but with a different icon.

Clickable Icons: Ubuntu Unity

To add an icon to the Unity Launcher in Ubuntu, you create a .desktop file in a similar manner to the Linux launcher you created before, but with a few more entries in the file. So let's create a new myscript.desktop:

```
[Desktop Entry]
Name=My Super Script
Exec=/usr/bin/php /home/rob/scripts/myscript.php
Icon=/usr/share/icons/Humanity/emblems/32/emblem-important.svg
Terminal=true
```

```
Type=Application
StartupNotify=true
Actions=Window;

[Desktop Action Window]
Name=Open me a new window please
Exec=/usr/bin/php /home/me/scripts/myscript.php -n
OnlyShowIn=Unity;
```

Don't forget to make it executable with chmod. This should work in its current location as with the previous Linux example. However, if you drag it to the Unity Launcher (or pin it while the script is running), it will remain there and add a new feature, the Action menu. Notice the Actions=Window line and the [Desktop Action Window] section in the preceding code. These define a new action (in this case, opening a new window, if our script had that capability via the -n flag), which is accessible by right-clicking the icon. Through this you can add any actions you want by, for example calling your script with different parameters, or even calling a completely different script (or other program) in the Exec line. If you want to automatically add Unity entries, or make them available to all users, I suggest the following articles.

Further Reading

- "Unity: Adding Items to the Dock" by Daan van Berkel

    - http://themagicofscience.blogspot.co.uk/2011/05/unity-adding-items-to-dock.html

- Unity Launcher Documentation and Guide at Ubuntu.com

    - https://help.ubuntu.com/community/UnityLaunchersAndDesktopFiles

All of the methods for starting scripts described here can be executed in any number of scenarios. You can use them directly from a command line, as part of a shell script, as a cron job, as a system call from other PHP (and non-PHP) scripts, as default file-type handlers, and so on. With appropriate precautions and permissions, you can even use these methods to call scripts from web-based PHP pages (there is usually a better and safer way to invoke them than via a web page, so I'll leave the details of implementing and securing it as an exercise for you if you really must do so).

Quitting Your Script

You've looked at starting your scripts, but what happens when it comes time to finish running them? Like web-based PHP scripts, CLI scripts will terminate happily when you hit the end of the script file and will tidy up all the resources used in the same way, closing resources such as database connections and releasing used memory. And again as with web scripts, if you want to end early, you can call the exit (or equivalent die) language construct as usual.

However, in the world of CLI scripts, this isn't considered very polite. Because CLI commands are designed to work together, often in chains of commands, most shell programs and scripts provide an *exit code* when they terminate to let the other programs around them know *why* they finished. Were they done? Did they encounter an error? Were they called incorrectly? Inquiring minds want to know.

It is particularly important to supply an exit code when your script may be the last item in a shell script, as the exit code of the shell script itself is taken to be the last exit code returned within it. You can make your PHP script provide an exit code simply by including it as a parameter to exit or die. An exit code is an integer, and there are several common exit codes to choose from:

- 0: Success. You've exited normally.

- 1: General error. This is usually used for application- or language-specific errors and syntax errors.

- 2: Incorrect usage.

- 126: Command is not executable. This is usually permissions related.

- 127: Command is not found.

- 128+*N* (up to 165): Command terminated by POSIX signal number *N*. For example, in the case of kill -9 myscript.php, it should return code 137 (which is 128+9).

- 130: Command terminated by Ctrl+C (Ctrl+C is POSIX code 2, so, using the previous example, 128 + 2 = 130).

- Any other positive integer is generally construed as exiting because of an unspecified error.

So, for instance, if you decide that the command-line arguments provided by your user are not in the correct format, you should terminate your script by using exit(2). If instead all goes well and your script continues to the end of its script file, you can let it exit by itself (or by calling exit without a parameter) because it returns status code 0 by default.

Further Reading

- "POSIX signals" section of the "Unix Signal" page on Wikipedia

    - http://en.wikipedia.org/wiki/Unix_signal#POSIX_signals

As with web scripts, you can register functions to be executed when your PHP script exits by using the register_shutdown_function() function. One use for this may be to check that all is well and evaluate which exit code should be returned. The exit code used as the parameter to exit or die within a registered shutdown function overrides the code used in the initial exit call that initiated shutdown. This means you can happily exit with exit(0) everywhere and then exit with exit(76) from your shutdown function if you detect that "the foo conflaganation isn't aligned with the bar initispations in your metaspacialatific object". Or similar. 76 is one of the general unspecified errors, so you should ensure that your program documentation details the actual meaning, and ideally output some informative text (ideally to STDERR) from your shutdown function to make sure the user knows what happened.

CHAPTER 4

■ ■ ■

Development Tools

So far we've outlined some of the basics of using PHP without a web server, but before we really get into the nitty-gritty details of developing useful nonweb software, we're going to take a slight detour into the world of PHP development tools.

This is for two reasons. First, before deciding which techniques and methods you are going to use (interactive CLI script or GUI interface), it is important to understand what tools are available to help support your choice of programming methodology. Second, you will often need to adopt a different workflow when developing a new type of software that you may not be familiar with, and you may need to find new tools to fit that new way of working.

In general, you can use the same development tools for general-purpose programming as you do for web development. After all, PHP syntax is the same wherever it's executed. The main differentiator is your workflow, and you may find yourself being more productive with different tools.

Of course, one of PHP's dirty secrets is that many PHP programmers don't use debuggers, unit testing, build systems, or code profilers, and in many cases don't even know what they are. Usually it's because many PHP scripts are developed as small, uncomplicated, low-risk projects by single developers, and the overhead of learning and deploying extra tools is an unnecessary burden (particularly for those without a formal computer science or programming education). Don't worry if you fall into this camp; we've all been there (and like to visit from time to time!).

However, when you start venturing into general-purpose programming, you'll find that the complexity of projects often increases. Rather than a selection of short-lived scripts with limited shared state executing in less than a second, you'll get into larger code bases with longer-running processes and more-complex dependencies. In such scenarios, the effects of bugs can be magnified, and tracking them down becomes increasingly hard. Code is revamped less often and can be relied upon by an organization and remain deployed for much longer, increasing the burden of maintaining code in the future. If you're not a regular user of the types of tools described in this chapter, you might find this the ideal opportunity to delve into the wider world of PHP development tools, and give yourself a good foundation on which to start building real software.

You'll look in turn at various classes of tools, and see some examples of, and links to, popular tools of each type.

PHP REPLs

When you want to test a few lines of PHP, your default instinct may be to create a new PHP file, save it, and then execute it with PHP. There is a faster and more interactive way, however. The PHP *interactive shell*, also known as the *PHP REPL*, is a quick and easy way to type in code and have it execute immediately. Unlike executing single lines of code by using php -r, the REPL (started by calling php -a) keeps the script's state (for example, contents of variables and objects) between each line that you type until you exit. You can use all of PHP's functions (although no libraries are loaded by default) and you can use include() or require() to include existing files of PHP code.

© Rob Aley 2016
R. Aley, *PHP Beyond the Web*, DOI 10.1007/978-1-4842-2481-6_4

This latter capability is useful for debugging the final output of a problematic script. Simply use include() to include your script, which will execute the script, and as long the script doesn't terminate prematurely, then you can use echo() or print_r() (or a similar command) to explore the state of the variables and other resources at the end of the run. Other brands of REPL are available and are listed later in this section.

Note that the REPL doesn't function in standard versions of Windows due to the lack of Readline library support, but it will work in Windows Subsystem for Linux (WSL).

By its nature, the PHP REPL can also be used as a CLI/shell in its own right, calling other PHP and non-PHP programs as you would, for instance, in a Bash shell. The following example is a capture of an interactive REPL session using the standard PHP REPL:

```
~$ php -a
Interactive mode enabled

php > # As we can type any valid PHP, I have added (valid PHP) comments
php > # directly to the REPL, rather than afterward in editing!
php >
php > # Let's start with some simple variable assignments:
php >
php > $a = 5;
php > $b = 6;
php >
php > # The REPL will throw Notices, Warnings, and Errors as appropriate,
php > # in real-time:
php >
php > $c = nothingdefined;
PHP Notice: Use of undefined constant nothingdefined - assumed
'nothingdefined' in php shell code on line 1
php >
php > # Just as with normal PHP source files, we can split commands across
php > # lines. The interpreter kicks in only when it hits the terminating
php > # semicolon :
php >
php > $d
php > =
php > 7
php > ;
php >
php > # The following shows that the state in the variables above has been
php > # kept :
php >
php > echo $a + $b + $c + $d ."\n";
18
php >
php > # Next, a more interesting example. Use the REPL instead of the
php > # shell to get the first line from a file :
php >
php > echo file('/proc/version')[0];
Linux version 4.4.0-38-generic (buildd@lgw01-58) (gcc version 5.4.0 20160609 (Ubuntu
5.4.0-6ubuntu1~16.04.2) ) #57-Ubuntu SMP Tue Sep 6 15:42:33 UTC 2016
php >
```

```
php > # Of course all of the usual protocol wrappers are available, so we
php > # can see what is happening in the world...
php >
php > $page = file('http://news.bbc.co.uk');
php >
php > echo $page[1];
<html lang="en-GB" id="responsive-news">
php >
php > # and maybe get a hash of that...
php >
php > echo md5 ( implode ( $page, "\n" ) ) . "\n";
c3e2fb06927099590aebb1ffcb3f0b5d
php >
php > # when we are done ...
php >
php > exit;
php >
php > # doesn't work, as it's just evaluated as PHP (and the REPL ignores
php > # exit/die calls). To exit the REPL, enter the word 'exit' on its own
php > # on a new line
php >
php > exit
~$
```

Sometimes you'll want to execute your commands within the environment of other scripts. For instance, you may have a script that declares constants, sets up database connections, and does other routine tasks that you normally include with include() at the start of your main PHP scripts. As noted earlier, you can include these files in the REPL too by using include(), but you may forget to do so and then wonder why things didn't work as they should. One facility PHP offers you, which applies not only to the REPL but to all forms of PHP execution, is the auto_prepend_file configuration directive. This tells PHP to execute a given file each time PHP is run before it starts to do anything else (such as executing the script you have asked it to execute). This can be set either in php.ini or via the -d flag on the command line. The following is an example of presetting some constants/variables. First, you create a script called initialize.php with the following content:

```
<?php

const FOUR = 4; # Declare a constant value

$five = 5; # Instantiate a variable with another value
```

Then, at the command line, start and run a REPL session as follows, using -d to execute the initialize.php script first:

```
~$ php -d auto_prepend_file=initialize.php -a
Interactive mode enabled

php > echo (FOUR + $five)."\n";
9
php > exit
~$
```

As you can see, the constant and variable you set up in the `initialize.php` file were available for use from the REPL without having to manually declare them. The `-d` flag is used here, but the option could be set in `php.ini` as well if you want to always use the same file. If you regularly use a few different initialization files like this, you can create shell aliases to commands by using the `-d` flag. For instance, you could add lines similar to the following to your `~/.bash_profile`:

```
alias php-clients="php -d auto_prepend_file=clientSetup.php -a"
alias php-inhouse="php -d auto_prepend_file=ourSiteSetup.php -a"
```

As well as the built-in PHP REPL explored earlier, numerous third-party REPLs are available, some of which include features such as a history of commands typed, tab-completion of commands, protection from fatal errors, and even abbreviated function documentation.

Toolbox	Boris
A small but robust REPL for PHP	
Main documentation and installation information	`https://github.com/d11wtq/boris`
Extension for Symfony and Drupal	`http://vvv.tobiassjosten.net/php/php-repl-for-symfony-and-drupal/`

Toolbox	phpa
A simple replacement for `php -a`, written in PHP	
Main web site, installation information, and documentation	`http://david.acz.org/phpa/`

Toolbox	PHP Interactive
A web-based REPL that allows better support for displaying HTML output. The project is an alpha release.	
Main web site	`www.hping.org/phpinteractive/`

Toolbox	Sublime Worksheet
An inline REPL for the Sublime Text editor	
Main web site	`https://github.com/jcartledge/sublime-worksheet`

Toolbox	phpsh
Developed at Facebook, this interactive shell for PHP features Readline history, tab completion, and quick access to documentation. It is no longer actively developed but still works fine.	
Main web site and documentation	`http://phpsh.org`
Installation information	`https://github.com/facebook/phpsh/blob/master/README.md`

Toolbox	**iPHP**
An extensible PHP shell	
Main web site	`https://github.com/apinstein/iphp`

Build Systems

Build systems are used for building and deploying software to development and/or live systems. They automate many of the repetitive tasks that occur when deploying a new revision of a software system. Build scripts and build systems originated with languages such as C, which required compilation before the software was able to run, and covered steps such as compiling and linking various software modules as well as managing source code dependency issues. Although PHP is not a compiled language, a build system can still be a great time-saver in performing tasks such as these:

- Gathering and managing assets (images, data files, and so forth)
- Packaging or moving scripts and assets
- Managing dependencies (often in conjunction with systems such as Composer)
- Archiving older versions or committing to source-control systems
- Running automated tests, static analysis, and other quality-control processes
- Running code minification or obfuscation processes
- Starting and stopping related services
- Refreshing and resetting your test environment
- Cleaning or initializing databases
- Generating documentation
- Notifying team members

Indeed, a build system can accomplish anything else needed to ensure that the latest version of your script is deployed successfully. In addition to saving time, a build system helps ensure consistency and prevent mistakes. As you'll no doubt know, trying to fix an obscure bug that occurred because you forgot to copy over the latest version of a minor data file isn't fun.

You can, of course, construct your own build system by using shell scripting (or even better, PHP CLI scripts!), which may suffice for small or simple projects. For larger or more-complex systems, an off-the-shelf build system may be a time-saver. Many such systems can cope with PHP, but one of the best for PHP work is Phing. *Phing* was built for PHP, can be easily extended with PHP classes, and has a wide range of PHP-related tasks already built in. Telling Phing what to do is a matter of creating simple XML files, which you can even create programmatically by using the PHP XML Writer extension if you need to.

Toolbox	Phing
The leading PHP build system, modeled on Apache Ant, a Java build system	
Main web site	`www.phing.info`
Installation info	`www.phing.info/trac/wiki/Users/Installation`
Main documentation	`www.phing.info/trac/wiki/Users/Documentation`
Tutorial	
"Deploy and Release your Applications with Phing" by Vito Tardia	`http://phpmaster.com/deploy-and-release-your-applications-with-phing/`

Continuous Integration

One step beyond build systems are *continuous integration* (CI) systems. Particularly useful in large, team-developed projects, CI systems allow multiple developers to continuously (or regularly) integrate their individual development work into the final complete software system. The CI system typically takes individual user commits from a version-control system and builds (or *integrates*) them into the final *product* along with other developers' work, usually testing and deploying the build as it goes. With CI systems, developers are often encouraged to make at least one commit each day, or more if possible.

In projects without CI, team members frequently develop on their own, and integrate their work with each other at the end of the process. In a large project with many developers, the integration stage is often lengthy and is a frequent cause of time (and money) overruns, as incompatibilities and problems are found and fixed late in the project. CI systems effectively remove this separate integration step, as integration is done from day one. Problems are revealed early on and fixed on an ongoing basis, with rewrites of incompatible code kept to a minimum. When the project is finished, the work of different developers or teams is more or less guaranteed to be interoperable and fully integrated into the project.

Further Reading

- An in-depth primer article on CI from software engineer Martin Fowler

  - `http://martinfowler.com/articles/continuousIntegration.html`

- "Continuous integration" on Wikipedia, with background, principles of CI, and links to CI software

  - `http://en.wikipedia.org/wiki/Continuous_integration`

There are a growing number of CI systems, most of which can cope with PHP projects. For smaller projects, CI systems can be "hand-rolled" with judicious use of existing build systems. Some of the more popular off-the-shelf ones for use with PHP are listed next.

Toolbox	Jenkins
A popular, versatile, and extensible open source CI server, with PHP support	
Main web site	http://jenkins-ci.org
Installation info	https://jenkins.io/doc/book/getting-started/installing/
Main documentation	https://jenkins.io/doc/
Tutorials	
PHPMaster tutorial on using PHP and Jenkins	www.sitepoint.com/continuous-integration-with-jenkins-1/
"Zero to Jenkins—PHP Continuous Integration" video by David Adams	www.youtube.com/watch?v=PklYO2vYIfc
Book	
Integrating PHP Projects with Jenkins, by PHPUnit creator Sebastian Bergmann	http://shop.oreilly.com/product/0636920021353.do
Other related resources	
Jenkins jobs template for PHP projects	http://jenkins-php.org/
Plug-in to allow you to capture code coverage reports from PHPUnit in Jenkins	https://wiki.jenkins-ci.org/display/JENKINS/ Clover+PHP+Plugin
Plug-in to allow you to use the Phing build system to build PHP projects in Jenkins	https://wiki.jenkins-ci.org/display/JENKINS/Phing+Plugin

Toolbox	PHPCI
A CI system designed specifically for PHP, written in PHP, which integrates easily with tools such as Composer, PHPUnit, and so on	
Main web site	www.phptesting.org/
Main documentation and installation info	https://github.com/Block8/PHPCI#phpci

Toolbox	Travis CI
The CI system integrated with GitHub. Supports PHP service.	
Main web site	http://travis-ci.org/
Main general documentation	http://about.travis-ci.org/docs/
Main PHP documentation	http://about.travis-ci.org/docs/user/languages/php/

Toolbox	Sismo
A continuous testing server (a subset of CI) written in PHP from Fabien Potencier, creator of the Symfony PHP framework	
Main web site, documentation and installation info	`http://sismo.sensiolabs.org/`

Toolbox	Criterion
Criterion is a continuous integration app built in PHP	
Main web site, documentation, and installation info	`http://romhut.github.io/criterion/`

Debuggers

A *debugger* provides an easy way for you to inspect the internal state of your application, often while it runs, at fixed points in the code, or after a crash. This can give you valuable insight into bugs, particularly those in long-running code or those relating to how external data affects variables, as well as direct flaws in your code. Debuggers can give you a *stack trace*, which shows the nested set of functions (or *stack*) your code is currently executing. They can also provide the current contents of variables, objects, and their members, the state of resource identifiers, and so on. Some additionally provide profiling capabilities (see the "Profilers" section later in this chapter). Numerous debuggers are available for PHP, and the most prolific (and arguably the most versatile) is Xdebug.

Toolbox	Xdebug
A versatile, comprehensive debugger and profiler	
Main web site	`http://xdebug.org/`
Installation info	`http://xdebug.org/docs/install`
Main documentation	`http://xdebug.org/docs/`
VIM client for Xdebug	`https://github.com/joonty/vdebug`
Atom client for Xdebug	`https://atom.io/packages/php-debug`
Sublime Text client for Xdebug	`https://github.com/martomo/SublimeTextXdebug`

Toolbox	phpdbg
Integrated into the PHP core since PHP 5.6, phpdbg is the new official PHP debugger.	
Main web site	`http://phpdbg.com/`
Main documentation and installation info	`http://phpdbg.com/docs`

Toolbox	MacGDBp
A Mac-only debugger, which sits on top of Xdebug	
Main web site	`www.bluestatic.org/software/macgdbp/`
Main documentation and installation info	`www.bluestatic.org/software/macgdbp/help.php`

Toolbox	Vulcan Logic Dumper (VLD)
An advanced tool by the author of Xdebug. It allows you to dump the opcodes for a script to aid in debugging	
Main web site, documentation, and installation info	`http://derickrethans.nl/projects.html#vld`
Article: "Print vs. Echo, Which One Is Faster?"—the age-old, irrelevant, debate solved by VLD	`http://fabien.potencier.org/article/8/print-vs-echo-which-one-is-faster`

Toolbox	Zend Studio debugger
The commercial Zend Studio IDE contains an integrated debugger.	
Main web site, documentation, and installation info	`www.zend.com/en/products/studio/`
Article: "Debugging a PHP CLI script" with Zend Studio by Kevin Schroeder	`www.eschrade.com/page/debugging-a-php-cli-script/`

Toolbox	PHP DebugBar
Displays basic debugging information as part of the PHP script output	
Main web site, documentation, and installation info	`http://phpdebugbar.com/`

Toolbox	Advanced PHP Debugger (APD)
The old official PHP debugger. It has not been updated for a few years.	
Main web site	`http://pecl.php.net/package/apd`
Main documentation	`http://php.net/manual/en/book.apd.php`

Testing and Unit Testing

Many strategies are used for testing all types of code, including PHP, and many books have been written on the subject, so I won't cover testing here except to make a couple of salient points and introduce a couple of PHP-related tools.

As your development projects increase in size (and in general-purpose programming, it's likely you will be creating much longer and more-complex scripts than when programming for the Web), testing becomes more and more important even for developers working on their own. Your ability to keep all the details of the code you've written in your head diminishes. The number of changes that, when made to one section of code, cause problems for other parts of the software, increase.

Many types of software testing methodologies exist, but unit testing in particular can help keep these things straight. For the uninitiated, *unit testing* involves creating tests for individual sections of code (such as functions, classes, and methods) that test the output of that portion of code against the specification/expected behavior for that code.

For instance, for a given function Foo(), you might write a test to check that it will always output values between 1 and 10 for any given input—except for the value bar, which should return the value –1. You can then use that function elsewhere and have confidence that it will always return a value within the specified range, no matter what you throw at it. If you later make a change to the way Foo() is implemented, your unit test will pick up if the range of output values Foo() gives has changed (for instance, if it now also outputs 0 and –2 in certain conditions), and it will fail the test. This will alert you to the fact that either you have a bug in the new code you put into Foo(), or your specification for Foo() has changed and you need to carefully check the places from which you've called Foo(), to make sure that the new range of output values won't cause issues elsewhere. Without such a test, it is easy to fail to notice the possible consequential effects of code changes, in particular on the way they may affect other potentially distant sections of code.

Before you start programming, though, it's important to consider the type of testing you intend to use, and to plan your code architecture/design accordingly. Some types of testing require a firm specification for the software from the start; others (such as unit testing) are made easier by structuring your code in certain ways to make tests easier to construct and maintain.

Further Reading

- "Test-driven development" on Wikipedia

  - http://en.wikipedia.org/wiki/Test-driven_development

- A reference for structuring PHP programs to make unit testing easier by using test-driven development: *The Grumpy Programmer's Guide to Building Testable PHP Applications* by Chris Hartjes

  - https://leanpub.com/grumpy-testing

- A 5-minute video introduction to test-driven development, also by Chris Hartjes

  - www.littlehart.net/atthekeyboard/2012/08/16/5-minute-tdd/

An assortment of popular PHP testing tools are listed here.

Toolbox	PHPUnit
The de facto standard for unit testing in PHP projects	
Main web site	http://phpunit.de/
Installation info	https://phpunit.de/manual/current/en/installation.html
Main documentation	https://phpunit.de/documentation.html
Tutorials	
"Let's TDD a Simple App in PHP" by Patkos Csaba	http://net.tutsplus.com/tutorials/php/lets-tdd-a-simple-app-in-php/
"Bulletproofing Database Interactions with PHPUnit Database Extension" by Jeune Asuncion	http://phpmaster.com/bulletproofing-database-interactions/
"Debugging PHPUnit Tests in NetBeans with Xdebug" by Rafael Dohms	http://blog.rafaeldohms.com.br/2011/05/13/debugging-phpunit-tests-in-netbeans-with-xdebug/
Video: "Leveraging 12 Years of PHPUnit" by Sebastian Bergmann (PHPUnit's author)	www.youtube.com/watch?v=AXZ1I5M6sHQ
Book	
The Grumpy Programmer's PHPUnit Cookbook by Chris Hartjes	https://leanpub.com/grumpy-phpunit

Toolbox	Codeception
Describes itself as "PHPUnit on steroids." Covers unit testing, acceptance testing, and functional testing, with a focus on ease of use.	
Main web site	`http://codeception.com/`
Installation info	`http://codeception.com/quickstart`
Main documentation	`http://codeception.com/docs/01-Introduction`

Toolbox	Enhance-PHP
A lightweight, open source PHP unit-testing framework written in PHP	
Main web site	`https://github.com/Enhance-PHP/Enhance-PHP`
Installation info	`https://github.com/Enhance-PHP/Enhance-PHP/wiki/Quick-Start-Guide`
Main documentation	`https://github.com/Enhance-PHP/Enhance-PHP/wiki`

Toolbox	atoum
A simplified unit-testing framework, aiming for simplicity and rapid implementation	
Main web site	`http://atoum.org/`
Main documentation and installation info	`http://docs.atoum.org/en/latest/`

Toolbox	SimpleTest
A simple unit-testing and web-testing framework	
Main web site	`www.simpletest.org`
Main documentation and installation info	`www.simpletest.org/en/overview.html`

Static Code Analysis

Static code analysis is the process of testing or examining code without executing it. The preceding examples of testing and debugging all involve running the code to look for bugs and issues. However, at times, checking the code for potential errors before executing it can be beneficial. Many simple errors such as bad syntax (misspelling function names, forgetting closing brackets, using nonexistent operators, and so on) can be picked up before running code. Code that takes a long time to run, or a test environment and data that takes a while to set up for each run, can benefit from being statically analyzed to catch glaring errors before a run starts. It can be particularly galling to happen upon a fatal error in a script `include()`'d at the end of an hour-long data analysis run that could have been caught before you even started! Of course, static analysis tools can't catch every kind of bug. They have no knowledge of the data your scripts will encounter or the environment in which they will run, or indeed your expectations of what the script will achieve.

A programming *lint* is a simple type of static code analysis tool. *Lint* was the name given to one of the first analysis tools for C many years ago, but it has become a generic term for these types of tools (as *Hoover* has become a generic term for *vacuum* in some areas). PHP has various lint tools, including one built right into PHP itself. To use the built-in lint, simply call `php -l yourfile.php`, and any syntax errors found will be printed to the terminal.

Other third-party lints and similar tools go beyond syntax checking, including features such as the abilitiy to check your code against particular coding standards that you may choose to use. Sticking to a given coding standard won't prevent bugs by itself, but can help code readability and maintainability, particularly if multiple developers are involved. It doesn't really matter which coding standard you use from the many available, but if you do use one, it is important that you use it consistently and across all of your code—and tools like these can help with that. Some tools, such as PHP Vulnerability Hunter, can look for code patterns that are indicative of particular faults (such as security vulnerabilities) but that aren't specific violations of a coding standard or a syntax error. The output of tools like these requires further consideration, as they are only indicators of potential problems. Whether a particular item of code, in your particular case, constitutes an actual security vulnerability will depend on the use case, the code surrounding it, and the environment it is executed in. That said, even if a code scanner detects something that isn't currently a security problem as your script is structured now, it may be worth changing that section (or adding strict unit tests to it) to ensure that any changes to related code in the future won't allow it to become exploitable then.

Further Reading

- How Etsy.com (PHP founder Rasmus Lerdorf's employer) implements static analysis for its PHP stack

    - `http://codeascraft.etsy.com/2012/08/10/static-analysis-for-php/`

- "PHP Static Analysis in Sublime Text" by Phil Sturgeon

    - `http://philsturgeon.co.uk/blog/2013/08/php-static-analysis-in-sublime-text`

- "Analyzing PHP Statically," a video by Julien Verlaguet, Facebook

    - `www.youtube.com/watch?v=gKWNjFagR9k`

Toolbox	PHPLint
A comprehensive PHP lint tool, available to download or use online	
Main web site, documentation, and installation info	`www.icosaedro.it/phplint/`
Online tool	`www.icosaedro.it/phplint/phplint-on-line.html`

Toolbox	PHP_Codesniffer
Pear package for detecting violations of a defined set of coding standards	
Main web site	`www.squizlabs.com/php-codesniffer`
Installation info	`https://github.com/squizlabs/PHP_CodeSniffer/#about`
Main documentation	`http://pear.php.net/manual/en/package.php.php-codesniffer.php`

Toolbox	PHP Depend

A static analysis and metric generation tool. Recommended for use with PHP Mess Detector (described next).

Main web site	`http://pdepend.org/`
Main documentation	`http://pdepend.org/documentation/getting-started.html`

Toolbox	PHP Mess Detector (PHPMD)

A spin-off tool that uses PHP Depend to look for bugs, suboptimal code, and more

Main web site	`http://phpmd.org/`
Installation info	`http://phpmd.org/download/index.html`
Main documentation	`http://phpmd.org/documentation/index.html`

Toolbox	PHPLOC

A simple tool that outputs a range of statistics about your code

Main web site	`https://github.com/sebastianbergmann/phploc`
Main documentation and installation info	`https://github.com/sebastianbergmann/phploc/blob/master/README.md`

Toolbox	PHP Analyzer

An advanced static analysis tool. Designed for use as part of a CI workflow but can be used as a stand-alone tool as well.

Main web site	`https://github.com/scrutinizer-ci/php-analyzer`
Installation info	`https://github.com/scrutinizerci/php-analyzer#installation`
Main documentation	`https://scrutinizer-ci.com/docs/tools/php/php-analyzer/`

Toolbox	PHP Vulnerability Hunter

An advanced white-box PHP web application fuzzer that scans for several classes of vulnerabilities via static and dynamic analysis. Primarily aimed at web sites, but can be used with some general classes of PHP software.

Main web site	`www.autosectools.com/PHP-Vulnerability-Scanner`
Main documentation	`www.autosectools.com/PHP-Vulnerability-Hunter-Guide`

Toolbox	PHP_CodeCoverage
An advanced tool for testing code coverage (the code that would be executed in a run).	
Main web site	https://github.com/sebastianbergmann/php-code-coverage
Main documentation and installation info	https://github.com/sebastianbergmann/php-code-coverage/#php_codecoverage

Going beyond basic lint-type capabilities and single-purpose scanning, several advanced open source and commercial analysis platforms are available for PHP that provide a much wider range of analysis and reporting capabilities, including various code quality metrics, code duplication analysis, security pattern analysis, and more, as well as integration with other tools such as unit-testing software and IDEs. These tools often have a significant learning curve and deployment/use cost (in terms of time and resources), and are more suited to larger projects, mission-critical projects, and projects with multiple developers. However, even when starting small with a single developer, if you honestly believe that your project will scale up, it may be worth considering using such a tool from the start to help minimize building up "technical debt" to be called in later in the project. Most enterprise-level commercial analysis platforms can deal with PHP, but for smaller projects, SonarQube is the leading open source platform.

Toolbox	SonarQube
An extensive open platform for managing code quality through code analysis	
Main web site	www.sonarqube.org
Installation info	http://docs.sonarqube.org/display/SONAR/Setup+and+Upgrade
Main documentation	http://docs.sonarqube.org/display/SONAR/User+Guide
PHP-specific plug-in	http://docs.sonarqube.org/display/PLUG/PHP+Plugin

Virtual Development and Testing Environments

When you develop for the Web, you usually control (or at least specify) the environment in which your PHP scripts are deployed (that is, your web server). When writing general-purpose software, this often isn't the case, particularly if you sell or otherwise distribute your software to others. You can specify operating systems and other software/hardware prerequisites for your software to match your own development environment, but it is often more desirable to make your software work on as wide a range of platforms as possible. This can raise issues when developing and testing, as you will require access to all the platforms that your users will use. We used to require many physical machines to run different operating systems and configurations. However, a modern solution for many cases is virtualization, running different platforms on the same hardware in *virtual machines*.

Many virtualization solutions are available, and one of the easiest (and cheapest) to use is VirtualBox from Oracle. Simply install VirtualBox, create and run a new virtual machine, and install an operating system as you would if you were setting up a physical machine from scratch. You can install most common operating systems including Linux and Windows variants; assign various levels of memory, processor, and disk space; and run many different virtual machines at the same time. You can also take *snapshots* of a virtual machine at a given time, and roll back to a particular snapshot when you need to. This is useful if your testing environment needs setting to an initial state (data, machine state, software state, and so forth) before each run. VirtualBox doesn't have all the bells and whistles of some virtualization environments and sometimes has lower-performance characteristics than those that run at a lower level. However, for many cases (including most software-testing scenarios), it performs well and is versatile.

Toolbox	VirtualBox
An easy-to-use virtualization system	
Main web site	`www.virtualbox.org`
Installation info	`www.virtualbox.org/manual/ch01.html#intro-installing`
Main documentation	`www.virtualbox.org/wiki/Documentation`

A note of caution: when using virtualization with commercial operating systems such as Microsoft Windows and macOS, you always need to be aware of licensing issues. Many commercial OSs require separate or additional licenses for virtual machines, even when you are using a fully licensed host operating system. In particular, the licensing requirements and costs for server variants can vary, depending on not just the number of virtual machines installed but the number of processor cores used by each virtual machine (a particular headache if you regularly vary the number of virtual cores provided to a given VM for testing purposes).

Virtualization can also be useful for development environments. It can be a pain to set up all your preferred tools on a new machine, or configure a machine to match a development environment specified for a team or company. Having your development environment as a portable virtual machine, or deploying a new virtual machine to a predefined recipe by using a tool such as Vagrant can make life a lot easier. You can also use a tool such as Ansible, which integrates well with Vagrant, to automate the deployment process (for instance, as part of a build step).

Toolbox	Vagrant
Creates and configures lightweight, reproducible, and portable development environments	
Main web site	`www.vagrantup.com`
Installation info	`www.vagrantup.com/docs/installation/`
Main documentation	`www.vagrantup.com/docs/`

Toolbox	Ansible
A simple-to-use automation tool useful in many areas of the development workflow	
Main web site	`www.ansible.com`
Installation info	`http://docs.ansible.com/ansible/intro_installation.html`
Main documentation	`http://docs.ansible.com`

Toolbox	Phansible
A tool to help you generate Ansible provisionings for PHP-based projects, using Vagrant	
Main web site	`http://phansible.com`
Main documentation	`http://phansible.com/docs/usage`

Further Reading

- "Make $ Vagrant Up Yours" by Juan Treminio, an article about Vagrant, Puppet, and PuPHPet.

    - `https://jtreminio.com/2013/06/make_vagrant_up_yours/`

Source/Version-Control Systems and Code Repositories

Version-control systems and *code repositories* help you to manage versions and branches of code, share and deploy code, and track errors and changes. These systems can be useful in most projects. Virtually all common version-control systems and code repositories work with PHP, including Apache Subversion (SVN), Git, Concurrent Version Systems (CVS), and others, and there are no PHP-specific reasons to recommend one over another. There are no particular PHP-specific tools to note here, other than to mention that most build systems (see the previous section) can be configured to work with most of these systems.

Several PHP libraries of note are in this area, a binding for the Git system, an API wrapper for the popular Git-based host GitHub, and a PECL package for interacting with SVN repositories. These libraries can be used in PHP-based build systems, for example.

Toolbox	PHP Git Bindings
PHP bindings for libgit2, the Git implementation used by GitHub, Microsoft, and others	
Main web site	`https://github.com/libgit2/php-git`
Installation info	`https://github.com/libgit2/php-git#installing-and-running`
Main documentation	`https://libgit2.github.com/libgit2/#v0.20.0`

Toolbox	Gittern
A library for reading/writing Git repositories that doesn't depend on the Git binary	
Main web site	`https://github.com/e-butik/Gittern`
Installation info	`http://gittern.readthedocs.org/en/latest/#installation`
Main documentation	`http://gittern.readthedocs.org/en/latest/`

Toolbox	PHP GitHub API
A simple object-oriented wrapper for the GitHub API	
Main web site and documentation	`https://github.com/KnpLabs/php-github-api`
Tutorial *"Talking to GitHub with PHP" by W.J. Gilmore*	`www.phpbuilder.com/columns/github/github-api-php_11-29-2011.php3`

Toolbox	GitElephant
An abstraction layer for Git written in PHP	
Main web site	`https://github.com/matteosister/GitElephant`

Toolbox	svn
PHP bindings for the Subversion revision-control system	
Main web site	`http://pecl.php.net/package/svn`
Installation info	`www.php.net/manual/en/svn.setup.php`
Main documentation	`www.php.net/manual/en/book.svn.php`

Further Reading

- Free Apress *Pro Git* book by Scott Chacon

    - `http://git-scm.com/book`

- A practical tutorial on using GitHub with a PHP project by Lorna Mitchell

    - `www.lornajane.net/posts/2012/do-open-source-with-git-and-github`

IDEs and Editors

Integrated development environments (IDEs) and *code editors* for PHP are plentiful, and you will likely have your own favorite for web-based PHP development. No IDEs or editors are currently specifically aimed at PHP CLI-based programming, but such code is syntactically compatible and similar to web-based PHP programming. You should have few problems using your existing PHP editing environment. Some additional features may not work correctly, such as web-based debuggers, or may require additional tinkering to use. A list of popular PHP IDEs is given in Appendix E at the end of the book.

Documentation Generators

Documentation generators (also known as *documentors*) automatically generate documentation from your source code. They do this by using the comments you put in the code and by picking up the syntactical structures in your code. They are useful for creating base documentation for programming APIs and technical documentation for other developers working on your code. The documentation provided usually requires further finessing or additional information in order to be truly useful and is usually of little use to end users of your software. However, such documentation provides a good overview of the code structure along with a useful reference for larger code bases, where finding the details of particular functions from the code itself can be time-consuming. Some IDEs and other programming tools can use the unmodified output from documentors to provide additional functionality, such as project-based context-specific help and autocompletions.

Toolbox	phpDocumentor
Popular and versatile PHP-based documentor	
Main web site	`www.phpdoc.org`
Installation info	`www.phpdoc.org/docs/latest/getting-started/` `installing.html`
Main documentation	`www.phpdoc.org/docs/latest/index.html`

Toolbox	phpDox
A fast, modern documentor that can pull in information from other static analysis tools	
Main web site	`http://phpdox.de/`
Main documentation and installation info	`http://phpdox.de/getting-started.html`

Toolbox	phpSimpleDoc
A simplified documentor that outputs HTML docs	
Main web site	`http://phpsimpledoc.tig12.net`
Installation info	`http://phpsimpledoc.tig12.net/user-guide/quick-start#toc_1`
Main documentation	`http://phpsimpledoc.tig12.net/user-guide`

Toolbox	Doxygen
A comprehensive and extensive documentor, which supports PHP but is not PHP specific	
Main web site	`www.stack.nl/~dimitri/doxygen/`
Installation info	`www.stack.nl/~dimitri/doxygen/manual/install.html`
Main documentation	`www.stack.nl/~dimitri/doxygen/manual`

Toolbox	Sami
The documentor created and used by the Symphony framework project for its API, although it is not Symphony specific	
Main web site	`https://github.com/FriendsOfPHP/Sami`
Installation info	`https://github.com/FriendsOfPHP/Sami#installation`
Main documentation	`https://github.com/FriendsOfPHP/Sami#configuration`

Profilers

Profilers let you measure and view the execution time and path of your code, usually with an aim to increase the performance of your scripts and remove code bottlenecks. Chapter 9 covers profilers in detail as we look further at script performance.

Other Tools

This section lists other tools that are useful for serious development but don't fit neatly into the preceding categories.

Toolbox	PHP Coding Standards Fixer
Attempts to fix your code to meet PSR standards	
Main web site, documentation, and installation info	`http://cs.sensiolabs.org/`

Toolbox	Composer dependency manager
The easy way to keep libraries consistent and up-to-date on a per project basis. See Appendix A for more information.	
Main web site	`http://getcomposer.org/`
Package repository	`https://packagist.org/`
Installation info	`http://getcomposer.org/doc/00-intro.md#installation-ni`
Main documentation	`http://getcomposer.org/doc/`
Tutorial *"Easy Package Management with Composer" by Philip Sturgeon*	`http://code.tutsplus.com/tutorials/easypackage-management-with-composer--net-25530`

Toolbox	PHP_Beautifier
Takes your PHP source code and formats it for readability by, for example, indenting code, adding new lines where needed, and formatting data structures	
Main web site	`http://pear.php.net/package/PHP_Beautifier`
Installation	`pear install PHP_Beautifier`
Main documentation	`http://beautifyphp.sourceforge.net/docs/`

Toolbox	PHPLighter
Takes your PHP source code and creates a syntax-highlighted HTML version. Uses advanced tokenization to highlight more features of code. Useful for reviewing and displaying code.	
Main web site	`https://github.com/brandonwamboldt/PHPLighter`
Main documentation and installation info	`https://github.com/brandonwamboldt/PHPLighter#usage`

Toolbox	PHP Refactoring Browser
A command-line refactoring tool for PHP that's still in early development	
Main web site, documentation, and installation info	`http://qafoolabs.github.io/php-refactoring-browser/`

Toolbox	phptidy
A tool for formatting PHP code for readability	
Main web site, documentation, and installation info	https://github.com/cmrcx/phptidy

Toolbox	Phabricator
An open software-engineering platform created at Facebook that includes many tools designed to help create better software. Written in PHP.	
Main web site, documentation, and installation info	http://phabricator.org/

CHAPTER 5

▓ ▓ ▓

User-Facing Software

After slugging through the preliminary information necessary to understand developing PHP in a nonweb context, you're now getting to the nitty-gritty of how to start communicating with your users without the rendering engine of a web browser.

Some software sits and happily runs without any interaction from humans. We'll call this *system software*, which is covered in Chapter 6. However, a large proportion of software requires interactivity with the user, and there are several ways of performing such interactions in PHP. From interactive command lines to fully fledged GUI-based software, it can all be done with PHP.

When choosing how your software interacts with humans, you need to focus on the needs of the user and put your own preferences to one side if at all possible. Command-line interactions are (usually) straightforward to code, and text is, well, just text, and it's what PHP excels at. However, many users, particularly nontechnical ones, shy away from text-based CLI software. Unless you are meticulous about your software structure and interface flow, text based input can

- Be prone to error

- Be hard to navigate

- Require mental agility on the part of the user

- Have low discoverability

- Be initially slower to use than a GUI

If you choose a text-based interface, make sure your target users will be happy with it. (You may be happy with it, but your users might not be like you!)

Text interfaces, because of the simplicity of coding, can often be a good choice for proof-of-concept and prototype software (particularly where the main benefits of the application are in what it does, not in how the user interacts with it). However, be aware that temporary interfaces have an uncanny way of "sticking around." Additionally, some nontechnical commissioning users (the words *pointy-haired boss* spring to mind here) can't see past an interface to the application beneath and may not be happy with your proposed project, even after you explain that the interface is temporary. This is understandable to some extent as, for most users, the application *is* the interface. It is all they see and use day in and day out. The changes to their files and the other functions performed just happen by "magic," of course.

Good user-interface design (whether for text-based interfaces or fully fledged GUIs) is a field of endeavor in and of itself, so get help from the professionals where you can, read some of the multitude of books available on the subject, or take a course. If you've ever looked at a piece of software and wondered how it got so popular while your preferred (much more functionally superior) software languished in obscurity, the answer is often at least partly due to good user-interface design.

© Rob Aley 2016
R. Aley, *PHP Beyond the Web*, DOI 10.1007/978-1-4842-2481-6_5

Command-Line Interfaces

Simple to code and easy to maintain, Command-Line based interfaces are useful in many situations. In the following sections we'll look at the code needed to interact with your users through the medium of text.

Command-Line Interface Basics

Although graphical interfaces seem to garner the most attention these days, there are still plenty of uses for text-based interfaces, particularly in environments with technically adept users. When creating a text based program to run on the command line, there are three primary considerations over and above the PHP you are already accustomed to:

- Getting keyboard input

- Outputting text (and graphics) to the screen

- Program flow control

Rather than learn about each one in isolation, you will instead look through a simple program that contains elements of each. Have a look through the following program, which is a screen-saver-type of routine that fills the shell with color via a wiggling snake-like cursor. Note that this script will work only in POSIX environments because of the use of shell escape-codes and the tput command.

```php
<?php

# First we will define some named constants.
# These are shell escape codes, used for formatting.
# Defining them as named constants helps to make our code more readable.

define("ESC", "\033");
define("CLEAR", ESC."[2J");
define("HOME", ESC."[0;0f");

# We will output some instructions to the user. Note that we use
# fwrite rather than echo. The aim is to write our output back to the
# shell where the user will see it. fwrite(STDOUT... writes to the
# php://stdout stream. Echo (and print) write to the php://output
# stream. Usually these are both the same thing, but they don't have to
# be. Additionally php://output is subject to the Output control &
# buffering functions (http://www.php.net/manual/en/book.outcontrol.php)
# which may or may not be desirable.

fwrite(STDOUT, "Press Enter To Begin, And Enter Again To End");

# Now we wait for the user to press Enter. By default, STDIN is
# a blocking stream, which means that when we try to read from it,
# our script will stop and wait some input. Keyboard input to the shell
# is passed to our script (via fread) when the user presses Enter.

fread(STDIN,1);

# We want the program to run until the user presses Enter again. This
# means that we want to periodically check for input with fread, but not
```

```
# to pause/block the program if there isn't any input. So we set STDIN to
# be nonblocking.

stream_set_blocking(STDIN, 0);

# In preparation for our output, we want to clear the terminal and draw a
# pretty frame around it. To do this, we need to know how big the terminal
# window currently is. There is no built-in way to do this in PHP, so we
# call an external shell command called tput, which gives information about
# the current terminal.

$rows = intval(`tput lines`);
$cols = intval(`tput cols`);

# We now write two special escape codes to the terminal, the first
# of which (\033[2J) clears the screen, the second of which (\033[0;0f)
# puts the cursor at the top left of the screen. We've already defined
# these as the constants CLEAR and HOME at the start of the script.

fwrite(STDOUT, CLEAR.HOME);

# Now we want to draw a frame around our window. The simplest way to draw
# "graphics" (or "semigraphics/pseudographics") in the terminal is to
# use box drawing characters that are included with most fixed-width fonts
# used in terminals.

# Draw the vertical frames by moving the cursor step-by-step down each
# side. The cursor is moved with the escape code generated by
# ESC."[$rowcount;1f"

for ($rowcount = 2; $rowcount < $rows; $rowcount++) {
  fwrite(STDOUT, ESC."[$rowcount;1f"."•"); # e.g. \033[7;1f• for line 7
  fwrite(STDOUT, ESC."[$rowcount;${cols}f"."•");
}

# Now do the same for the horizontal frames.

for ($colcount = 2; $colcount < $cols; $colcount++) {
  fwrite(STDOUT, ESC."[1;${colcount}f"."•");
  fwrite(STDOUT, ESC."[$rows;${colcount}f"."•");
}

# And finally fill in the corners.

fwrite(STDOUT, ESC."[1;1f"."•");
fwrite(STDOUT, ESC."[1;${cols}f"."•");
fwrite(STDOUT, ESC."[$rows;1f"."•");
fwrite(STDOUT, ESC."[$rows;${cols}f"."•");

# You can see the full range of box drawing characters available at
# http://en.wikipedia.org/wiki/Box-drawing_character
# They are just "text" like any other character, so you can easily copy
# and paste them into most editors.
```

51

```
# $p is an array [x,y] that holds the position of our cursor. We will
# initialize it to be the center of the screen.

$p = ["x"=>intval($cols/2), "y"=>intval($rows/2)];

# Now for our first element of flow control. We need to keep the program
# running until the user provides input. The simplest way to do this is to
# use a never-ending loop using while(1). "1" always evaluates to true, so
# the while loop will never end. When we (or the user) are ready to end
# the program, we can use the "break" construct to step out of the loop
# and continue the remaining script after the end of the loop.

while (1) {

# Each time we go through the loop, we want to check if the user has
# pressed Enter while we were in the last loop. Remember that STDIN is
# no longer blocking, so if there is no input, the program continues
# immediately. If there is input, we use break to leave the while loop.

  if (fread(STDIN,1)) { break; };

# We will step the position of the cursor, stored in $p, by a random
# amount in both the x and y axis. This makes our snake crawl!

  $p['x'] = $p['x'] + rand(-1,1);
  $p['y'] = $p['y'] + rand(-1,1);

# We check that our snake won't step onto or over the frame, to keep
# it in its box!

  if ($p['x'] > ($cols-1)) { $p['x'] = ($cols-1);};
  if ($p['y'] > ($rows-1)) { $p['y'] = ($rows-1);};
  if ($p['x'] < 2) { $p['x'] = 2;};
  if ($p['y'] < 2) { $p['y'] = 2;};

# We want a pretty trail, so we need to pick random colos for the
# foreground and background color of our snake that change at
# each step. Colors in the terminal are set with yet more escape
# codes, from a limited palette, specified by integers.

  $fg_color = rand(30,37);
  $bg_color = rand(40,47);

# Once chosen, we set the colors by outputting the escape codes. This
# doesn't immediately print anything, it just sets the color of
# whatever else follows.

  fwrite(STDOUT, ESC."[${fg_color}m"); # \033[32m sets green foreground
  fwrite(STDOUT, ESC."[${bg_color}m"); # \033[42m sets green background

# Finally we output a segment of snake (another box drawing character)
# at the new location. It will appear with the colors we just set, at
# the location stored in $p
```

```
fwrite(STDOUT, ESC."[${p['y']};${p['x']}f"."•");

# Before we let the while loop start again, we need to do one more
# very important thing. We need to give your processor a rest.
# If we just continued our loop straightaway, you would find your
# processor being hammered, just for our relatively simple program.
# Our snake would also consume the screen at super-speed!
# usleep pauses execution of the program, so others can use the
# processor or the processor can "rest." Every little bit helps the
# responsiveness of your machine, so even if you need your program
# to loop as fast as possible, consider even a small usleep if you can

    usleep(1000);
};

# If this line of code has been reached, it means that we have 'break'd
# from the while loop.

# To be a good citizen of the terminal, we need to clean up the screen
# before we exit. Otherwise, the cursor will remain on whichever line
# our snake left it, and the background/foreground colors will be
# the last ones chosen for our snake segment.

# The following escape code tells the terminal to use its default colors.

fwrite(STDOUT, ESC."[0m");

# We then clear the screen and put the cursor at the top left, as we
# did earlier.

fwrite(STDOUT, CLEAR.HOME);
```

This program should demonstrate the three basics listed earlier:

- *Getting keyboard input*: You can read from STDIN in the same way you would any other PHP stream.

- *Outputting text (and graphics) to the screen*: You can output to STDOUT (or use echo/print), control the appearance and cursor with escape characters, and use block drawing characters to make semigraphics/pseudographics.

- *Program flow control*: A while(1) loop is useful for keeping a program running, with break to continue flow outside the loop. It's important to use usleep or sleep to stop your process from hogging a processor.

Advanced Command-Line Input

The previous section showed how to use fread() to read keyboard input. This is suitable for simple programs, but if you are looking to create a more complex interface to allow users to issue commands, then you may want to look at the Readline extension, which you can use to implement a shell-like editable command-line program. Unfortunately, for Windows users, the Readline library works only under Linux and Unix. Nothing comparable is available for the Windows platform unless you use the experimental Windows Subsystem for Linux (WSL), which does support Readline. The Readline library is used by PHP itself for the php -a interactive REPL.

The following example script shows how to implement a simple bespoke command-line type of interface with the Readline library:

```php
<?php

# Create arrays to hold our command history and list of valid commands.

$history = array();

$validCommands = array();

# Define some valid commands (I imagine we're programming a command-line
# interface to killer robot here...you know, typical day-to-day stuff)

$validCommands[] = 'kill';
$validCommands[] = 'destroy';
$validCommands[] = 'obliterate';
$validCommands[] = 'history';
$validCommands[] = 'byebye';

# We want to enable tab-completion of commands, which allows the user to
# start typing a command and then press Tab to have it completed, as
# happens in Bash shells and the like. We need to provide a function (via
# readline_completion_function) that will provide an array of possible
# function names. This can be based on the $partial characters the user
# has typed or the point in the program we are at, or any other
# factors we want. In our case, we'll simply provide an array of ALL of
# the valid commands we have.

function tab_complete ($partial) {

  global $validCommands;

  return $validCommands;

};

readline_completion_function('tab_complete');

# We now enter our main program loop. Note that we don't include a usleep,
# as readline pauses our program execution while it waits for input from
# the user.

while (1) {

# We call readline with a string that forms the command prompt. In our
# case, we'll put the date & time in there to show that we can change
# it each time it's called. Whatever the user enters is returned. This
# one simple line implements most of the readline magic. At this stage,
# the user can take advantage of tab-completion, history (use up/down
# cursor keys), and so on.
```

```
$line = readline(date('H:i:s')." Enter command > ");
```

```
# We need to manually add commands to the history. This is used for
# the command history that the user accesses with the up/down cursor
# keys. We could choose to ignore commands (mistyped ones or
# intermediate input, for example) if we want, although we'll add
# everything our users enter in this example.
```

```
readline_add_history($line);
```

```
# If we want to programmatically retrieve the history, we can use a
# function called readline_list_history(). However, this is
# available only if PHP has been compiled using libreadline. In most cases,
# modern distributions compile it using the compatible libedit library
# for licensing and other reasons. So we will keep a parallel copy of
# the history in an array for programatic access.
```

```
$history[] = $line;
```

```
# Now we decide what to do with the users input. In real life, we may
# want to trim(), strtolower(), and otherwise filter the input first.
```

```
switch ($line) {

    case "kill":

        echo "You don't want to do that.\n";

        break;

    case "destroy":

        echo "That really isn't a good idea.\n";

        break;

    case "obliterate":

        echo "Well, if we really must.\n";

        break;

    case "history":
```

```
# We will use the parallel copy of the command history that we
# created earlier to display the command history.
```

```
        $counter = 0;
```

```php
        foreach($history as $command) {

          $counter++;

          echo("$counter: $command\n");

        };

        break;

    case "byebye":

# If it's time to leave, we want to break from both the switch
# statement and the while loop, so we break with a level of 2.

        break 2;

    default :

# Always remember to give feedback in the case of user error.

        echo("Sorry, command ".$line." was not recognised.\n");
  }

};

# If we reached here, outside of the while(1) loop, the user typed byebye.

echo("Bye bye, come again soon!\n");
```

You may have noticed that I chose to use byebye as the command to quit the program. This was not just a whimsical choice on my part, but illustrates the need to think about discoverability. If you were presented with this program, without seeing the previous source code, and asked to close it, you likely would try quit, exit, end, and so on, before resorting to a good old Ctrl+C. In a GUI interface, you would have no such problems when faced with a Bye-Bye! button. With text-based input, it is best to stick to common and memorable formats for commands, provide visual guidance and clues where possible, and aid in discoverability with good documentation, a help command, and user training.

Further Reading

- Readline extension in the PHP manual

    - www.php.net/manual/en/intro.readline.php

Working with STDIN, STOUT, and STDERR

The PHP CLI SAPI automatically opens the standard streams for you when your script starts, so there is no need to issue commands such as fopen('php://stdin', 'r'). You can treat these streams just like any other PHP stream and start using them straightaway. You saw some examples earlier, but here are a few more to illustrate the many options available:

```php
<?php

# Get one line of input from STDIN

echo ('Please Type Something In : >');

$line1 = fgets(STDIN);

echo ('**** Line 1 : '.$line1." ****\n\n");

# Get one line of input, without the newline character

echo ('Please Type Something Else In : >');

$line2 = trim(fgets(STDIN));

echo ('**** Line 2 : '.$line2." ****\n\n");

# Write an array out to STDOUT in CSV format.
# First, create an array of arrays...

$records[] = ['User', 'Full Name', 'Gender'];
$records[] = ['Rob', 'Robert Aley', 'M'];
$records[] = ['Ada', 'Augusta Ada King, Countess of Lovelace', 'F'];
$records[] = ['Grete', 'Grete Hermann', 'F'];

echo ("The following is your Data in CSV format :\n\n");

# ...then convert each array to CSV on the fly as we write it out

foreach ($records as $record) {

  fputcsv(STDOUT, $record);

};

echo ("\n\nEnd of your CSV data\n");

# Pause until the user enters something starting with a number

echo ('Please type one or more numbers : >');

while (! fscanf(STDIN, "%d\n", $your_number) ) {

  echo ("No numbers found :>");

};

echo ("Your number was $your_number\n\n");

# Send the text of a web page to STDOUT
```

```
echo ("Press enter for some interwebs :\n\n");

fread(STDIN, 1); # fread blocks until enter pressed

fwrite(STDOUT, strip_tags( file_get_contents('http://www.cam.ac.uk') ) );

# Send an error message to STDERR. You can just fwrite(STDERR,...
# if you want, or you can use the error_log function, which uses the
# defined error handling routine. By default for the CLI SAPI this is
# printing to STDERR.

error_log('System ran out of beer. ABORT. ABORT.', 4);
```

The error logged on the last line of the preceding code will usually appear in your shell along with the other output, because that is where most shells put STDERR by default. If you want to check that it did come via STDERR rather than STDOUT, the following Bash command will highlight any STDERR output (denoted by the 2>) in red. It uses escape codes to color the error (31 sets the color to red, 07 reverses it, and then 0 clears it).

```
~$ php script.php 2> >(while read errors; do echo -e "\e[07;31m$errors\e[0m" >&2; done)
```

In short, you can use the standard streams in any number of ways, often treating them as standard file pointers or streams.

CLI Helper Libraries

Some prewritten libraries and components can take some of the effort out of creating interactive console software. I've listed three common ones in this section. As with most libraries of this type, they are quite "opinionated" in how your program should be structured, so do look thoroughly through the documentation of each before choosing which best suits your project.

The Symfony Console (part of the Symfony framework project) is well-tested and stable; as with most Symfony components, it is well-documented and supported. If you are familiar with the Symfony framework, the code style should be familiar to you, but it is equally at home with other frameworks (it is used for the Laravel framework's Artisan Console tool, for instance). The Webmozart Console toolkit is a refactored version of the Symfony Console component so has similar features but a different coding style. It is also currently still in beta. Finally, the Hoa Console is perhaps the most distinct of the three, with a coding style that focuses on real-world tasks and is arguably easier to get to grips with as a developer.

Toolbox	Symfony Console
The Console component of the Symfony PHP framework project	
Main web site	https://github.com/symfony/Console

Toolbox	Webmozart Console
A (beta) Console component refactored from the Symfony Console	
Main web site	https://github.com/webmozart/console

Toolbox	Hoa\Console library
A Console library aimed at industrial and research use	

Main web site	`https://github.com/hoaproject/Console`

Partial GUI Elements—Dialog Boxes

Later in this chapter you will look at systems for producing complete graphical interfaces, but an intermediate stage can be used for simpler programs that need to only occasionally interact with or notify the user (for instance, popping up a warning or a graphical request for input). PHP allows us to use several methods of calling or creating visual display elements, as discussed in this section.

Dialogs Invoked from the Shell

Various shell commands invoke graphical elements onscreen. You can call shell commands in various ways from PHP, including using `shell_exec` or backticks as in the following example. See Chapter 7 for more details and possibilities. These shell dialog commands include `notify-send`, `zenity`, and `kdialog`..

notify-send

On Debian-based systems, `notify-send` pops up a notification "bubble" on a user's screen. Exactly how it appears depends on the distribution, but it is usually a system-standard notification similar to those displayed when you get new e-mail or a system event occurs. It uses `lib-notify` from the Gnome project, which may need to be installed (`sudo apt-get install libnotify-bin`). Call it from PHP as follows:

```php
<?php

# With shell_exec...

shell_exec('notify-send -i error "Flange Error" '.
  '"An error occurred with the Flange Grommet. Flange 2.0 not found."');

# or with backticks...

$command = 'notify-send -i info "Flange Completed" '.
  '"Flange has been Grommeted. See  manual for de-grommeting info"';

`$command`;
```

The `-i` flag allows you to specify an icon. You can either provide the full path to an image, or reference a standard icon (usually found in a location such as `/usr/share/icons/`) as we have done in the preceding example.

Use `man notify-send` to find out the various options available to customize the notification.

Ubuntu Unity users note: the flag `-t` allows you to specify a time-out after which the notification disappears. However, this flag is ignored in Ubuntu Unity; instead, the duration of the notification depends on the length of its text. Setting `-t 0` in Unity turns the notification "bubble" into an alert box that requires the user to explicitly close it instead.

zenity

zenity allows you to display common dialog boxes, from calendars to color pickers. Based on GTK+, it allows various formatting and content options, and returns the user input back for use in your script. zenity is installed in most Gnome-based systems.

```php
<?php

# Execute zenity using backticks. Zenity returns the user's input as text
# that we collect into a string variable. Let's use it to pop up a
# calendar, then tell the user what day of the week it is.

$day = `zenity --calendar --text="Choose a day" --date-format="%d %b %Y"`;

if ($day) {
echo('The date chosen is a '.date('l', strtotime($day))."".\n");
};

# Now we'll show a file selector and then show an "info" dialog to tell
# the user the size of the file selected.

$filename = trim(`zenity --file-selection`);

if (file_exists($filename)) {

$command = 'zenity --info --text "The size of the file chosen is  '.
filesize($filename).' bytes."';

`$command`;

};
```

The full range of dialog boxes available include a color selector, various notification dialogs, text inputs, a progress meter, and more.

kdialog

kdialog is the equivalent of zenity for KDE desktops.

Further Reading

- The full list of dialog boxes and options available in zenity
  - https://help.gnome.org/users/zenity/
- More information and tutorial on kdialog
  - http://techbase.kde.org/Development/Tutorials/Shell_Scripting_with_KDE_Dialogs

Windows Dialog Boxes

A useful PECL package allows you to access the Win32 API from PHP. The API provides access to create common Win32 dialog boxes. You will look further at this library in Chapter 8, when you learn how it can be used to interact with the Windows Registry.

Toolbox	win32std
Set of standard Windows API functions	
Main web site	http://pecl.php.net/package/win32std
Main documentation and installation info	README file within the download
Alternative documentation	http://wildphp.free.fr/wiki/doku.php?id=win32std:index

Static HTML Output

PHP is, of course, excellent for creating HTML output—that is its original *raison d'etre*, after all. HTML can be useful for displaying information, charts, data, and so forth at the end of a CLI run, and you can use PHP's built-in HTML tools to do this. Usually, HTML display occurs via a web server such as Apache, so it may not be immediately obvious how to create and display HTML from CLI scripts. The end goal is to create one or more HTML files to display your output and save them to disk, to be displayed by a local web browser.

You can probably imagine creating this HTML in strings and sequentially writing out to disk in a similar manner to creating other text/data files. Luckily, PHP provides us with a neat trick called *output buffering* that allows us to pretend we are sending out HTML in the normal web server environment, making the process somewhat quicker. This allows us to use facilities such as intermingling blocks of HTML with code, echo'ing and print_r'ing data and so on, but instead of sending it out to a web server, PHP captures it for us and allows us to write it down to disk en mass. This can be particularly useful if you have existing reporting or templating code from a web-based project that you want to easily reuse from the command line. The following example demonstrates how to tell PHP to start collecting output, create some output ourselves, save it to disk, and finally open it in a local web browser:

```php
<?php

echo("This text will go to STDOUT (your terminal) as normal\n");

# Start buffering our output rather than sending it to STDOUT

ob_start();

# Echo and print write to the php://output stream. By default,
# php://output writes to STDOUT, which is why echo normally prints stuff
# back to the terminal. ob_start() captures the php://output stream,
# however, we can still write to STDOUT directly (rather than via echo) if
# we want to tell the user what we're up to.

fwrite(STDOUT, "Starting HTML Generation...\n"); # displayed in terminal

# So we create our HTML as we would if we were "on the web"
```

```php
echo('<html>');

print("<head><title>My HTML Page</title></head>\n");

?>
<body>
<h1> Intermingle Some HTML</h1>
<p>In the traditional PHP Way</p>
<p>
<a href-"http://www.php.net">An Important Link</A>
<?php

echo('</body></html>');

fwrite(STDOUT, "Finished HTML Generation\n"); # displayed in terminal

# ob_get_contents() creates a string with everything buffered so far.

$ourHtml = ob_get_contents();

# We can continue with buffering if we need to, or in this case we
# end "ob_end_clean"ly. If we ob_end_flush() instead, then the contents of
# the buffer would be pushed to php://output, which after ending the
# buffering is STDOUT, which we don't want in this case.

ob_end_clean();

# Now that we've ended buffering...

echo ("This Text will go to our terminal via STDOUT\n");

# Finally, we want to save the buffered HTML to a file. Let's create
# a unique temporary file name ....

$filename = tempnam(sys_get_temp_dir(), 'my_report_').'.html';

# and write the HTML string to it.

file_put_contents($filename, $ourHtml);

# Finally, we want to open a web browser to view the HTML "report" we
# just created. Here we use the helper command "see" (available on
# most Debian-based distros) to open the default viewer for the filetype
# (HTML). The command "open" achieves the same thing on other platforms.
# On Windows, you can omit the helper command and just "execute" the
# $filename (i.e. `$filename`) and Windows will open the default viewer
# (browser) for that filetype.
#
# You can also specify a particular browser if you want,
# e.g. `firefox $filename`.

`see $filename`;
```

Further Reading

- "Output Buffering Control" section in the PHP manual

    - www.php.net/manual/en/book.outcontrol.php

Complete Graphical Interfaces

Many users expect full graphical user interfaces (GUIs) these days, with very good reason. GUIs, when done right, are good for discoverability and ease of interaction. They can provide intuitive human-friendly ways of presenting data and information and are ideal for event-based programming.

Most GUI programs are written to use *widget toolkits* (also known as *GUI toolkits*). These are toolkits or frameworks that provide code for the building blocks of GUIs: windows, forms, buttons, lists, mouse interactions, menus, events, and more. There are many widget toolkits; some are low level and platform specific (such as the Windows API for Windows, or Carbon for macOS), some are higher level and cross-platform (such as GTK+ and QT), and some are language specific (such as Swing for Java and LCL for Object Pascal). Wikipedia has a fairly comprehensive list.

Further Reading

- "List of widget toolkits" on Wikipedia

    - http://en.wikipedia.org/wiki/List_of_widget_toolkits

Two approaches exist in PHP for using these toolkits to make graphical interfaces. The first is via *direct bindings*: your PHP script invokes the toolkit directly via a library or PHP extension. The second is via a *helper application*: your PHP script tells the helper application what it wants to display by using an intermediate language such as HTML or XML User Interface Language (XUL), and the helper application deals with calling the necessary elements of the toolkit (or its own code) and displays the interface for you. The former is the traditional way of writing graphical applications, and the latter is more akin to the web approach (where the browser is the helper application to which your scripts send HTML). Both approaches have pros and cons. In this section, you'll look at current implementations of both methods.

Understanding GUI and Event-Based Programming

It's worth spending a few moments at this point talking about one of the main differences between GUI apps and, for instance, command-line programming. Most GUI programming is *event-based* programming, which can sometimes take a while to get your head around if you haven't programmed using this style before.

With a GUI program, you typically start programming "sequentially" as normal by opening a window or form and populating it with buttons, text, images, data, or whatever. At this stage, your program then goes into a waiting loop, usually waiting for the user (or sometimes the system) to do something. The program may be waiting for the user to click a button, enter some text, select an option, or wait for a new item of data to arrive. Each of these things is called an *event*, and you typically can't predict the order in which events will happen. So your code binds these events to functions or methods, and the GUI toolkit calls these as the relevant events occur. If you've done much JavaScript programming in the browser, this will feel familiar to you.

This means that your code is often executed out of sequence, and so keeping abreast of state becomes much more nuanced than in command-line scripts and even PHP web scripts, which usually run sequentially from top to bottom. The most common way of dealing with event based programs is to use object-oriented programming (OOP) techniques. Indeed, the rise of GUI software drove the rise in OOP (or followed from it, depending on who you talk to). It's still perfectly possible to use traditional "imperative" style programming, of course, particularly if you are careful around issues such as state and scope, but if you intend to do a lot of GUI programming and aren't familiar with OOP, you may be doing yourself a favor if you pick up an OOP primer and have a quick flick through.

Further Reading

- "Object-oriented programming" on Wikipedia

  - http://en.wikipedia.org/wiki/Object-oriented_programming

- "Introduction to PHP OOP" by Lorna Mitchell

  - www.lornajane.net/posts/2012/introduction-to-php-oop

- "Object-Oriented PHP for Beginners" by Jason Lengstorf

  - http://net.tutsplus.com/tutorials/php/object-oriented-php-for-beginners/

Web programming is, of course, event-based in a sense: you typically present an HTML page to the user, wait for the user to click a button or link, and handle that "event" with a different HTML page (or another run through of the same script with different parameters). Each of your HTML pages (or the PHP scripts that generate them) is in some way equivalent to the individual functions or methods called in your GUI scripts, and your web server (such as Apache) is equivalent to the waiting loop in your GUI program that holds things together and reacts to your events. The difference is that in web-based programming, with PHP in particular, you operate on a shared-nothing (or almost nothing) basis. Each script execution or HTML page fetch is deliberately separate from another unless you otherwise act to share some state (for example, via sessions, cookies, and databases). In GUI programming, you are typically operating from within the same script set under one process, and thus it is a share-(almost)-everything architecture. Once you have your head around this concept, you will find it much easier to plan and map out your software. Now let's look at some of the GUI toolkits available.

wxPHP

Started in 2005, *wxPHP* has recently gained steam and is the most active of the widget library bindings listed here. wxPHP provides bindings for wxWidgets, a cross-platform library of native widgets that supports Linux, Windows, and macOS. The latest builds are available directly from the wxPHP GitHub repository, followed by releases on the main site. wxWidgets is a library based primarily on C++, but has bindings for a wide range of other languages, and is well supported, comprehensive and extensive, and under active development. Some observers have criticized many wxWidget applications as having a bland, corporate look (think "lots of gray"), but it is perfectly possible to create attractive interfaces with it too. The wxPHP web site has assorted screenshots of applications created with the PHP bindings.

A quick word about documentation; the documentation (class references, for example) provided by wxPHP are fairly perfunctory. They are automatically generated each time a new version of the bindings is built and basically just list which widgets and properties are supported. A better source of useful information is the official wxWidgets documentation, as well as the wxWidgets wiki. Between them they provide full details about what each widget does along with guides and tutorials. These are not PHP specific, but generally useful anyway regardless of the language you are using. You should probably consider the wxPHP documentation as a simple reference as to whether a particular widget or method has been implemented in PHP.

Further Reading

- Official wxWidgets documentation

  - `http://wxwidgets.org/docs/`

- Official wxWidgets wiki

  - `http://wiki.wxwidgets.org/`

Once installed, creating applications is fairly straightforward. Windows (often called *forms* or *frames*) can be built up programmatically by adding buttons, boxes, inputs, and such directly from your PHP script. For more-complex layouts, this can be a tedious way to design the interface. Luckily, wxFormBuilder (available from the software repositories on most Debian-based Linux distros) is a graphical layout tool for wxWidgets that lets you design an interface by dragging and dropping elements onto your window, and it now supports outputting the necessary PHP code to use your design from within your program. You can also use it to manage events, specifying which functions to execute when, for instance, a button is clicked. With the addition of wxFormBuilder, wxPHP is branding itself as a leading PHP rapid application development (RAD) environment, with good reason.

Let's have a look at some sample wxPHP code. This will help you understand how a GUI application is typically structured in PHP and how it differs from a typical web application. Although the following code is wxPHP specific, many GUI toolkits follow the same kind of object-oriented, event-based structure. The following code was written by, and is reproduced with, the kind permission of the wxPHP project. The inline comments are mine.

```php
<?php

# Each frame or window is designed by extending the wxFrame class and
# adding graphical elements like buttons, menus, text boxes, and so on,
# as well as any functions to react to "events" like mouse clicks and
# window closes.

# We'll create a class "MainFrame" that describes our application's window

class MainFrame extends wxFrame
{

# We'll add a function that destroys the frame object when we quit.

  function onQuit()
  {
    $this->Destroy();
  }

# We'll add a function to display an "about" dialog to display some
# information about the application

  function onAbout()
  {

# "wxMessageDialog" is one of the many components or "widgets"
# available in the toolkit. This saves you from having to create a
# new frame/window to display your message.
```

```php
    $dlg = new wxMessageDialog(
      $this,
      "Welcome to wxPHP!!\nBased on wxWidgets 3.0.0\n\n".
      "This is a minimal wxPHP sample!",
      "About box...",
      wxICON_INFORMATION
    );

# Show the dialog box we create above.

    $dlg->ShowModal();
  }

# Add a constructor function. This function is run when we create our
# application window by creating a new object from this class.

  function __construct()
  {

# This calls the constructor function from the wxFrame class that
# we have extended, creating a frame with the title
# "Minimal wxPHP App" in the default position on screen, with
# the initial size of 350 x 260 pixels. Note that this frame is
# not visible by default, it's just created in memory at the
# moment. This means that we can add things to it and fully
# prepare it before we show it to the user, rather than the
# user seeing a blank window that then suddenly fills with
# buttons etc.

    parent::__construct(null, null, "Minimal wxPHP App",
    wxDefaultPosition, new wxSize(350, 260));

# We're going to add menus to our window with various options,
# which means first adding a menu bar into which we put the menus.

    $mb = new wxMenuBar();

# Now we add the menus. First a "File" menu with a "Quit" option

    $mn = new wxMenu();
    $mn->Append(2, "E&xit", "Quit this program");
    $mb->Append($mn, "&File");

# And now a "Help" menu with an "About" option.

    $mn = new wxMenu();
    $mn->AppendCheckItem(4, "&About...", "Show about dialog");
    $mb->Append($mn, "&Help");
```

```
# Note the menu and options above all have "&"" symbols in. This
# comes before the letter that should be used for keyboard
# shortcuts. Using a widget toolkit like this means that you don't
# have to write your own code for managing things like keyboard
# shortcuts, saving you time and effort and creating a consistent
# experience for your users.

# Finally add the menu bar to the frame.

    $this->SetMenuBar($mb);

# Let's add a source-code editing box to the frame, which is
# another one of the available widgets in the toolkit and has
# functionality like syntax highlighting, smart indentation etc.

    $scite = new wxStyledTextCtrl($this);

# The final widget we're going to add is a status bar at the
# bottom of the window.

    $sbar = $this->CreateStatusBar(2);
    $sbar->SetStatusText("Welcome to wxPHP...");

# At the start of this class we defined a couple of functions, one
# to show an about box, and one to quit the app. On their own
# they won't do anything; we need to connect them to the menu
# options we created earlier. More specifically, to the
# "wxEVT_COMMAND_MENU_SELECTED" event, which is called when the
# user selects something from the menu.

    $this->Connect(2, wxEVT_COMMAND_MENU_SELECTED, array($this,"onQuit"));

    $this->Connect(4, wxEVT_COMMAND_MENU_SELECTED, array($this,"onAbout"));

  }
}

# We've now designed our frame and populated it with widgets and functions
# but at this stage in the code it doesn't yet exist. We need to create
# a new object using our class, which will bring it to life and call
# the constructor function above.

$mf = new mainFrame();

# The frame now exists, it is populated with widgets, and the functions
# are all hooked up to the events. However, it is hidden, so we need
# to make it visible.

$mf->Show();
```

```
# At this point, we need to let wxWidgets take over and run the show.
# Calling wxEntry lets wxWidgets manage the application, wait for and
# react to events, and call the functions that we've previously specified.
# As you can see, we need to have specified all of our application's code
# before we get to this point.

wxEntry();

# If we reach this point, it means that our application has quit (either
# the user has closed it or something in our code has closed it), and
# we can either do any tidy-up necessary or just quit.
```

With wxPHP installed, the preceding code can be saved as myapp.php, for example, and executed in the same manner as any other PHP CLI script (for example, by calling php myapp.php).

As you can see, one of the main differences from procedural web scripts is that we generally don't execute code as we go along. Everything is defined up front, usually in classes, and executed as needed in reaction to user input. This is why object-oriented code is particularly suited to GUI and event-based programming, as it provides a model that maps more naturally to code that is usually executed "out of sequence," and the visual metaphor of windows and widgets relate naturally to the programming metaphor of classes and objects.

The preceding example is simple and not particularly useful. To see an example of a full, useful application written with wxPHP, have a look at the Phar GUI project listed in the next Toolbox. This is an open source Phar file explorer (see Chapter 10 for information about Phar files) written by the wxPHP project maintainer. It demonstrates the anatomy of a larger application and also demonstrates the use of the wxFormBuilder application for designing the graphical interface.

Toolbox	wxPHP
RAD-type toolkit for wxWidgets	
Main web site	www.wxphp.org
Main documentation and installation info	www.wxphp.org/docs and https://github.com/wxphp/wxphp#table-of-contents
Interface design tool	https://github.com/wxFormBuilder/wxFormBuilder
Version built for Raspian (Raspberry Pi)	www.wxphp.org/news/raspberry-pi-raspbian-binary-build
Phar GUI tool	https://github.com/jgmdev/phar-gui

PHP-GTK

PHP-GTK is an official PHP extension that provides direct bindings to the GTK+ widget toolkit from PHP. The first version was released in 2001, and the project has enjoyed some success. However, activity on the project has waned in recent years, and activity came to an almost complete lull between 2010 and 2015. In 2015, activity picked up and new beta versions were released, although at the time of writing nothing has happened with the project in 2016. That said, the stable releases of code are mature and reasonably complete and stable, and it is a relatively easy toolkit to start with. There is a reasonably large tooling environment for GTK+ in general, such as the Glade interface layout tool.

Advantages of PHP-GTK include the following:

- Provides direct binding to the GTK+ toolkit

- Fast and complete control over the toolkit elements

- Officially supported PHP project

- Availability of tools such as Glade for help with interface design and layout

- Cross-platform

- PHP compilers such as PriadoBlender, Roadsend PHP, and bcompiler offer some support for PHP-GTK

- Various additional GTK components are available through the PHP Extension and Application Repository (PEAR)

Disadvantages include the following:

- Lack of activity on the project raises questions on its future direction (if any).

- GTK+ doesn't look native on all platforms; the look and feel of GTK+ apps is most at home on Linux-type OSs.

- GTK+ itself is less popular than it once was, although as a project it is still active and progressing.

Toolbox	PHP-GTK
Official PHP GUI toolkit	
Main web site	`http://gtk.php.net/`
Main documentation and installation info	`http://gtk.php.net/manual/en/html/index.html`
GitHub repository	`https://github.com/php/php-gtk-src`
Mailing list archives	`http://marc.info/?l=php-gtk-general`
Worldwide community site	`http://php-gtk.eu/`
Brazilian portal	`www.php-gtk.com.br`

Toolbox	Glade
GTK+ visual interface design tool that can be used with PHP-GTK	
Main web site	`http://glade.gnome.org/`
Main documentation and installation info	`https://wiki.gnome.org/action/show/Apps/Glade`
Glade and PHP-GTK tutorial	`http://gtk.php.net/manual/en/tutorials.helloglade.php`

Local Web Server and Browser

One general technique that has been employed with varying degrees of success when creating local PHP apps is to deploy the whole web stack locally on each PC. This means installing a copy of PHP and Apache (or Nginx, or similar) and accessing the PHP web pages over a local port (for example, http://127.0.0.1:80) in a web browser.

Advantages of this approach include the following:

- Reuse existing web code and web skills, mostly as is

- Cross-platform

The disadvantages are numerous, however:

- Heavy resource overhead for the web server.

- Non-native experience.

- Must be secured to stop external access.

- Web servers can be temperamental if not properly tuned to the system they are deployed on.

- Large maintenance overhead.

- Larger vector for security exploits.

- Performance hit of using the verbose HTTP for interaction between the UI and the back end.

- Cross-browser compatibility issues occur in the same way as on the Web, unless a particular browser is deployed or required.

In general, this is definitely one to avoid if at all possible, certainly for public distribution of software. It may be worth considering if you have existing web applications you need to deploy in short order on local machines that you have responsibility for and control over. If you are going to go down this route, it is worth considering deploying an existing stack "solution" that has already ironed out some of the issues involved in local deployment of web stacks. A handy list of LAMP-type stacks—Linux/Apache/MySQL/(PHP|Perl|Python) — can be found on Wikipedia, and likewise a comparison of WAMP (Windows/AMP) stacks can be found there too. Remember that while the solution is generally cross-platform, the setup and fine-tuning of the web stack can vary a lot across OSs, depending on exactly what you are trying to achieve and the complexity of your application.

Further Reading

- List of AMP-type stacks (including LAMP and WAMP) on Wikipedia

  - http://en.wikipedia.org/wiki/List_of_Apache%E2%80%93MySQL%E2%80%93P
    HP_packages

PHP's Built-in (Testing) Web Server

Since v5.4, PHP has come equipped with a built-in web server, primarily designed for testing purposes. It is intended to be used locally by single users rather than on the public Web, so it lacks the performance, security, and resource management controls of a full-fledged web server such as Apache or Nginx, and is not extensible by means of modules and the like. Nevertheless, a lightweight server like this makes more sense for local apps than the Apache-based solution described previously, where these extra features aren't generally required. That said, it still has a longer than desirable list of disadvantages.

Advantages of the built-in server include the following:

- Reuse existing web code and web skills, mostly as is
- Cross-platform
- No extra server to deploy beyond PHP itself

The following disadvantages remain:

- Non-native experience.
- Must be secured to stop external access.
- The PHP developers have explicitly stated that it was designed specifically for the testing/development environment.
- Performance hit of using the verbose HTTP for interaction between the UI and back end.
- Cross-browser compatibility issues occur in the same way as on the Web, unless a particular browser is deployed or required.
- Not all features of servers such as Apache are included, so some rewriting of the web app may be required if these are needed.

Toolbox	PHP built-in web server
PHP's own built-in test web server	
Main web site and documentation	`http://php.net/manual/en/features.commandline.webserver.php`
Installation info	Installed as part of standard PHP installation
"Taking Advantage of PHP's Built-in Server" by Vito Tardia	`www.sitepoint.com/taking-advantage-of-phps-built-in-server/`

WebSocket and Browser

A variation on the preceding web server/browser scenarios is using WebSocket, part of the evolving HTML5 specification designed to allow two-way communication and push-type data flows in the browser. LAMP-type stacks and the PHP built-in web server don't, by default, handle WebSocket connections. The specification is relatively new, and you'll need to deploy a dedicated WebSocket server or a PHP WebSocket server library (usually based on spawning PHP CLI processes to handle communications). Beyond those issues, the pros and cons are roughly the same as those discussed for traditional web server communications. Due to the "push" ability of sockets, communications may be quicker and less frequent.

Toolbox	Ratchet
Popular PHP WebSocket library that uses ReactPHP	
Main web site	`http://socketo.me/`
Installation info	`http://socketo.me/docs/install`
Main documentation	`http://socketo.me/docs`

Toolbox	whippy.php
A pure PHP WebSocket server	
Main web site	`https://github.com/rthrfrd/whippy.php`

Toolbox	Web Socket Service
A PHP package to handle WebSocket accesses using child processes	
Main web site	`www.phpclasses.org/package/7259-PHP-Handle-Web-socket-accesses-using-child-processes.html`

SiteFusion

SiteFusion is a GUI solution based on Mozilla XULRunner. *XULRunner* is the Mozilla technical platform on which applications such as Firefox and Thunderbird are currently built, and it is a general-purpose XUL/HTML/JavaScript runtime. Rather than providing a totally local solution, SiteFusion focuses on the client/server scenario. A local XULRunner application in installed on the client PCs, but the PHP application code lives on the server running under custom SiteFusion server software. It is possible to install the client and server on the same machine, but many of the cons listed previously in the "Local Web Server and Browser" section apply to this configuration. SiteFusion exposes XUL as the primary method of building the interface, which although similar to HTML still has a learning curve. HTML can, of course, be used because XUL has the browser element, but SiteFusion doesn't provide any abstraction of the HTML/DOM to assist working with the contents of the browser element. Some HTML tags can be used directly within XUL code (outside the browser element), but Mozilla advises against this for various reasons. SiteFusion's main target market (and the area in which it is definitely worth considering) is with client/server apps, where central control over the application is desired and it is deployed on a local network within one organization.

The advantages of SiteFusion are as follows:

- Native experience

- Cross-platform

- Designed for client/server applications

- Stable, mature project with ongoing development

Disadvantages include the following:

- Responsiveness can be subject to network delays.

- Not ideal for local-only installations.

- XUL is less common than HTML, so you have less documentation, support, toolkits, and so forth, although HTML components can be run in the browser element, and some JavaScript tools/components will operate in/on the XUL interface.

Comprehensive tutorials and documentation can be found on the SiteFusion web site.

Toolbox	SiteFusion
XUL-based client/server PHP GUI system	
Main web site	`http://sitefusion.org/`
Installation info	`http://sitefusion.org/10`
Main documentation	`http://sitefusion.org/tutorials`

WinBinder

WinBinder provides PHP direct bindings for the Windows API. Thus, it works only on Windows-based platforms (or under Windows compatibility layers such as Wine on Linux). The current status of the project is unknown, the web site is still functioning, and the files are available for download. However, the community forum has been closed down, the last version was released in 2010, there are no news posts, and the system appears to support only older Win32-style interfaces.

Toolbox	WinBinder
Windows API-based GUI toolkit	
Main web site	`http://winbinder.org/`
Main documentation and installation info	`http://winbinder.org/manual.php`

Adobe AIR

An alternative to a web browser for LAMP stack or PHP test server deployments, *Adobe AIR* lets you create local HTML/JavaScript applications that run using Adobe AIR (formerly Adobe Integrated Runtime). While Adobe envisions you creating your whole application in Flash, ActionScript, HTML, and JavaScript, and allows privileged access to the file system, offline storage, and more, you can easily hook up your "web" application to PHP scripts in the same way a browser would. In essence, the AIR app is your browser. This provides a better visual environment than a browser, but still has most of the same drawbacks as listed previously. Adobe has also recently withdrawn support for Linux, although it does now support mobile and e-reader platforms. In the latter case, you may not be able to run the PHP portion of your app locally.

Toolbox	Adobe AIR
Runtime supporting HTML and JavaScript apps that can replace a browser	
Main web site	`www.adobe.com/products/air.html`
Main documentation and installation info	`www.adobe.com/devnet/air/documentation.html`

NW.js

Similar in concept to Adobe AIR, *NW.js* (formerly node-webkit) allows you to create HTML and JavaScript apps with elements of the Chrome browser (namely, the scripting and rendering engines). You can use NW.js to create a custom browser for your local or remote PHP app. As an open project based on an actively developed browser, it may be a safer and more standard option than Adobe's offering.

Toolbox	NW.js
Runtime supporting HTML and JavaScript apps that can replace a browser	
Main web site	`http://nwjs.io/`
Main documentation and installation info	`https://github.com/nwjs/nw.js`

Electron

A newer alternative to NW.js, *Electron* (formerly Atom Shell) is the JavaScript app runtime developed by GitHub to power its Atom editor. Like NW.js, it uses parts of Chrome, but instead of the Node version of the JavaScript engine, it uses io.js, a fork of Node that is now more actively developed. Electron itself is newer and less mature than NW.js, but is rapidly closing the lead and is now more stable in some areas.

Toolbox	Electron
Runtime supporting HTML and JavaScript apps that can replace a browser	
Main web site	`http://electron.atom.io/`
Main documentation and installation info	`http://electron.atom.io/docs/`

PHP-Qt

PHP-Qt is an extension to provide PHP bindings for the popular cross-platform QT widget toolkit. This project last released code in 2007 and was abandoned in 2009. It is mentioned here only for completeness. The code is still available for download and may be of interest for someone attempting to develop a similar solution.

Toolbox	PHP-Qt
Defunct project to provide bindings for the QT toolkit.	
Information	`http://en.wikipedia.org/wiki/PHP-Qt`

PHP/TK

PHP/TK is a project last updated in 2004, proving bindings for the Tcl/Tk X-Windows interface toolkit. As with PHP-Qt, it is mentioned here only for completeness.

Toolbox	PHP/TK
Bindings for the TCL/TK toolkit	
Main web site	`http://php-tk.sourceforge.net/`

CHAPTER 6

System Software

In the previous chapter, you looked at user-facing software—software that the human user interacts with directly. In this chapter, you are going to look at what I call *system software*—software that does things (generally) without a human driving it.

To write system software, you typically need to create a *daemon*, which is a continuously running process. Once you've created the daemon, you need to implement its primary function. Some daemons work continuously (measuring, monitoring, communicating, and so on), whereas others wait and work in response to events (network connections, system changes, and user actions). You'll look at how to create a daemon in PHP and set it working continuously. You will then look at how to take that basic daemon and instead of working continuously, make it just spring into life to react to certain events that occur in your system.

In the user-facing software from the previous chapter, the software is typically used by one person or process at a time. System software, on the other hand, often serves many clients at the same time. A *client* in this context may be a network client (for example, a web browser for a web server), a user process (a GUI client accessing your API server), a file (a log file for a logging server), or something similar. While doing so, it needs to remain *responsive*—one client shouldn't have to wait while another client's request finishes. Think how backed up the Web would get if Apache could serve only one web page at a time! To manage concurrent tasks in PHP and maintain a responsive daemon, you can use task dispatch and management systems, which you will look at in the final part of this chapter.

Daemons in PHP

A *daemon* is a program that runs, usually continuously, as a background process. It often doesn't interact directly with users, but performs background tasks or responds to system events or calls from other software, network requests, or other machine-to-machine events. Examples of programs that run as daemons include Cron (which waits in the background and executes tasks based on the current time), and Apache (which sits and waits for calls from remote machines for web resources). Daemons usually can be characterized as follows:

- Run permanently (or for a long time, or until a predetermined event occurs),

- Start up at boot time

- Perform useful tasks

- Are owned by root or a (nonhuman) system user

© Rob Aley 2016
R. Aley, *PHP Beyond the Web*, DOI 10.1007/978-1-4842-2481-6_6

However, these criteria don't universally apply to all daemons. The only concrete thing daemons have in common is that they don't have a controlling terminal (tty), and thus are deemed to be running in the background. Without a tty, the software cannot get user input from the keyboard or display output back to the user via the terminal (though there are other ways to directly and indirectly interact with a user). Although consuming minimal resources was traditionally a key trait of background processes, that is not now commonly the case. Software "servers" such as database management systems and web servers run as background daemons but often consume large (or even all) of the system's resources and often have machines dedicated just to running them. So it may be best to think of daemons as any permanently running software that doesn't usually directly interact with the user.

Creating a Daemon

To create a daemon in PHP, you use the PHP process control extension, or PCNTL, which is available only on Unix/Linux-type systems. On Windows, you can use the win32service PECL extension to control Windows services (a.k.a. daemons), including turning your own PHP script into a service. This extension is only in beta and documentation is sparse, so we don't cover it here.

Toolbox	win32service extension
Beta extension that allows you to create and control Windows services	
Main web site	`http://pecl.php.net/package/win32service`
Main documentation and installation info	`http://php.net/manual/en/book.win32service.php`
Example of a PHP script as a service	`http://php.net/manual/en/win32service.examples.php`

Most precompiled versions of PHP include the PCNTL extension, but if not, you will need to recompile PHP by using the `--enable-pcntl` option, or install the extension by using your package manager. See Appendix A for details.

The outline process for creating a daemon is as follows:

1. Run a process (PHP script). We call this the *parent process*.

2. From the parent, fork (copy) a child process.

3. The parent process then exits. The child process is now parentless.

4. init adopts the parentless child process. init is the original process started by the kernel when it boots and is the ancestor of all processes.

5. Dissociate (detach the child) from the terminal you started the parent in. This is so that

    • None of your output appears in the terminal

    • Killing the terminal won't kill your child process

    • The process is truly running in the background

6. To dissociate (detach), you need to do the following:

    • Move the child process into its own POSIX process session.

    • Fork it once again (into the grandchild process) and kill the child process.

    • Close any file descriptors such as STDIN that may tie it to the terminal.

   Once all this is done, you will be returned to the command prompt in the terminal (assuming that's where you started your original parent process from), and your (grandchild) daemon will be running on its own. You will be able to interact only indirectly with your daemon from now on.

   Finally, assuming that the daemon is to run continuously (or for a set period of time) rather than just completing a task and exiting, the process will need to enter a loop where it will continuously cycle and, for instance, await events or perform continuous tasks. It's probably also wise to give it the ability to exit upon demand.

   This may sound like quite a long and involved process, but it is fairly straightforward in PHP. The following script follows this process and outlines the basics:

```php
<?php

# We start by forking this script, which creates the child process.

$pid = pcntl_fork();

# The child process will start running from here and will be a copy of the
# parent process, which includes all opened resources, variable values, and
# so on, with the sole exception of the $pid variable above, which is not
# set for the child. The parent process will keep running from here as
# well, with the process ID of the child process assigned to $pid.

# If for some reason a child process could not be forked, for example,
# the system is low on memory, $pid will be set to -1.

if ($pid == -1) { exit("Could not fork the child process"); };

# If $pid is set to a process ID, then we must be the parent, and
# should exit.

if ($pid) { exit(0); };

# As the parent has exited above, the following code is now executed
# solely by the child process.

# We detach from the TTY (terminal) by becoming the "session leader"
# (instead of the TTY being leader. This starts a new POSIX session) ...

if ( posix_setsid()  === -1 ) {
  exit("Could not become the session leader");
};

# ... and then by forking again, to create a grandchild process

$pid = pcntl_fork();

if ($pid == -1) { exit("Could not fork child process into grandchild"); };

# Exit the child process, leaving only the grandchild beyond this point.

if ($pid) { exit(0); };
```

```
# Now to finally dissociate from the TTY and run in the background, we
# need to close our input and output streams to it. These are
# automatically defined and opened in the CLI SAPI, so will always need to
# be closed.

if (!fclose(STDIN)) { exit('Could not close STDIN'); };
if (!fclose(STDERR)) { exit('Could not close STDERR'); };
if (!fclose(STDOUT)) { exit('Could not close STDOUT'); };

# STDOUT is now closed; if you echo or print anything or interpolate HTML
# after this point, your script would crash. Likewise, any error messages
# would have nowhere to go, and any inadvertent attempts to read input
# would end badly. So instead we will re-create these three streams, but
# with sensible destinations. When we fclose the standard streams, and
# because you cannot redefine a constant, PHP simply assigns the standard
# streams to the next three new file descriptors opened (whatever they
# are called and whereever they point to). Thus the following also acts
# to protect any other streams you may open from "pollution" caused by
# accidental writes to those standard streams.

$STDIN = fopen('/dev/null', 'r');
$STDOUT = fopen('/dev/null', 'w');
$STDERR = fopen('/var/log/our_error.log', 'wb');

# We are now a free-floating daemon, fully detached from our TTY!

# Now we go into our main loop and do something useful.

# We set a variable that will allow us to escape from the loop if we
# want to shut down our daemon.

$stayInLoop = true;

while ($stayInLoop) {

    # do useful stuff here, like listening for connections,
    # monitoring things, or whatever else your daemon does.

    # When it's time to exit, set $stayInLoop = false at some point in the
    # loop, and this loop will be the last. If you need to exit before the
    # loop finishes, you will need to call break and do any necessary
    # tidying up. Here, we will end if it's a Tuesday, looping only once.

    if (date('l') == 'Tuesday') { $stayInLoop = false; };

    # For this example, we're going to execute a cli program called
    # notify-send to periodically pop up a notification to say hello,
    # which we looked at in Chapter 4.

    `notify-send 'Hello, The daemon is alive!'`;
```

```
# The following line adds a "sleep" to each cycle of the loop. If we
# didn't do this, our daemon would (try to) consume 100% of the CPU
# time as it constantly cycles and evaluates the conditions for
# looping. You can adjust the time it sleeps for, depending on the
# "responsiveness" required of your daemon. Giving it a break for even
# a few 100 or 1000 milliseconds (using usleep) helps to maintain
# overall system responsiveness.

    sleep(15); # Loop every 15 seconds
};

# We've exited our loop, so do any cleanup required here

`notify-send 'The Daemon is now finished. Bye Bye.!'`;

# And then exit

exit(0);
```

Although this code doesn't do anything particularly useful, it provides an outline of the basic steps involved in creating a PHP daemon and shows how simple it can be. You can combine it with the other techniques outlined in this book to create some useful systems and networking tools that run permanently in the background.

You need to keep several important issues in mind when writing daemons in PHP, to ensure that they keep running as expected.

First, when you fork a process as we have done to create a child process, the child is an almost exact copy of the parent, including the state of variables and resources. This means that if you do anything in the parent script before forking, it will be replicated in the state of the child. A common gotcha, particularly if forking multiple daemons from the same script, is setting up database connections in the parent before forking. The children will then share the same resource identifier as the parent and the other children (that is, they share exactly the same connection), and as soon as one of them closes the connection (for example, by exiting), the database will become unavailable to all of the others. On the other hand, this doesn't apply to, say, variables. If you set the variable $foo = 6; in your parent, when each child starts, $foo == 6 will be true, but if you alter it in one child, it will not alter in the others, as they are separate variables (just set to the same value at the start). Technically, the resource identifiers in the database example are also separate identifiers in each child; they just happen to point to exactly the same external database connection.

Second, resource usage and garbage collection are important to handle correctly for very long-running scripts, such as daemons. PHP has traditionally had a "designed to die" model; for instance, it wasn't until recently that garbage collection was turned on by default. In web scripts, you usually don't have to worry too much about resource usage, because short-running scripts typically don't use much, and PHP will clean up after you when your script exits. In long-running scripts, PHP's garbage collection can do only so much (and may do it at inconvenient times), so you will need to manage your resources carefully. This is particularly pertinent if you repeatedly create new variables, objects, resource handlers, and so on, or rely on high responsiveness from your script. See Chapter 9 for a detailed look at performance, garbage collection, measuring/minimizing resource usage, and generally keeping scripts up and running.

Finally, some platforms have standard practices for daemons, which help everything to get along smoothly. You may wish to consider those applicable to your platform. These can include things such as setting your working directory to / (for example, chdir /), and using init scripts to start and stop your daemon. These vary from platform to platform and are not PHP specific, so are beyond the scope of this book.

Further Reading

- "Getting into Multiprocessing," a discussion of forking

  - www.hackingwithphp.com/16/1/3

Network Daemons Using libevent

In the previous section, you used a fairly basic while(1) { } event loop to keep your daemon running and responding to events or doing useful work. The advantage of that approach is that it is very simple for basic needs and is implemented natively in PHP with no external dependencies. The downside, however, is that it leaves you to implement all the details, and the complexity increases as your project grows. One popular alternative to consider is libevent, a library that provides a framework for dealing with event-based programming. This library can be accessed in PHP though two PECL modules:

- *pecl-libevent*: This is an older module, and is fairly simple and straightforward to use. However, it doesn't support libevent2 (only 1.*x* versions, 1.4.0 or above), and thus has fewer features

- *pecl-event*: This is a complete rewrite of the previous PECL module of the same name, abandoned in 2004. It is currently actively developed and supports libevent2. This has more options, including specific classes tailored for HTTP, DNS, SSL, and other types of event connections. Pecl-event is also cross-platform, and so can be used on Windows systems as well. For these reasons, this is the module we will use in the following examples.

Toolbox	pecl-event
The libevent extension	
Web site and installation	https://pecl.php.net/package/event

Libevent describes itself as "a library that provides a mechanism to execute a callback function when a specific event occurs on a file descriptor or after a time-out has been reached." In layman's terms, this means that libevent will execute a function of your choice either at predetermined time intervals or when a particular file descriptor event occurs. *File descriptors* in PHP cover not just events occurring on actual files, but anything that can be treated as a file or stream. This includes network sockets and system streams such as STDIN. In fact, due to a problem with epoll (a Linux kernel event notification system, used by libevent) compatibility, libevent typically cannot be used for file events (detecting file accesses and modifications, and so forth) on many platforms. Because of this, we will additionally look at inotify in the next section for use with file events. Indeed, you should consider libevent for only network/stream type events, which is where it really shines.

Libevent also offers event buffering, so in demanding environments it will queue events for you to process at your leisure, and you won't risk missing something because your script was off doing something else. This is particularly important in a nonmultitasking environment like PHP. Note that libevent deals only with responding to events, not creating a daemon in the first place, so you will still need to use code from the previous section to turn your script into a daemon before using Libevent to do the work. Alternatively, it will happily run in nondaemonized CLI scripts as well.

The following example shows how to use the pecl-event module to call libevent to act as a simple HTTP server. For brevity, the following example runs as a standard CLI process. You can daemonize it by using the techniques discussed in the previous section if you need to.

```php
<?php

# Before we start doing any actual work, we first define a series of
# functions that will provide responses to our "events"; in this case
# http requests. The real magic of libevent occurs at the end of this
# script.

function techInfo($req) {

# This is our first response function. The object $req passed in is
# the current http request/connection.

# First we will set a "Content-Type" output header to tell the web
# browser to expect plain text rather than HTML. If we were outputting
# HTML, we would still need to send a header, but the event library
# does this for us if we don't add one ourselves.

  $req->addHeader ( 'Content-Type' , "text/plain; charset=ISO-8859-1",
    EventHttpRequest::OUTPUT_HEADER );

# Next we'll gather some information about the request, and format
# it into a string to send back to the web browser.

  $replyText .= 'Command : ' . $req->getCommand() . "\n";

  $replyText .= 'Host : ' . $req->getHost() . "\n";

  $replyText .= 'Input Headers : ' .
          var_export($req->getInputHeaders(),true) . "\n";

  $replyText .= 'Output Headers : ' .
    var_export($req->getOutputHeaders(),true) . "\n";

  $replyText .= 'URI : ' . $req->getUri() . "\n";

# To send a reply back, we create an "EventBuffer" containing the
# reply contents, in our case, the $replyText above.

  $reply = new EventBuffer;

  $reply->add($replyText);

# Finally, we send our EventBuffer to the browser, with an HTTP
# status of 200-OK to confirm everything happened correctly.

  $req->sendReply(200, "OK", $reply);

};
```

```php
function closeServer($req) {

# Our next function allows the visitor to shut down the server by
# simply visiting a URL. We'll send them a message before we shut down
# to let them know.

  $reply = new EventBuffer;

  $reply->add("Ok 1337 haxor, you've killed the server...");

  $req->sendReply(200, 'OK', $reply);

# We then call the exit method of the event base, to exit the event
# loop, which we'll look at toward the end of the program.

  global $base;

  $base->exit();

};

function notFound($req) {

# This function handles the case where we can't find a resource.
  $req->sendError(404, 'Does not appear to be here. Sorry.');

};

function cat($req) {

# This function is one of the most important on the internet. It
# returns a picture of a cat. You will need a cat picture named
# cat.jpg in the same directory for this to work, but that shouldn't
# be too difficult to arrange...

# As we're returning a binary image file, we need to set the
# appropriate mime-type output header.

  $req->addHeader ( 'Content-Type' , "image/jpeg" ,
    EventHttpRequest::OUTPUT_HEADER );

# Get the contents of the image file ....

  $cat = file_get_contents('cat.jpg');

  # and add them to a new EventBuffer ...

  $reply = new EventBuffer;

  $reply->add($cat);
```

```
# Finally, deliver the cat to an appreciative audience ....

  $req->sendReply(200, "OK", $reply);

};

function genericHandler($req) {

# This function will handle any requests that the previous functions
# haven't. We'll use the opportunity to serve up an HTML page with a
# title and a picture of a cat. The <img> tag will cause the browser
# to make a second call, which will be routed to the cat() function
# above to deliver the image file.

  $replyText = '<html><head><title>'.$req->getUri().'</title></head>';
  $replyText .= '<body><h1>Picture of cat</h1><br>';
  $replyText .= '<img src="/images/cat.jpg">';
  $replyText .= '</body></html>';

  $reply = new EventBuffer;

  $reply->add($replyText);

  $req->sendReply(200, "OK", $reply);

};

# Now we've defined all of our functions for delivering content, we need
# to actually set up our server.

# First we create an "EventBase," which is libevent's vehicle for holding
# and polling a set of events.

$base = new EventBase();

# Then we add an EventHttp object to the base, which is the Event
# extension's helper for HTTP connections/events.

$http = new EventHttp($base);

# We'll choose to respond to just GET and POST HTTP requests.

$http->setAllowedMethods(
  EventHttpRequest::CMD_GET | EventHttpRequest::CMD_POST);

# Next we'll tie the functions we created above to specific URIs using
# function callbacks.

$http->setCallback("/info", "techInfo");
$http->setCallback("/close", "closeServer");
$http->setCallback("/notfound", "notFound");
$http->setCallback("/images/cat.jpg", "cat");
```

```
# Finally, we'll add a default function callback to handle all other URIs.
# You could, in fact, just specify this default handler and not those
# above, and then handle URIs as you wish from inside this function using
# it as a router function.

$http->setDefaultCallback("genericHandler");

# We'll bind our script to an address and port to enable it to listen for
# connections.

$http->bind("0.0.0.0", 12345);

# Then we start our event loop by using the loop() function of our base. Our
# script will remain in this loop indefinitely, servicing http requests
# with the functions above, until we exit it by killing the script or,
# more ideally, calling $base->exit() as we do in the closeServer()
# function above.

$base->loop();
```

To try out this script, place one of your many cat pictures in the same directory, calling it cat.jpg, and then run the script. Open a web browser and navigate to http://localhost:12345, whereupon you should be greeted by a cat. To get some information about your connection, go to http://localhost:12345/info. To shut down the server, go to http://localhost:12345/close.

This is a fairly simple example, but it demonstrates the basic structure of an event-driven program. The Event library (via libevent) can respond to a wide variety of event types, and helpers for a number of network-style responders are included.

A listing of other daemon/event tools, frameworks and information is presented next.

Toolbox	PHP Simple Daemon
A stable, production-ready PHP daemon library	
Main web site	https://github.com/shaneharter/PHP-Daemon
Main documentation and installation info	https://github.com/shaneharter/PHP-Daemon#php-simple-daemon

Toolbox	Kellner framework
Asynchronous, scalable I/O framework for PHP based on libevent	
Main web site	https://github.com/fhoenig/Kellner
Main documentation and installation info	https://github.com/fhoenig/Kellner#readme

Toolbox	Nanoserv
Network-oriented server daemon framework for PHP	
Main web site	http://nanoserv.si.kz/
Main documentation	http://nanoserv.si.kz/doc/

Toolbox	phpDaemon
Asynchronous server-side PHP framework for web and network applications using libevent2	
Main web site	`http://daemon.io/`
Main documentation and installation info	None, see example code at `http://daemon.io/#outofbox`

Further Reading

- Socket programming tutorials, useful for adding socket-based network capabilities to your daemons

  - `http://christophh.net/2012/07/24/php-socket-programming/`

  - `www.binarytides.com/php-socket-programming-tutorial/`

  - `www.adayinthelifeof.nl/2010/07/30/creating-a-traceroute-program-in-php/`

- Reddit thread linking to many network utilities written in PHP

  - `www.reddit.com/r/PHP/comments/s9t3k/im_trying_to_find_really_unique_mindboggling_php/`

File Monitoring Daemons Using inotify

Daemons that respond to events in the file system are often useful. Example uses include the following:

- *File conversion daemons*: The daemon monitors a particular folder. When a file of a specified type is added to that folder, the daemon converts it into another format automatically.

- *File sync daemons*: The daemon watches one or more folders, and automatically syncs any changes with an external storage service or device.

- *Change notification daemons*: Want to know when someone else updates your important files? Get a daemon to watch them and report back to you!

- *File search services*: A daemon watches the file system and indexes files as they are created or modified, for rapid searching later.

And of course, there are many more uses for daemons that can watch for file and directory events. As noted previously, libevent can be used to monitor individual files for changes, though this doesn't work on all platforms and monitoring directories is more complicated.

Step forward inotify. Inotify provides a simple way to monitor a file or directory (or entire file system if you want). Available in Linux-type systems, it talks directly to the kernel to get file-system events as they happen, and buffers them for your script to deal with.

Inotify can be accessed in two ways from your PHP script. The first is by using the inotify PECL extension to directly interact with it. The second way is to call one of the `inotify-tools` command-line programs from your script. By default, the inotify extension allows you to monitor either one file or one directory under one watch. So, if you want to recursively watch all of the subdirectories of a given directory, you need to traverse the directory tree and set up watches for each directory (as well as watching for the creation of new directories and setting up a watch for each of those as well). If you are interested in monitoring only a couple of files or a couple of directories, then using the PECL extension is a straightforward way to do this while staying within PHP. On the other hand, if you want to recursively watch one or more directories and their subdirectories (or an entire file system), then the command-line tool inotifywait is usually easier to use, as it will automatically recursively set up the watches for you.

Using the inotify PECL Extension

The following script is an example of using the PECL extension, as a daemon, to monitor the current directory for any file access or modify events, and to pop up a notification bubble:

```php
<?php

# Turn this script into a daemon (see the start of this chapter for info)

$pid = pcntl_fork();

if ($pid == -1) { exit("Could not fork the child process"); };

if ($pid) { exit(0); };

if ( posix_setsid()  === -1 ) {
    exit("Could not become the session leader");
};

$pid = pcntl_fork();

if ($pid == -1) { exit("Could not fork child process into grandchild"); };

if ($pid) { exit(0); };

if (!fclose(STDIN)) { exit('Could not close STDIN'); };
if (!fclose(STDERR)) { exit('Could not close STDERR'); };
if (!fclose(STDOUT)) { exit('Could not close STDOUT'); };

$STDIN = fopen('/dev/null', 'r');
$STDOUT = fopen('/dev/null', 'w');
$STDERR = fopen('/var/log/our_error.log', 'wb');

$stayInLoop = true;

# Let the user know we are now up and running

`notify-send -i face-glasses 'File monitoring daemon started'`;

# We create an inotify instance to use

$inotify = inotify_init();
```

```
# We then add one or more "watches" to the instance. Each watch gives
# inotify a file or directory to monitor, and tells it which events to
# watch for. In this case, we want to watch the directory the script is in
# (which PHP provides in the magic constant __DIR__ ), and we want to look
# for file accesses (IN_ACCESS) or (|) file modifications (IN_MODIFY).
# This is a "bit mask" of events, which will discuss later.

$watch = inotify_add_watch($inotify, __DIR__, IN_ACCESS | IN_MODIFY);

# Once our watch is set up, it will keep running, so we can enter our
# usual program loop and wait for inotify to tell us when an event occurs

while ($stayInLoop) {

# We now call inotify_read to get an array of file events that our
# watch has spotted. inotify_read blocks execution until an
# event occurs, so if nothing is happening, our script will sit and
# wait at this point until it does.

  $events = inotify_read($inotify);

# inotify_read returns an array of events. Often this may just be an
# array with one event on a nonbusy file/directory. However, multiple
# events may occur at the same time, and inotify queues events while
# your program is doing other things (like processing previous events)
# so you should always be prepared to handle multiple events. So we
# loop through the $events array...

  foreach ($events as $event) {

# The "mask" value tells us which type of event (or events)
# have occurred

    $type = $event["mask"];

# "name" gives us the file or directory name of the event

    $filename = $event["name"];
# We'll compose a human-readable string to present to the user

    switch ($type) {

      case IN_ACCESS :
        $what = "accessed";
        break;

      case IN_MODIFY :
        $what = "modified";
        break;
```

```
        case (INACCESS+IN_MODIFY) :
          $what = "accessed and modfied";

    };

# We'll now pop up a notification bubble with the event details

    `notify-send -i document '$filename was $what'`;

# Finally, if a file called bye.txt was accessed or modified,
# we'll exit our loop and exit the daemon.

    if ($filename == 'bye.txt') { $stayInLoop = false; };
  };

};

`notify-send -i face-raspberry 'File monitoring daemon stopped'`;

exit(0);
```

In this script, we tell inotify the types of events we are interested in by creating a *bit mask*. You can think of bit masks in the following (simplified) way:

- Each possible event type is represented by a constant (for example, IN_ACCESS or IN_MODIFY).

- Each constant is an integer (for example, echo IN_ACCESS; prints 1, echo IN_MODIFY; prints 2).

- Each integer is chosen so that adding any combination of these integers together always gives a unique number. (Technically, the numbers are powers of 2.)

- echo IN_ACCESS+IN_MODIFY; prints 3. No other addition of any of the constants will give 3. So if in your event the mask value is 3, you know that both IN_ACCESS and IN_MODIFY occurred in that event.

Further Reading

- Full explanation of bit masks on Wikipedia

- http://en.wikipedia.org/wiki/Mask_%28computing%29

In the preceding example, you use inotify_read() to get details of file events that have occurred. inotify_read() is a blocking function causing your script to pause. If you want to occasionally check for events, but not cause your script to block if none have happened, you can treat the inotify instance as a stream (the inotify_init() function returns a standard file descriptor). In this way, you can, for instance, use stream_set_blocking() to make it a nonblocking stream.

Further Reading

- Example of accessing inotify as a stream, in the PHP manual

  - http://php.net/manual/en/function.inotify-init.php

Using the inotifywait Command

The second way to call inotify is by *shelling out* to the inotifywait shell command. The following example sets up a watch to look for any file modifications or deletions anywhere in the file system under the /home directory. For brevity, I've shown this as a simple CLI script. You can use the previously shown technique for turning it into a daemon as necessary. Ensure that the inotifywait command is installed first (sudo apt install inotify-tools).

```php
<?php

# Create the command-line string to execute inotifywait with the options
# we want. In this case, we use the following options :
#
#   --csv : Returns the output in easy-to-parse csv format
#   -q : Suppresses any messages and shows only the event output
#   -r : Run in recursive mode, so all subdirectories are included
#   -m : Run in "monitor" mode, which simply means it runs continuously
#   -e : Specifies which events to listen for (modify and delete)
#
# Finally, we give it the directory to watch (/home). This could be just
# '/' if you want to watch the whole file system.

$command = 'inotifywait --csv -q -r -m -e modify -e delete /home';

# Because we want to start displaying the events as they happen, rather
# than after the command finishes (as it won't finish), we can't use
# methods like backticks or shell_exec() to run the script. Instead we use
# popen() to treat it like a file stream.

$handle = popen($command, 'r');

# read each line of output as it occurs

while ($line = fgets($handle)) {

# The data is in CSV format (as we used --csv), so parse it into
# a PHP array

  $event = str_getcsv($line);

# Output details of the event to the shell

  echo 'A '.$event[1].' event occured in Directory '.$event[0];
  echo ' on file '.$event[2]."\n";

};
```

inotifywait automatically sets up watches on all subdirectories when you use the -r recursive option. However, on a large file system, this can take several seconds or more when it starts for the first time. See the man page for inotifywait for all the possible options. Read the next chapter for details on popen() and other ways to interact with shell commands from PHP.

Inotify Limits

Although inotify is a versatile tool, be aware of a couple of limits. First, as I've noted, setting up recursive watches can take some time, during which events will not be listened for. Second, the default limit for the number of *watches* (directories or subdirectories) is usually set to 8192. You will need to increase this in /proc/sys/fs/inotify/max_user_watches if your file system has more directories. Finally, although inotify buffers notifications for you while your script is busy, that buffer has a finite size. Thus, if the task that your script performs in response to events takes a long time (for example, file type conversion), you may wish to farm out that processing to external scripts to allow yours to get back to responding to events quicker. See the following section on task dispatch and management systems for ways to do this.

Task Dispatch and Management Systems

Earlier in this chapter, you looked at how to fork new processes, and in the next chapter you'll look at how to execute or call, and talk to, other external commands. These examples should give you some good ideas of how to create worker tasks to carry out processing in parallel with your main PHP scripts. In many cases, rolling your own task/worker dispatch and management scripts is a good idea, but there are also many times when it may be more prudent to use something already written by an expert. Luckily, in these cases, you can take advantage of any one of a number of excellent task dispatch and management systems that work with PHP. A few of the more common and useful systems are listed in this section, but first we'll look at one particular system—Gearman—which has fantastic PHP bindings and good community support, and is an ideal task system to cut your teeth on.

Gearman and PHP

The PHP manual describes Gearman (www.php.net/manual/en/intro.gearman.php) as follows:

> *Gearman is a generic application framework for farming out work to multiple machines or processes. It allows applications to complete tasks in parallel, to load balance processing, and to call functions between languages. The framework can be used in a variety of applications, from high-availability web sites to the transport of database replication events.*

In essence, Gearman is a middleman between your main scripts and your worker scripts. Your main scripts can fire off tasks to Gearman, and Gearman will allocate those tasks to workers when they become available. It will then monitor the workers and report their progress back to the main script along with the results of the task. You can have multiple Gearman servers for redundancy, and you can operate everything in a distributed manner across many machines. You simply tell your main scripts where your Gearman server(s) are, and start firing off tasks. You don't even have to wait for the results of the tasks if you don't want to, and you can register callback functions to handle results from multiple tasks as they come in. To configure the worker scripts, you tell them where the Gearman server(s) are and specify which tasks that particular script can handle, and add a little code to feed back progress during the task if you wish. You then fire up your worker scripts, and they sit and wait for tasks to come in.

To help you visualize the possibilities available with Gearman, Figure 6-1 shows a multimachine setup with redundant Gearman servers.

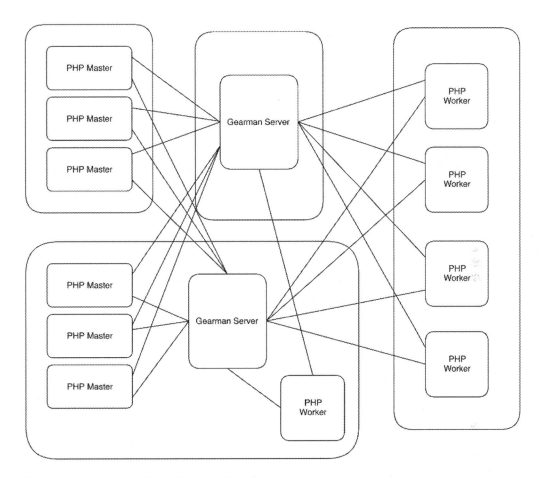

Figure 6-1. *Example with multiple machines/masters/clients/servers*

In this particular network, we have six PHP master scripts running on two machines. Each master is connected to two Gearman server instances, one running on its own machine and one on a shared machine. In turn, there are five PHP worker scripts, four running on their own machine and one on the shared machine. All of the worker scripts are also connected to both of the two Gearman server instances. In this setup, you can see that if one of the Gearman server instances is unavailable, the system would continue to run, because all components are connected to both server instances at the same time, and so can use either. Likewise, if one or more master or worker scripts are unavailable, work still happens as the Gearman server instances dish out the jobs to the remaining scripts. And the best thing of all is that Gearman takes care of this "fallback" system for you. You simply point your masters and workers at the Gearman servers, and Gearman deals with routing the jobs appropriately.

You can, of course, run it all on the same machine, and this is a common configuration. This makes it suitable for using Gearman to support parallel computations in PHP where there is no need for extra hardware but where PHP's single-threaded operation hampers full utilization of the machine.

Further Reading

- "Using Gearman from PHP" by Lorna Mitchell

  - www.lornajane.net/posts/2011/using-gearman-from-php

- "Queues Are Your Friend" (section in "5 Things You Should Check Now to Improve PHP Web Performance") by Gonzalo Ayuso, gives example PHP/Gearman code

  - http://php.dzone.com/articles/5-things-you-should-check-now

- "Introduction to Gearman—Multitasking in PHP" by Alireza Rahmani Khalili

  - www.sitepoint.com/introduction-gearman-multi-tasking-php/

- "Installing gearmand, libgearman, and pecl gearman extension for PHP from Source" by Hasin Hayder

  - http://hasin.me/2013/10/30/installing-gearmand-libgearman-and-pecl-gearman-from-source/

Other Task Dispatch Systems

A couple of other common task dispatch systems with PHP bindings are listed next. If none of them quite meet your needs, you can use the interprocess communication techniques described in the next chapter as the basis for creating your own. We will also look at simulating multithreading in PHP in Chapter 9.

Toolbox	Beanstalkd
A simple, fast task dispatch system	
Main web site	http://kr.github.com/beanstalkd/
Main documentation and installation info	https://github.com/kr/beanstalkd/wiki
PHP libraries	https://github.com/kr/beanstalkd/wiki/client-libraries

Toolbox	php-resque
A PHP task queue based on Redis. A port of the GitHub Ruby-based Resque.	
Main web site	https://github.com/chrisboulton/php-resque
CLI tool for managing php-resque workers	https://github.com/wa0x6e/Fresque

Further Reading

- "Offline Processing in PHP with Advanced Queuing" by Christopher Jones

  - https://blogs.oracle.com/opal/entry/offline_processing_in_php_with

■ ■ ■

## CHAPTER 7

Interacting with Other Software

Few pieces of software run in total isolation. Most talk to various other processes and programs on your system. This is particularly true on open source systems (where licensing is less of an issue), because there is often little point in reinventing the wheel when, with minimal effort, you can simply call upon other existing software and libraries to perform tasks that are already a "solved problem."

Although you may have come across some of these methods when programming for the Web, there is generally less call for interactions when your script will execute and be gone in the blink of an eye. Various methods are used for invoking and interacting with other software. The primary use for these methods is interacting with non-PHP software, but because these methods are language agnostic, they can, of course, be used for communication between two or more scripts written in PHP.

Starting External Processes from PHP, or Shelling Out

Before your script can start talking to another process, that other process has to start running. You can manually start another piece of software at the same time as your PHP script, but often it is useful for the PHP script itself to start the other software when it needs to. This is often referred to as *shelling out*.

Numerous functions are available in PHP to achieve this, each doing it in a slightly different way:

- `exec()`: Executes a program and sends the text output to the user.

- `passthru()`: Executes a program and sends the binary output to the user.

- `system()`: Executes a program and gathers the output for use by PHP.

- `shell_exec()`: Executes a command via a shell and gathers its output for use by PHP.

- Backtick operator (for example, `` `command` ``): identical to `shell_exec()`.

- `pcntl_exe()`: Executes a program in the current process space (that is, it stops the current PHP script and replaces it with the specified program).

- `popen()`: Executes a program and opens a file pointer (identical to the pointers returned by `fopen()`, for example) to read or write to the process via STDOUT or STDIN. Can only read or write, not both.

- `proc_open()`: Like `popen()`, but with more control. Allows both reading and writing at the same time. Not as simple to use as `popen()`.

Which method you choose depends on what you intend to do with the newly opened process and how you want to talk to it. If you're not sure from the preceding descriptions which function is appropriate for your use, the following "Further Reading" list gives some pointers, information, and examples of implementations that should give you some direction.

© Rob Aley 2016
R. Aley, *PHP Beyond the Web*, DOI 10.1007/978-1-4842-2481-6_7

Further Reading

- "Cookbook" recipes for using the previously listed functions

  - http://pleac.sourceforge.net/pleac_php/processmanagementetc.html

- "Proc_Open: Communicate with the Outside World," tutorial by Timothy Boronczyk

  - www.sitepoint.com/proc-open-communicate-with-the-outside-world/

- "Shelling Out Sucks" by Stefan Karpinski, an article on the downsides of calling external programs via an intermediate shell

  - http://julialang.org/blog/2012/03/shelling-out-sucks

When calling external scripts, remember that using untrusted user input in command names or options is a recipe for a bad security day! The escapeshellarg() function can protect you from some inadvertent mistakes, but won't stop you from executing "bad" functions or files.

Further Reading

- Sanitizing shell arguments by using escapeshellarg() in the PHP manual

  - www.php.net/escapeshellarg

Talking to Other Processes

Once you have other processes up and running, PHP supports various ways to talk to them, which you'll look at in this section. These methods mainly apply to processes that have been started up by other means, or which your script has started and disassociated itself from. If you've used popen() or proc_open() to run them, you can simply communicate via PHP streams as normal. You can still use the following methods as well, though, if you need additional channels of communication.

Semaphores

A basic form of interaction between programs is negotiation over shared resources. If you have a data source, peripheral, data set, or any other kind of resource that you want only one program to access at a time, you need some form of communication between the programs to decide who is using it and to work out when they have finished with it. Since the advent of System V, Unix has had the concept of *semaphores* to manage this process. PHP embodies their use in the sysvsem extension, which is usually already compiled into most PHP distributions on Unix and Linux systems. Semaphores are like a flag that gets passed around, and only the program holding the flag can access the resource. The following code shows an example of passing a semaphore. Open two shell windows and run the script in each one. You will see the scripts getting and releasing the semaphore, such that at any one time, only one script will have the semaphore.

```php
<?php

$process = getmypid();

$semaphore = sem_get('123456', 1, 0666, 1);

if (!$semaphore) { echo("Couldn't get semaphore\n"); exit;};
```

```
while (1) {

  sem_acquire($semaphore);

  echo ($process." has the semaphore\n");

  sleep(rand(0,5));

  if (!sem_release($semaphore)) {

    echo("Couldn't release semaphore\n");

    exit;

  };

  echo ($process." has released the semaphore\n");

};
```

First you get the pid (process ID) of your script to be sure you are running different processes. Next, you create a semaphore by using sem_get() and return an ID for that semaphore (you can run multiple semaphores for different reasons at the same time, so the ID is important). If another script has already created it, this will just return the ID. Note that all of your scripts/programs that want to share a particular semaphore must use the same parameters for the sem_get() function (or its equivalent in another language); otherwise, a new semaphore will be created. The first parameter for sem_get() is a unique integer key that identifies the semaphore (this is different from the ID returned by the sem_get() function, which is PHP's internal resource ID for the semaphore and will vary from script to script for the same semaphore). The second parameter is the number of unique users permitted to hold the semaphore at any one time. This allows you to, for instance, allow two (or more) people to "hold the flag" at the same time, which can be used to place an upper limit on the number of simultaneous users of a resource. The third parameter specifies the standard Unix permissions (as you would use with chmod, for instance), and the fourth parameter specifies whether to automatically release the semaphore if the request goes away.

Once you have your semaphore set up, you then enter a loop. Each time through the loop you try to get the flag with sem_aquire(). This is a blocking function, which means that your program will sit and wait until the semaphore is available and you can grab it. Once you have it, the program will continue. You sleep for a random time (in "real life" you would do something useful with the resource you are protecting with the semaphore), and then release it back again. At this point, the next waiting process will pounce in and "grab the flag," as you go back to the start of the loop and try to acquire it again.

It's important to note that semaphores work on the honor system. Every program is expected to implement and respect the semaphore. The system itself doesn't know about or enforce semaphores, so a rogue program can simply nip in and use the resource regardless of who is "holding the flag." Thus semaphores shouldn't be used for any systems that you don't absolutely control (or don't mind if unentitled software grabs your resource), and only where all programs want to share the resource. There is also little protection against deadlocks, whereby one program gets the semaphore and fails to release it due to an error with that program. The final parameter of the sem_get() function does allow for the automatic releasing of the semaphore if the request disappears (for example, if the process crashes or the semaphore is closed in the current script with sem_remove()), but this may not protect against the process simply hanging.

The sem_get() function requires a unique integer key to identify the semaphore, and this key (like a telephone number) must be known to all of the programs in advance. If you are having trouble deciding on a key or sharing it, take a look at the ftok() function, which generates a key based on the pathname to a known file and a project identifier.

Further Reading

- ftok() in the PHP manual

  - http://php.net/manual/en/function.ftok.php

When you have your semaphores running, you can check their status from the shell with the command ipcs -s, which will show details of all the semaphores on the system. While semaphores don't directly allow you to exchange data with other programs, they can be used to facilitate communication via other means, such as shared files or shared memory segments, which you'll look at next.

Further Reading

- "Semaphore Functions" section in the PHP manual

  - www.php.net/manual/en/ref.sem.php

- "What Is Wrong with PHP's Semaphore Extension" by Jonathon Hill

  - http://jonathonhill.net/2012-12-08/what-is-wrong-with-phps-semaphore-extension/

Shared Memory

Shared memory is a simple and widely supported method of passing data between two or more processes, and it really is as simple as it sounds. A process can create a segment of memory, with a key as a unique ID, assign standard Unix-type permissions to it, and then it and other processes can read, write, and delete data from that segment as necessary (and as permissions allow).

Shared memory is probably the fastest way of sharing information between two processes. There is no disk I/O or database access, for instance, to slow you down and no intermediate message broker to spend time processing and distributing the information. The downside is that you have to manage the whole process yourself, although this isn't as hard as it sounds.

Shared memory is supported in two extensions, the System V sysvshm extension (part of the semaphore extension, like sysvsem described in the previous section) and the more recent shmop extension. We will look at the latter, as it is based on the C shm API, which makes it easier to share data with non-PHP programs (unlike the former, which uses its own proprietary data format, making it hard to share with anything other than PHP). The shmop extension is also usually faster than sysvshm as it stores its data in a raw form. As with semaphores, this extension is not available on Windows.

Like files, shared memory can become corrupt if multiple processes try to write to it at the same time. In our next example, we don't need to worry about locking the shared memory segment, as only one process will be writing to it; we won't include any locking code for brevity and clarity. Where locking is an issue, you can use the semaphore method outlined in the previous section to ensure that only one process writes to the memory segment at a time. Using multiple memory segments at the same time by the same or different processes doesn't require locking, as long as only one process is writing to a specific segment at a given time.

It's time to look at an example of shared memory in action. The following are two scripts. The first script, generator.php, generates an array of three random numbers every second, encodes them as JSON, and puts them into a shared memory segment. The second script, display.php, retrieves that data and outputs it to the terminal. To try these, open two terminal windows and run one in each at the same time.

generator.php

```php
<?php

$segment = shmop_open('1234456', 'c', 0755, 1024);

for ($counter=0; $counter < 20; $counter++) {

$jsonArray = json_encode(

  array(rand(0,50000),
  rand(0,2000),
  rand(5000,100000))

);

$jsonArray = str_pad($jsonArray, 1024-strlen($jsonArray), ' ');

$dataSize = strlen($jsonArray);

$bytesWritten = shmop_write($segment, $jsonArray, 0);

if (!$bytesWritten) { echo("Error - couldn't write to memory\n"); };

if ($dataSize != $bytesWritten) {
  echo("Error - couldn't write all data to memory\n");
};

sleep(1);

};

shmop_delete($segment);

shmop_close($segment);
```

display.php

```php
<?php

$segment = shmop_open('1234456', 'c', 0755, 1024);

while (1) {

  sleep(1);

  $size = shmop_size($segment);
```

```
$jsonArray = shmop_read($segment, 0, $size);

echo("Fetched $size bytes of data at ".date("H:i:s").
". Our random numbers are :\n");

print_r(json_decode(trim($jsonArray)));

};
```

Let's look through `generator.php`. First you create a shared memory segment by using `shmop_open()`. This takes four parameters; the first is a unique integer key to identify this segment, and as with semaphores, it must be unique and shared with the other processes that are going to access your shared memory segment. (As noted in the preceding "Semaphores" section, you can use `ftok()` as one way of generating and sharing a unique ID.) The second parameter is the mode in which you'll open the segment. The options are as follows:

- `a`: Open for read-only access on existing segment

- `c`: Create a new segment, or open for read and write if it already exists

- `w`: Open for read and write access on existing segment

- `n`: Create a new segment, or fail if it already exists

Note that this read-only access applies only to the process you are in. Another process can open the segment for writing (if it has write permissions—as detailed later in this section).

The third parameter to `shmop_open()` specifies the permissions for the memory segment, in octal. These are the same as Unix file permissions (that you assign using `chmod`, for example). These apply only to segments that have not already been created and are ignored for existing segments. The last parameter is the size, in bytes, of the shared memory segment. You should ensure that the segment will be big enough for the data you want to put into it (otherwise, your data will be truncated when writing), but not larger than necessary (otherwise, you will waste memory that could be being used by other processes). Once created, `shmop_open()` returns an identifier that you can use to refer to this segment, which you place in `$segment`. Note that this is an internal PHP resource identifier, and is different from the unique key used as the first parameter for `shmop_open()`.

Once you have created your memory segment, you perform a loop 20 times and then mark the segment for deletion and close it. In the loop, you create an array of three random numbers and encode it into a JSON string called `$jsonArray`. You then pad this with spaces up to 1024 by using `str_pad()`. This padding is important, as a memory segment isn't like a variable in PHP; it has a fixed size. If you store a five-character string in the segment, for example, and then store a three-character string instead, you will find that when you try to read it, you will have the last two characters of your initial string on the end of your three-character one. Thus, if you are going to be repeatedly using the same segment, you need to find a way to clear any extra space in the segment that you aren't using at that moment, or find a way to pass the length of data that you have written to the other process so that it reads only the correct amount of data. One common way to do this is to write the length of your string to the memory first (always in, say, the first 4 bytes of memory) and then write the actual data. The receiving process reads the length data first and then reads only the required number of bytes from the remaining data in the segment. The other way, as we are doing here, is to always fill the segment completely. You do this by `str_pad()`ing your data with spaces up to 1,024 bytes, and then `trim()`ing off the spaces on the receiving end.

Once you've padded $jsonArray, you get its size (in this case, it should always be 1,024) and write it to the memory segment by using shmop_write(), which returns the number of bytes it has successfully written into $bytesWritten (hopefully, 1,024 if all went well). shmop_write() takes three parameters. The first is the $segment PHP resource identifier, the second is the string to write to memory, and the third is the offset. The offset specifies where in the memory segment you want to start writing the data. In our example, you want to start at the beginning, so you use 0. If you were using the first 4 bytes, say, to write the data size, then your second shmop_write() writing the actual data would start with an offset of 5.

After you've done the writing, you check to see that you managed to write (that $bytesWritten isn't -1) and that you managed to write all of the data (you didn't try to write more than 1,024 bytes in this case).

Once you've been through our loop 20 times (sleeping for a second each time to keep things readable in the output!), you mark the memory segment for deletion and close it. You'll come back to those last two lines in a moment.

Now let's look at our other script, display.php. You open the shared memory segment with shmop_open() in exactly the same way as our first script. Because you use the c mode, which creates the memory segment, it doesn't matter which of our scripts you open first. You could have used the a read-only mode if you knew that generator.php was running first (or were willing to wait for it).

After the segment is open, you continually loop (sleeping for a second each time as you know the generator.php script will update the segment only once a second), getting and displaying the contents of the memory segment.

To get the contents, you use shmop_read(). This takes three parameters: the first is the $segment PHP resource identifier, the second is the offset where you will start reading, and the third is the amount of data you want to read. In this case, you want the entire segment, so you start at the beginning (offset = 0) and read to the end (1,024 bytes along). If you want to read to the end of the segment but don't know its size, you can use shmop_size() to find it as in this example, although in this case it's superfluous, as you already know it will be 1,024.

Once you have your data, which should be the $jsonArray string padded with spaces, you trim() off the spaces and json_decode() the string back into an array that you print_r() out.

Now let's return to the last two lines of generator.php, calling shmop_delete() and shmop_close(). Shmop_delete() doesn't actually delete the memory segment; instead, it marks it for deletion. This means that no new processes can open the memory segment, but existing processes that have already opened it can continue to access it. It remains accessible until all of those existing processes close it (or exit), at which point it will be deleted.

You can see this deletion process in action by running these two scripts. generator.php exits after 20 seconds, and display.php keeps running forever (due to the while(1) loop). After generator.php exits, you will notice that display.php keeps outputting the same three random numbers each time. This is because although you've marked the memory segment for deletion in generator.php, display.php still has it open and so it can still read it (albeit getting the same value each time, as nothing is updating it). If you kill display.php and start it again (without starting generator.php), you will find that it now reads nothing, as the memory segment was deleted when the previous display.php process (the last one using it) exited.

The other peculiarity is that you call shmop_delete() *before* you call shmop_close(). If you close it first, PHP will not have the internal reference anymore and so won't know which memory segment to mark for deletion. Once you have called shmop_delete(), you can't do anything else within your script to the memory segment other than closing it. You must have appropriate permissions to be able to mark a segment for deletion. You should ensure that you mark your memory segments for deletion at some point before all of your processes are finished with it. Otherwise, you will end up with a *memory leak*—memory is allocated and thus can't be used by other programs, lowering the amount of available memory to the system as a whole.

Of course, the shmop functions deal only with transferring the data between processes. Understanding or parsing the data is left as an exercise for the programmer. If the application you are communicating with doesn't dictate the format (for instance, if you are developing the system yourself rather than trying to hook into an existing system), then you will need to decide on a suitable format. Although you used JSON to encode your array into a string in the preceding example, you could also use PHP's serialize() and unserialize() functions if you knew you would be sharing the data only with other PHP scripts. If you think, however, that your software may be interacting with programs written in another language in the future, sticking to language-independent encodings such as JSON or XML is a wiser choice.

Although it should be obvious, remember that any data in memory is volatile. It won't be there if your system crashes, if the memory segment is deleted (usually when one or more programs exit), or after a reboot. Write anything critical to disk as well.

Further Reading

- shmop "Shared Memory" section in the PHP manual

  - http://php.net/manual/en/book.shmop.php

- SimpleSHM, an abstraction layer for shmop to simplify getting and setting shared memory

  - https://github.com/klaussilveira/SimpleSHM

PHP Message Queues

Message queues provide an easy way for multiple processes to interact. At its simplest, one process adds messages to the queue, and another takes them off. The queue is usually maintained by an intermediate process or the OS itself. Queues make a programmer's life easier than, say, messaging using shared memory, because the programmer doesn't need to worry (too much) about timing and synchronization, and there is usually no need for locks. The sending process can fire off a message and forget about it (if it wants to), and the receiving process can sit around and wait for a message to arrive (or do other things and check back for the messages later). Numerous message queue APIs and extensions are available to PHP, and you will look at most of them later in this chapter. In this section, you'll learn about the sysvmsg message queue, which is part of the semaphore extension presented in the previous section. This is a basic but useful message queue system, and has the advantage that it is usually compiled into most PHP distributions (except Windows) and it doesn't require any third-party APIs, daemons, or libraries.

Let's jump right in with an example. You're going to modify our random-number generator scripts from the previous section to use a message queue. Our first script, generator2.php, is going to fire off 20 messages, each with three random numbers, in quick succession and then exit. Our second script, display2.php, will pull those messages out at its own pace (one per second) and display them.

generator2.php

```php
<?php

$queue = msg_get_queue('1234456', 0666);

for ($counter=0; $counter < 20; $counter++) {

  $phpArray = array(rand(0,50000), rand(0,2000), rand(5000,100000));
```

```php
  if (!msg_send($queue, 3, $phpArray, true, true, $errorCode)) {

    echo("Error - couldn't send message - code $errorCode\n");

  };

};
```

display2.php

```php
<?php

$queue = msg_get_queue('1234456', 0666);

while (1) {

  sleep(1);

  if (!msg_receive($queue, -4, $realType, 1024, $phpArray, true,
0, $errorCode)) {
    echo("Error - Couldn't receive message - code $errorCode\n");
  };

  echo("Fetched message at ".date("H:i:s").". Random numbers are :\n");

  print_r($phpArray);

};
```

If you run generator2.php first, you will see it complete and exit almost straightaway. You can then wait as long as you like before running display2.php, hours or days even, as the messages will happily sit there in the queue (unless you turn off your computer). When you do run it, you will see the random numbers appearing, one set every second. If you use Ctrl+C to kill the script before it has read all 20 messages, you can simply start it again and it will pick up where it left off, until all 20 have been displayed. At that point, it will sit and wait for any new messages to appear in the queue. If you run generator2.php again in another terminal while display2.php is sitting and waiting, you will see display2.php spring into life again almost immediately and start displaying the new set of numbers you just generated.

So let's look at how these scripts work. They should seem similar to, but simpler than, the earlier shared memory examples. In each script, you first open the message queue with the msg_get_queue() function. This either creates, or, if it already exists, opens the message queue. You supply the function with a unique integer key as the first parameter to indicate which queue you want to use. (See the notes on the ftok() function in the preceding "Semaphores" section regarding generating unique keys.) The second parameter represents standard Unix permissions for the queue. The function returns a unique ID for $queue that you use with the msg_send() and msg_receive() functions. This ID is an internal PHP resource ID and is different from the queue key specified earlier.

In `generator2.php` you then generate a PHP array of random numbers as before, and you put this array into the queue with the `msg_send()` function. You do this 20 times in quick succession and then exit. This function takes several parameters:

- `queue`: This is the $queue resource identifier.

- `msgtype`: This is an arbitrary integer that specifies the type of message. You can choose to assign your messages an integer corresponding to any kind of criteria you want, and then when receiving messages, you can filter by this type field. For instance, you can choose to receive the next message of type 3, or the next message of any type. This can be useful, for instance, to assign a priority to messages and then use that to deal with them in order of priority at the receiving end.

- `message`: This is the actual message to send. This should be a string, *unless* you have the next parameter (`serialize`) set to `true`, in which case you can pass a variable or object of any type that PHP can serialize into a string. In our example, for instance, you pass a PHP array directly to the `msg_send()` function without calling any kind of encoding function on it first (for example, `json_encode()` or `serialize()`), because you have the next parameter set to `true`.

- `serialize`: If this is set to `true`, this will automatically call the session module serialization mechanism to serialize the message into a string. This is usually the `serialize()` function (unless you have chosen to use the WDDX serializer or something similar). If you are planning to pass data to non-PHP programs by using the message queue, you should not use this automatic serialization (which is unique to PHP) and instead use another encoder such as `json_encode()` or format your data as XML, for instance, depending on which formats the programs you are communicating with will accept.

- `blocking`: If the queue is full and you try to send a message, the `msg_send()` function will *block*. This means it will sit and wait for space to become available in the queue and hold up your script until that happens. If you set this parameter to `false`, the function will return `false` instead of blocking, set the `errorcode` parameter to MSG_ EAGAIN (to indicate you should try again later), and let the script continue to run. In this case, it is your responsibility to remember the message and try to send it again because the `msg_send()` function will forget all about it.

- `errorcode`: This parameter stores any error code generated in case of an error. If an error occurs, the function will return `false` as well as setting this code.

So in our example, you use `msg_send()` in blocking mode to send the PHP array $phpArray as your message, assigning it as a type 3 message (which is purely arbitrary in this case), using automatic serialization of the array into a string and catching any error codes in $errorCode.

Now you look at our `display2.php` script. After calling `msg_get_queue()` to join the queue, you start a continuous loop (using `while(1)`) that will try to read a message from the queue each time you go through the loop. You've added a `sleep(1)` 1-second delay to space out the message requests and show that the timing of the requests isn't important (you can change this to another value, and it will work just as well, or indeed remove it completely and grab all the messages without delay). To get a message, you use `msg_ receive()`, which takes the following parameters:

- `queue`: The $queue resource identifier.

- desiredmsgtype: The type of message you want to receive. If this is 0, you will get the next message in the queue. If it is set to a positive integer (say, 5), you will get the next message that was sent using 5 as the type parameter in msg_send(). If it is a negative integer (say, –3), you will get the next message in the queue with the lowest type that is less than or equal to the absolute (non-negative) value of this parameter. For example, if you specify –3, you will get the first message with type 1, 2, or 3 (and if there are multiple messages with these types, you take the first message that has type 1, and then when all the 1s are gone, you take the first with type 2, and so on).

- msgtype: This is the message type that you have received. This is useful when you specify a negative value for desiredmsgtype to get a message from a range of types, and want to see the type of message that you were given.

- maxsize: This specifies the maximum size (in bytes) of the message that you are willing to receive. If the message that you would receive is bigger than this size, the msg_receive() function will either return false and not return a message at all, or if MSG_NOERROR is set in the flags parameter, it will instead truncate the message and return just the first maxsize bytes. Be aware that the msg_receive() function allocates a block of memory equal to maxsize before it tries to read the message. This means that even if the message is small (for example, 10 KB), your script will crash if you specify too large a size here (for example, 1 GB when you have only 512 MB of memory free).

- message: This is the message you receive. If the unserialize parameter is set to true, any PHP types such as arrays or objects will be unserialized and returned as the correct type. If false, you will receive the message as a (potentially serialized) string.

- unserialize: If true, the contents of message will be automatically unserialized.

- flags: You can specify the following flags:

  - MSG_IPC_NOWAIT: If there are no suitable messages to receive, by default msg_receive() will block the execution of the script and sit and wait for a new message to arrive. If you set this flag, the script will not block, will return the integer value for MSG_ENOMSG, and your script will continue.

  - MSG_EXCEPT: If you ask for a message of a particular type by using a positive integer for desiredmsgtype and you set this flag, you will get a message of *any* type *except* the one you have specified.

  - MSG_NOERROR: Stops errors when the message is too big (see the previous msgtype entry for details).

- errorcode: If an error occurs, the msg_receive() function returns false and this parameter is set to the relevant error code.

So in our example, you ask for a message that has a maximum 1,024 bytes and a type of –4 (that is, its type is 1, 2, 3, or 4). Our generator2.php script creates messages of type 3, and all are less than 1,024, so they will all match and be returned. $realType will be set to 3, and $phpArray will contain our data as an array because you have set unserialize to true. You haven't set the MSG_IPC_NOWAIT flag, so if there are no messages, your script will block at the msg_receive() command waiting for new messages.

You can use `msg_queue_exists()` to check that a message queue exists before trying to use it, and `msg_remove_queue()` to destroy a queue when you are done with it. To get more information about a queue, you can call `msg_stat_queue()`, which returns an array with the following keys:

- `msg_perm.uid`: The UID (user ID) of the process that owns (created) the queue

- `msg_perm.gid`: The GID (group ID) of the process that owns (created) the queue

- `msg_perm.mode`: The file access mode (permissions) of the queue

- `msg_stime`: The time that the last message was added to the queue

- `msg_rtime`: The time that the last message was removed from the queue

- `msg_ctime`: The time that the queue was last changed (either a message was added or removed)

- `msg_qnum`: The number of messages currently in the queue

- `msg_qbytes`: The maximum size in total of the message queue, in bytes

- `msg_lspid`: The PID (process ID) of the process that last added a message to the queue

- `msg_lrpid`: The PID of the process that last removed a message from the queue

The maximum size of the queue (all of the messages in the queue at any one time) can be read from this array as `msg_qbytes`. This is often set at 16 KB. If you want to change this value, on Linux you can change the file `/proc/sys/kernel/msgmnb` to a higher value (in bytes). Remember that you need to do that on any system that you deploy on and need to have root privileges to do so.

The message queues you've used are *bidirectional*. This means, assuming each process has the appropriate permissions, each one can both add *and* remove messages from the queue. When doing this, you need to be sure that you don't inadvertently remove messages that you have added yourself before the other process has had a chance to do so (for example, by using the message type field to specify the intended recipient). Alternatively, you can open two message queues and use one for sending and one for receiving in your process (and vice versa in the other process). It is particularly important to keep things straight in this regard, when you start adding more than two processes to your queue, bearing in mind that the number of processes that can join your queue is limited only by your available system resources.

Further Reading

- "Message Queues" section in the PHP manual

  - `www.php.net/manual/en/ref.sem.php`

Third-Party Message Queues

As you can see, the sysvmsg message queue system is a simple and easy built-in way to pass asynchronous messages between processes. It provides only basic queue functionality and does have it limits (not being supported on Windows is a major one). If you have more-advanced requirements, you might want to check out one of the other messaging systems available with PHP bindings. A list of some of the more common ones follow. Between them, they cover just about any messaging need. Be aware that some of the systems are definitely not for beginners, and all require the deployment of additional software or libraries.

Toolbox	0MQ

An extremely fast and comprehensive messaging transport layer, with support for many languages and OSs. Quite advanced and not suited to beginners.

Main web site	`http://zero.mq`
Installation info	`www.zeromq.org/bindings:php`
Main documentation	`https://github.com/mkoppanen/php-zmq/wiki`
Example code from Rasmus Lerdorf	`http://talks.php.net/show/phpuk2012/16`

Toolbox	SAM for IBM MQTT

An extension aimed at producing a simple extensible API for multiple messaging platforms. Currently only IBM's MQTT is supported.

Main web site	`www.php.net/manual/en/intro.sam.php`

Toolbox	RabbitMQ

A messaging system that implements the widely supported AMQP messaging standard, a widely supported cross-platform messaging protocol

Main web site	`www.rabbitmq.com`
Third-party PHP libraries	`www.rabbitmq.com/devtools.html#php-dev`
Tutorial *"Integrating PHP with RabbitMQ" by Alvaro Videla*	`www.slideshare.net/old_sound/integrating-php-withrabbitmqzendcon`
Book *I'm British so I Know How to Queue by Stuart Grimshaw*	`https://leanpub.com/im_british_so_i_know_how_to_queue`

Toolbox	Apache ActiveMQ Apollo

A part of the ActiveMQ Java-based messaging system, supporting the STOMP, AMQP, MQTT, OpenWire, SSL, and WebSocket messaging protocols. Designed for enterprise systems.

Main web site	`http://activemq.apache.org/apollo`
PHP libraries for STOMP	`http://stomp.github.io/implementations.html`

Toolbox	PHP-Queue

A unified PHP front end for different queuing back ends

Main web site	`https://github.com/miccheng/php-queue`
Main documentation	`https://github.com/miccheng/php-queue#getting-started`

Further Reading

- "Publishing Queue Messages from PHP Using Different Backends" by Artur Ejsmont

    - http://artur.ejsmont.org/blog/content/publishing-messages-from-php-
      to-different-message-queue-backends

APC Cached Variables

You may be aware of the Alternative PHP Cache (APC) system from your web work with PHP. This can be used to cache variables in memory, which can then be accessed by different scripts. Unfortunately, this works only on the Web, as the cache operates per process. When running through a server such as Apache, PHP operates under the Apache process, which is a set of one (or more) long-running processes. With the PHP CLI SAPI, the converse is true. Each run of each script creates its own process, which terminates when the script terminates. APC can be enabled for CLI, but at the end of each script run, the cache will be destroyed, and each process has its own cache. This can occasionally be useful for memory-based caching in long-running, single-process programs (for example, system daemons), but even then you may still decide that a dedicated memory-caching system such as Memcached may be better, as it can cope with unexpected restarts of the process. For these reasons, this book doesn't cover the APC. If you are using a web-based solution, you can find more information in the PHP manual.

Further Reading

- "Alternative PHP Cache" section in the PHP manual

    - www.php.net/manual/en/book.apc.php

Virtual Files—tmpfs

tmpfs is a file system that allows you to create and use files stored in memory. This type of system is often called a *RAM disk*. These virtual files act and operate like normal files on disk, and can thus allow your processes to communicate by reading and writing data in files as you would with normal on-disk files. The advantages tmpfs brings are twofold: it's fast, and everything is temporary. Because the files are held in memory, there is no mechanical hard disk to wait for, so I/O is quick. And because the files are held in memory, they are only temporary and will disappear upon a reboot if you haven't already deleted them. A further advantage is that, being standard files, they aren't a PHP-specific technology, and so can be accessed from other software as needed.

I won't go into specific details of how to use them to communicate between processes, as I assume that you are familiar with accessing standard disk-based files from PHP and creating and reading appropriate file formats. You can access files on a tmpfs file system in exactly the same way as normal files and streams. The fact that they are in memory is transparent to your PHP script.

To create a tmpfs file system on Linux, you first create a directory on disk to use to "attach" the memory device to your file system. You then mount the memory device at that location and start using it.

```
mkdir /home/rob/myMemoryDrive

sudo mount -t tmpfs /mnt/tmpfs /home/rob/myMemoryDrive

php -r "file_put_contents('/home/rob/myMemoryDrive/test.txt','Hello');"
```

```
cat /home/rob/myMemoryDrive/test.txt

sudo umount -a /mnt/tmpfs

cat /home/rob/myMemoryDrive/test.txt
```

In this script, you create a directory at /home/rob/myMemoryDrive to attach the memory device, and then mount it there. You execute a line of PHP to demonstrate creating a memory file as you would any other file, and then cat the file, which should output *Hello*. Finally, you umount the device and try to cat the file again, but as you'd expect, the file is gone; it is never saved to physical disk. You can mount tmpfs devices by using the mount command as shown in this example each time you boot your system or whenever you want to use them, or you can add an entry into your fstab file to have one automatically created each time your system boots. Whichever way you mount the device, when you shut down or reboot, always remember that it, and all of the files within it, will be destroyed.

As tmpfs operates in the same way as a normal file system, you need to make sure that you set the relevant file permissions to allow all of your applications to access it (or prevent access by those who shouldn't be able to meddle with it). Also bear in mind that memory swapping to disk may occur if your system becomes short of memory, so your data may temporarily touch your hard disk in these cases, and under certain conditions may be recoverable from disk after that. Always consider the security implications of any messaging system you choose.

If you are considering communicating by using tmpfs instead of physical hard disks for performance reasons, you should also bear in mind that modern operating systems (including modern Linux) can use aggressive in-memory caching for disk access. This means that the operating system transparently caches oft-read disk-based files to dynamically allocated unused memory (usually without you even knowing) to increase apparent physical disk performance. In these cases, you might not see the performance improvements that you may expect when reading some files from, and traversing directory trees on, a tmpfs memory disk. Writes to disk and seldom-accessed files aren't usually cached, so tmpfs may still give you the wins you are expecting in those cases.

Virtual Files—Windows RAM Disks

In Windows, there is no built-in way to create a memory-based file system. Assorted third-party software exists to create RAM disks, but it is not standardized. Most of it requires a GUI interface for setting up the disk manually on each system.

Further Reading

- List of third-party RAM disk software on Wikipedia

  - https://en.wikipedia.org/wiki/List_of_RAM_drive_software#Microsoft_Windows

Standard Streams

You looked at the standard streams (STDIN, STDOUT, STDERR) and how to use them in previous chapters. It should now be obvious that you can use them to communicate with other processes via shell piping and I/O redirection. If you start the processes you want to talk to from within PHP by using proc_open() or popen(), PHP is automatically using the standard streams when reading and writing to the other process.

Linux Signals

It is possible to crudely use Linux signals to communicate between processes, although this is generally used for parent-child control. See Chapter 8 for more information on Linux signals.

Task Dispatch and Management Systems

One common use of messaging systems is to manage worker processes and dispatch tasks. If you want to use a prebuilt solution, have a look at the "Task Dispatch and Management Systems" section in Chapter 6.

CHAPTER 8

■ ■ ■

Talking to the System

So far you've looked at software that communicates with your users, via text-based or graphical interfaces, and system software that doesn't need to talk to users at all. One thing that both types of software have in common is the need to deal with the underlying system that it sits on top of. That system is a structure containing the file system, operating system, hardware interfaces, and various system-level services. When programming for the Web, you typically don't interact with hardware, lower-level aspects of the system, and so on. Indeed, in many cases, you specifically take steps to prohibit your users from doing so!

In contrast, dealing with printers, sound cards, and other hardware is a common requirement when constructing many types of software, and interfacing with system-level services is often a necessity. You will work with portions of the file system from web pages, but with offline software, you usually have the freedom and resources to work with a wider range of file formats, larger file sizes, and more-privileged files. In this chapter, you'll look at some of the ways to interact with these resources, both from within PHP and with the aid of helper applications, as well as some of the issues to consider when doing so.

File-System Interactions

Software commonly needs to interact with many types of data files—from images to text files, formatted documents to videos, structured data to configuration files, and many more. PHP has built-in functions for reading, writing, parsing, and displaying many types of data files, and between PEAR, PECL, Composer, and third-party libraries, even more types are covered. On many systems, particularly Unix variants, helper applications can also be called to further extend the range of file types covered. In fact, there are very few file types that you will struggle to deal with in PHP, and those tend to be proprietary formats with closely guarded specifications. If you stick to open formats, and in particular standards-based formats, you will invariably find the tools you need in the PHP ecosystem.

Data Files and Formats

Appendix B contains a reference list of functions, libraries, and helpers available for a wide range of common formats. Remember that where a particular version of a format doesn't appear in Appendix B, it is often usable using the functions for the generic format it is based on (for example, many XML-based formats are perfectly amenable to being manipulated by the generic XML tools listed). Always keep in mind that data files are a large vector for security exploits, and even where software is operated locally by trusted users, those users may inadvertently try to open files from malicious sources. Always treat external data as potentially tainted, and treat unvetted extensions/helpers as if they have potential security vulnerabilities.

© Rob Aley 2016
R. Aley, *PHP Beyond the Web*, DOI 10.1007/978-1-4842-2481-6_8

Dealing with Large Files

When you don't have a limit on the time your script can run, you can work with bigger files than you may be used to when using PHP on the Web. In general, you can deal with large files in the same way as you would smaller files. However, one big problem you may run into is memory usage. It's important to understand the way that PHP uses memory when loading and processing files so that you can make appropriate choices in your code. Many of the libraries for handling particular file formats listed in Appendix B deal with opening and processing large files efficiently on your behalf, so this section is most relevant when you do your own file processing, or use a library that requires you to pass it raw data (rather than a file name).

First let's look at simple methods for reading in a file in one go. PHP has two easy-to-use functions for doing this: file() and file_get_contents(). The former reads the file into an array, and the latter into a single string:

```php
<?php

$filename = 'bigfile.csv';

echo("Size of file : ".filesize($filename)." bytes\n");

$memory1 = memory_get_usage();

$file_array = file($filename);

$memory2 = memory_get_usage();

$file_string = file_get_contents($filename);

$memory3  = memory_get_usage();

echo("Memory used by array : ".($memory2-$memory1)." bytes\n");

echo("Memory used by string : ".($memory3-$memory2)." bytes\n");
```

Running this script on a sample large file I had lying around elicited the following output:

```
Size of file : 186097433 bytes
Memory used by array : 296969824 bytes
Memory used by string : 186097588 bytes
```

So you can see that reading the file (about 177 MB) into a string adds an overhead of 155 bytes, which is not too bad. However, reading this file into an array adds an additional 105 MB to the original size of the file! In PHP, arrays are versatile data structures; they "*can be treated as an array, list (vector), hash table (an implementation of a map), dictionary, collection, stack, queue, and probably more*" (according to the PHP manual). However, this versatility comes at a price, and that is the additional memory used for storing the structure information. So before loading the file, consider whether the processing you are going to do on the data can be done on a string, or whether the extra overhead of an array is worth it for the manipulation capabilities. If you can use a traditional array or hash-like structure without the versatility of the PHP array type, but with a lower resource overhead, look into the PHP Standard PHP Library (SPL). The SPL contains a range of "traditional" data structures that may be more optimized for your use case.

Further Reading

- "Standard PHP Library (SPL)" section in the PHP manual

  - www.php.net/manual/en/book.spl.php

Sometimes, no matter what type of data structure you read your file into, there isn't enough memory available on the system, you hit a memory limit imposed for your script, or you just need to keep memory usage low in general. Often processing of a data file can be done on a line-by-line (or chunk-by-chunk) basis, and PHP allows you to read in a file piece by piece rather that in one go. Assuming you discard the data you've read before you read some more (unset it, overwrite it, or write it out to a file, for example), then you will use just enough memory to store that one line or chunk. Let's look at an example:

```php
<?php

$filename = 'bigfile.csv';

$memory1 = memory_get_usage();

$file_string = file_get_contents($filename);

$memory2  = memory_get_usage();

unset($file_string);

$memoryBase = memory_get_usage();

$file_handle = fopen($filename, 'r');

while ($line = fgets($file_handle)) {

  $memoryCurrent = memory_get_usage();

  if ($memoryCurrent > $memoryBase) { $memoryHigh = $memoryCurrent;};

};

echo("Memory used by single string : ".($memory2-$memory1)." bytes\n");

echo("Max memory used when reading by line : ".
  ($memoryHigh-$memoryBase)." bytes\n");
```

On my sample file, this gave the following output:

```
Memory used by single string : 186097768 bytes
Max memory used when reading by line : 9000 bytes
```

This illustrates the extreme differences in memory usage by the two different techniques.

If you're working with files that are, or may be, greater than 2 GB, you should also be aware that some file-system functions may not return the correct (or any) result for files bigger than that on many platforms. This is because these platforms use a 32-bit integer, PHP's integer type is signed, and 2 GB is the largest size that can be represented by a signed 32-bit integer.

This affects functions such as `filesize()`, `stat()`, and `fseek()`. You can, of course, access external commands to replace some of these functions; for instance, `wc -c` on Linux returns the number of bytes in a file for all files supported by the operating system. On 64-bit Linux, with a recent version of glibc installed, you can compile PHP with the `D_LARGEFILE_SOURCE -D_FILE_OFFSET_BITS=64` flag for better large-file support, though be aware that if you are writing scripts for distribution, this obviously won't be an available option for all.

In all of these examples, remember that your script has to work within any memory limit you or PHP has imposed. By default, the PHP CLI SAPI turns off the memory limit. You can type `php -r "echo(ini_get('memory_limit'));"` at the command line to see the default memory limit (–1 means no limit). From within your script, `ini_get('memory_limit')` will tell you the current maximum, and `memory_get_usage()` will tell you what you're currently using.

Handling memory usage when dealing with large amounts of data is something that often trips programmers up. As you've seen, understanding how the various functions you use operate can help you process that data more efficiently and help minimize memory use.

Understanding File System Functions

PHP has numerous file system–related extensions. Many are part of the PHP core or compiled into most PHP distributions and contain hundreds of useful functions. Most of them operate in a simple straightforward manner, allowing you to get and set file and directory information and manipulate files and the file system as you would expect. We won't cover most of them here, as I'm sure many will be familiar to you from your web projects and they are covered well in the PHP manual.

Further Reading

- "File System Related Functions" section in the PHP manual

  - `www.php.net/manual/en/refs.fileprocess.file.php`

Many of these functions ape command-line programs that you may be used to, such as `chmod`, `mkdir`, `touch`, and so on, and operate broadly as you might expect. However, a difference arises in longer-running scripts that revolves around PHP caching file-system information to increase performance, which you'll look at next.

The PHP File Status and realpath Caches

On the Web, speed is king. PHP operates two information caches to speed up access to the file system. The first is the *file status cache*, which caches information about a given file (for example, whether it exists, whether it is readable, its size and type, and so on). The second is the *realpath cache*, which caches the actual, real path for a given file or directory (expanding symlinks, relative paths, `.` and `..` paths, `include_paths`, and so on). Information is added to the cache automatically by PHP each time it encounters a new file, and is then used by any number of functions the next time they attempt to look at that same file. With a web page that's gone in the blink of an eye and little that may have happened on the file system, this is often a good trade-off for increased performance.

However, the chances that the details of a file or path may change while your script runs obviously increase with the length of time that your script takes to execute. Therefore, PHP gives us a couple of options for working with these two caches. The following example shows the file status cache in action, and how to use `clearstatcache()` to clear it:

```php
<?php

# Create a file and add some text to it

$filename = 'test.txt';

$handle = fopen($filename, 'w+');

fwrite($handle, 'test');

# The following should print 4

echo stat($filename)["size"]."\n";

# Now write some data to the file, increasing the file size.

fwrite($handle, 'more test');

# Intuitively, the following command should print 13 as the file is now
# bigger than before. However, it still prints 4, because the filesize
# value for this file is now cached.

echo stat($filename)["size"]."\n";

# If we clear the cache ....

clearstatcache();

# then the next line should print 13 as expected

echo stat($filename)["size"]."\n";

fclose($handle);
```

The realpath cache operates in a similar way, and can be cleared by calling clearstatcache(true)—that is, by calling it with true as the first parameter. You can also clear the cache for just one particular file by calling clearstatcache(true, 'myfile.txt'), where the second parameter is the file name (and the first must be set to true, that is, you must also clear the realpath cache).

Of course, clearing these caches may not be necessary in your application, and doing so has performance implications. Consider each file access on a case-by-case basis.

Working with Cross-Platform and Remote File Systems

While most file system–related functions in PHP are platform agnostic, you may find yourself writing your own functions to deal with files, or at the very least handling file names and paths from assorted platforms. The useful Pathogen library takes away some of the pain of dealing with the various representations of file names and paths across platforms.

Toolbox	Pathogen
A general-purpose library for working with file paths and schemas. Works with Unix and Windows path formats, URIs, and more.	
Main web site	`https://github.com/eloquent/pathogen`
Main documentation and installation info	`https://github.com/eloquent/pathogen/#installation-and-documentation`

More and more remote, cloud, and pseudo file systems are beginning to appear. Many users now use platforms such as Dropbox and Amazon S3, and interact with other services through common protocols including WebDAV, SFTP, and the like. Most of these services have PHP extensions or API examples available, but the Flysystem abstraction library aims to render many of these unnecessary by providing a generic API for handling remote file systems.

Toolbox	Flysystem
A file-system abstraction library that allows you to easily swap the local file system for an assortment of remote ones	
Main web site	`http://flysystem.thephpleague.com/`

Accessing the Windows Registry

The *Windows Registry* is a structured, hierarchical database that Windows and other applications use to store configuration information. Although not used universally by all applications, most store some information in the Registry, and the operating system itself uses it extensively. You can access the Registry from PHP too, allowing you to check and set configuration information both for your own applications, and if you have the right permissions, other applications and the OS itself. To do this, you need to use the win32std extension with PHP.

Toolbox	win32std
Set of standard Windows API functions	
Main web site	`http://pecl.php.net/package/win32std`
Main documentation and installation info	See README file within the download
Alternative documentation	`http://wildphp.free.fr/wiki/doku.php?id=win32std:index`

▓ **Caution** Incorrectly changing or altering the Registry can cause a wide range of problems with individual applications, as well as systemwide problems. In short, you can bork your machine if you do it wrong. Learn how to back up and restore the Registry *before* you start playing. Or play around in a disposable VM first before you use a production machine (and even then, backing up your production machine is still a good idea!).

Before you continue, you should understand the layout of the Registry. The Registry is divided into *keys* and *subkeys*. Each subkey stores either a configuration value or further subkeys, in a directory/tree-like structure. Windows operates a permissions system based on users and keys/subkeys. Details of what information goes where and the specifics of the permission system are beyond the scope of this book.

Further Reading

- "Understand How the Windows Registry Works," by Dan Gookin, a *For Dummies* quick guide to the layout of the Registry

  - www.dummies.com/computers/operating-systems/windows-xp-vista/ understand-how-the-windows-registry-works/

- A slightly more in-depth article on Wikipedia

  - http://en.wikipedia.org/wiki/Windows_Registry

- Fairly comprehensive, official Registry documentation

  - http://msdn.microsoft.com/en-us/library/ms724871.aspx

Let's look at an example of reading a value from the Registry. You're going to get the e-mail address that is stored for use with the Firefox Crash Reporter software, which appears in the Registry at HKEY_CURRENT_ USER\Software\Mozilla\Firefox\Crash Reporter\Email:

```php
<?php

# We first have to "open" a key before we can do anything with it.

$keyHandle = reg_open_key('HKEY_CURRENT_USER',
    'Software\Mozilla\Firefox\Crash Reporter');

if ($keyHandle) {

  $email = reg_get_value($keyHandle, 'Email');

  echo ("Crash Reporter Email  : $email\n");

  reg_close_key($keyHandle);

} else { die ("Couldn't open Registry key"); };
```

In addition to accessing a subkey directly, you can loop through (or *enumerate*) a particular subkey. For instance, let's check out what printers you have installed:

```php
<?php

$keyHandle = reg_open_key('HKEY_CURRENT_USER',
  'Software\Microsoft\Windows NT\CurrentVersion\PrinterPorts');

if ($keyHandle) {

  $subkeys = reg_enum_key($keyHandle);

  foreach ($subkeys as $index => $subkey) {
```

```
    echo "Printer $index is $subkey \n";

  };

  reg_close_key($keyHandle);

} else { die ("Couldn't open Registry key"); };
```

Here you use reg_enum_key() to get a list of the subkey names. You could use reg_enum_value() in a similar way to get a list of the values for the subkeys instead. To visually browse the Registry, you can use the Windows application regedit.exe. This will give you a feel for the locations of various subkeys. However, be aware that many subkeys are either seemingly duplicated for the same app but in different areas (usually for settings that are made per machine rather than per user), or hidden in completely unintuitive locations (such as many of the operating system keys). The latter is usually due to either bad design or backward-compatibility. In any case, if you need specific information, consult the official developer documentation for the application or for Windows itself to determine exactly where that information is located (and what, exactly, it means).

Reading from the Registry is a fairly benign activity. It's hard to mess up your system by checking values (unless you act on bad or wrong information). Writing to the Registry, on the other hand, is much more dangerous, and the win32std extension makes it simple to live life dangerously!

The following example opens the subkey with reg_open_key() as in the preceding example, and then uses reg_set_value() to write to it. If the subkey doesn't already exist, it will be created for us. If it does already exist, the value will be updated.

```
<?php

$keyHandle = reg_open_key('HKEY_CURRENT_USER',
  'Software\My Php Software Co\My Software\login');

if ($keyHandle) {

  reg_set_value($keyHandle, 'username', REG_SZ, 'rob');

  reg_close_key($keyHandle);

} else { die ("Couldn't open Registry key"); };
```

The third parameter to reg_set_value() (in this case, REG_SZ) is the data type of the value passed in the fourth variable. You can find all of the data types the Registry supports at http://en.wikipedia.org/wiki/Windows_Registry#Keys_and_values.

In summary, accessing the Registry in this way provides a powerful way to store software configurations and credentials, and allows wide-ranging access to Windows OS and application-specific information. The downsides, aside from general criticisms of the Registry design and layout itself, are that it is platform dependent, and it is easy to damage your system if you aren't careful. Make those backups now, before you start playing.

Linux Signals

On Unix and Linux systems, *signals* are a method that the operating system (possibly at the behest of a user) can use to send, well, *signals* to a process. The OS interrupts the normal execution flow of the process to deliver the signal, allowing the process to act on the signal immediately (if it wishes to do so). A wide range of signals can be passed, including requests to terminate, error condition signaling, and polling notifications.

Common signals have been codified in the POSIX standards, a full list can be found on Wikipedia, and the list supported by PHP can be found in the PHP manual:

Further Reading

- "POSIX signals" on Wikipedia

    - http://en.wikipedia.org/wiki/Unix_signal#POSIX_signals

- PHP-supported signals in the PHP manual

    - www.php.net/manual/en/pcntl.constants.php

- *Signaling PHP* by Cal Evans, a whole book just about signals!

    - https://leanpub.com/signalingphp

You can listen and respond to these signals from your PHP scripts by using the PCNTL extension. The following script demonstrates how to do this. It uses a PHP feature called *ticks*, which allows a callback function be executed after every *N* statements. You don't need to do anything with ticks; you simply need to enable them (using a declare construct) so that they are available to the PCNTL functions to use as they deem fit.

```php
<?php

# Enable ticks every 1 `tick-able` statement

declare(ticks = 1);

# Declare a variable that will control whether our program keeps running.

$keepRunning = true;

# Output our PID (Process ID) so that we can use it in a kill command in
# another terminal to terminate the correct (this) script
# (e.g. ~$ kill 123456 )

echo("My PID is ".getmypid()." if you wanna kill me. I dare ya!\n");

# Now we create a function to handle signals when they come in.

function signalHandler($signal)
{

  # $signal contains the signal that was received
  # Always remember that this function can be called from any point in
  # the script, so be careful if relying on the state of the program

  switch ($signal) {

    case SIGINT:

        # SIGINT is sent when a user wants to interrupt the process.
        # From the terminal this is usually by pressing Ctrl+C
```

```
                echo ("No, you may NOT interrupt me. The cheek of it.\n");

                break;

        case SIGTERM:

            # Similar to SIGINT, SIGTERM is sent when a user requests
            # termination of the process, but is a slightly "stronger"
            # request.

            echo("Well, if you REALLY insist, let's go. Bye!\n");

            # set $keepRunning to false so that we exit at the start of
            # the next loop

            global $keepRunning;
            $keepRunning = false;

            break;
    };
};

# Before we start the main body of our program, we need to tie the
# handler function we just created to the signals that we want it to
# handle.

pcntl_signal(SIGINT, 'signalHandler');
pcntl_signal(SIGTERM, 'signalHandler');

# Any signals received from now will be processed by the signalHandler
# function.

# Let's now enter a loop and do some work

while ($keepRunning) {

  echo("Yawn, nothing happening...\n");
  sleep(5);

};

# If we reached this point, then we must have exited the loop.
# That means that we must have received the SIGTERM signal as
# we haven't built any other means to exit the loop!

echo("That's it, you've stopped me. I hope you're happy.\n");
```

Run this script and try pressing Ctrl+C. Normally, your PHP script would exit as PHP handles SIGINT by default by exiting the script. However, we've handled it and refuse to close the script, so you will get a terse message and the script will continue! This is generally an impolite thing to do, as the user (or system) has requested to interrupt the process. If you want to be a good citizen, at this point you could choose to close or temporarily pause the process, or prompt the user ("We're still computing your Foobar value, are you sure you want to exit?"). If you still have some critical processing to do, it may be worth telling the user that you got their signal and will shut down in a moment, to save the user from trying other methods to kill the script. Run the script again, take note of the process ID (PID) shown (for example, 123456), and in another terminal window, type kill 123456. The kill command, by default, sends the SIGTERM signal to request that the process terminates. In the first terminal window, you should see your PHP script "gracefully" exiting, printing a couple of messages as it goes.

If you run the script once more, and this time use kill -9 123456 to try to stop the script, you should see it stop dead in its tracks without outputting any messages. This is because the -9 flag tells kill to send the SIGKILL signal. We haven't handled this signal, because it is one of the few that we can't, and on POSIX systems it causes the process to terminate immediately. This is useful if a process isn't responding to any other signals and you need to end it. However, it can be dangerous as the process doesn't have a chance to do any cleanup, such as closing files and releasing resources, and so can lead to errors such as file corruption and resource leaks. If your system handles SIGTERM events, but may take a little while to clean up after itself, it is worth letting the user know that shutdown is in progress; otherwise, the user may resort to a SIGKILL, thinking your process has just hung.

Sending Signals

It is possible to dispatch signals from your PHP scripts as well. This can be used to (crudely) communicate with other scripts, as well as to control processes if your script has sufficient permissions. To send a signal, simply use the misleadingly named posix_kill() function. This function lets you send any PHP-supported signal, not just those used to kill a process. To use it, you need to know the PID of the process you want to talk to (for example, 123456), and then you simply call posix_kill(123456, SIGINT), for example.

Linux Timed-Event Signals

Sometimes we want our scripts to do something every so often—for example, check the status of a resource, do some cleanup, or update a log file. There are a couple of ways to achieve this. The simplest is by using the sleep() or usleep() functions to sit and wait for a number of seconds/microseconds before performing a task. This is not always of use, because when you call sleep(), the script simply stops and waits for that amount of time rather than continuing to do other useful work. In the previous section, you briefly looked at PHP ticks that enable you to run a callback function every *N* (potentially useful) statements. This allows you to do useful work between calls to the callback function, but there is no guarantee on how long those statements will take to execute, so we can't wait for a specific length of time. In fact, PHP has no internal way of keeping track of time in this way. However, by using POSIX signals, which you looked at in the previous section, you can ask the system to set an "alarm" for a certain number of seconds into the future. When this alarm goes off, the system will interrupt PHP with a POSIX signal, which you can handle to run your callback function.

The previous section explained how to listen for and process Linux signals. If you haven't read that section yet, I recommend you do so now to fully understand the example that follows:

```php
<?php

# We enable ticks for pcntl to use as before.

declare(ticks = 1);

$keepRunning = true;

# This is the function that we want to execute every 5 seconds.
```

```php
function takeABreak($signal) {

    echo("\n\n ======== HAVING A BREAK, BE BACK SOON ========");

    sleep(3);

    echo("\n\n ======== BREAKS OVER, BACK TO WORK! ======== \n\n");

    # We need to request an alarm again each time.

    pcntl_alarm(5);

};

# This is a function to gracefully exit our program

function timeToGo($signal) {

    global $keepRunning;

$keepRunning = false;

};

# In a moment we will ask the system to set an alarm, but before that
# we will register the callback function that will happen when the
# alarm goes off, i.e. when the system sends us a SIGALARM signal

pcntl_signal(SIGALRM, "takeABreak", true);

# Just to show that we can handle any and all signals with more than
# one callback function, we'll also register a different handler for
# the SIGINT/SIGTERM signals

pcntl_signal(SIGINT, 'timeToGo');
pcntl_signal(SIGTERM, 'timeToGo');

# Once we have got a callback function registered, we can go ahead and
# ask the system to set an alarm for us. The alarm works only once, so
# you'll notice this call to pcntl_alarm is repeated at the end of the
# callback function to set the alarm again

pcntl_alarm(5);

# Now we enter our main work loop

while ( $keepRunning ) {

    echo('...doing work...');

    usleep(50000);

};
```

```
# If we get here, then we've had the SIGINT or SIGTERM signals

echo("\nBye Bye, see you tomorrow.\n");
```

If you run this script, you will see '...doing work...' printed to the screen every half a second. Every 5 seconds, your alarm callback function will kick in and pause the work for 3 seconds, before the work resumes.

There are a few important concepts to understand when using alarm signals:

- The alarm callback function interrupts the normal script execution. The normal script does not continue to run in the background while the alarm function is executing (it is not multithreaded).

- The alarm function can kick in at any point in your script. If you modify the state of the script (for example, setting global variables, using resources and connections), your script should be able to handle that new state at any point in its execution.

- You do not know how long your main script, or any part of it, will take to run in advance. This is affected by things like load on the system and resources, user interactions, and so on. Thus you should not set alarms that assume anything about the progress of the underlying script.

- Only one alarm can be set at a time. Any further calls to `pcntl_alarm()` will cancel the first alarm, although it will also return the number of seconds left on the previous alarm.

- You can cancel an alarm by calling `pcntl_alarm(0)`, which again returns the number of remaining seconds on that alarm.

- Any `SIGALRM` that is received will have the side effect of exiting any system calls that happen to be in progress, such as calls to `sleep()`. Thus you should ensure that your script can tolerate such interruptions (or your alarm callback function should repair/reset any possible damage to the state of the script).

- If at any point you want your main script to wait until the next alarm occurs, you can call `pcntl_sigwaitinfo(array(SIGALRM))`, which will pause execution until the alarm occurs.

Printing (to Paper)

As much as we may wish to work in a paperless office, sooner or later we still have to artfully spill some toner onto a sheet of A4 or legal. PHP has a printing extension, but it is problematic because it is Windows only, it officially supports only versions up to Windows 2000 (although it generally works with versions up to Windows 7), and the required DLL file no longer comes standard with PHP. The printing extension also is no longer detailed in the PHP manual. For those reasons, we don't cover it in this book. It is still available on PECL, and the archived PHP manual address for detailed information is given next.

Further Reading

- PECL web site for the printer extension

  - `http://pecl.php.net/package/printer`

- Printer extension in the archived PHP manual

  - `web.archive.org/web/20140711163854/http://php.net/manual/en/book.printer.php`

Instead, we're going to look at a different way to print from PHP that will generally work across all platforms with some tweaks: creating and printing PDF files from PHP.

You're going to use a free PDF library written in PHP call FPDF. No installation is necessary; you simply require() the fpdf.php file in your script and start using it. Once you've used it to create a PDF file, you then need to print it. The easiest way to do this is to open it with the system's default PDF viewer, which will act as a print preview, allowing the user to then print it as a normal file. An alternative is to print it directly in the background without opening up a preview, which is done in a similar way.

Toolbox	FPDF
PDF creation library written in PHP	
Main web site	www.fpdf.org
Documentation	www.fpdf.org/en/tutorial/index.php

Let's look at an example in Linux first:

```php
<?php

# Load the fpdf.php library

require('fpdf.php');

# Create a new PDF object and start a new page

$pdf = new FPDF();

$pdf->AddPage();

# Add an image. Here we can use PHP's http wrapper to include a web image

$pdf->Image('http://static.php.net/www.php.net/images/php.gif',10);

# Now we'll set the font and add a header, plus some other text

$pdf->SetFont('Arial','B',24);

$pdf->Cell(0,30,'An Important Report','B',1,'C');

$pdf->SetFont('Arial',null,10);

$pdf->Cell(0,12,'Lots of really important text goes here. Etc.', null, 1);

# Generate a unique temporary file name

$filename = tempnam(sys_get_temp_dir(), "rep").'.pdf';

# Save the PDF to that temporary file

$pdf->Output($filename, 'F');
```

```
# Finally open the PDF for "print preview" in the default viewer

`xdg-open $filename`;
```

This generates a PDF report and opens it in your default PDF viewer for printing by the user. open and gnome-open also perform the same task as xdg-open on many Linux distros, which is to examine the file and open the appropriate registered viewer.

If, instead, you would rather send the report directly to the printer yourself without displaying it to the user, replace the last line with this:

```
`lp $filename;`
```

The lp (or *line printer*) command prints text, PDF, or PostScript files. Unless you specify otherwise, it sends the file to the system's default printer. You can change which printer is used and other settings; man lp at the command line will give you all the options.

For Windows, the preceding example script will run with a change to the last line. To open the PDF with the default viewer, use

```
`start $filename;`
```

Printing in the background is dependent on the PDF viewer installed, as there is no equivalent of Linux's lp command. For Adobe Acrobat, you can use the following, with the path changed as appropriate:

```
`"C:\Program Files (x86)\Adobe\Reader 11.0\Reader\AcroRd32.exe" /t "$filename"`
```

This opens Acrobat, loads the file, minimizes the window, and prints it. The downside is that the minimized window is still visible and doesn't close after printing. There is also no control over which printer is used; the command uses the default printer. For Foxit Reader, you can similarly do this:

```
`"C:\Program Files (x86)\Foxit Software\Foxit Reader\Foxit Reader.exe" /t "$filename" "Oki
C830DN"`
```

This has a couple of advantages over the Adobe version. Foxit doesn't open a window, even minimized, and you can specify the printer to use in the second parameter. Printing files other than PDF documents can usually be done in a similar manner, by calling an external print handler.

Audio

There are a number of useful libraries in PHP for dealing with audio. These can be used to make and record sounds, play back audio, and create effects and manipulate audio streams. Some of the more popular are listed here.

Toolbox	PHP-FFMpeg
PHP bindings for the FFmpeg audio/video recording, conversion, and streaming library	
Main web site	https://github.com/alchemy-fr/PHP-FFmpeg
Main documentation and installation info	https://github.com/alchemy-fr/PHP-FFmpeg#installation

Toolbox	OGG/Vorbis extension
An extension to read and manipulate OGG/Vorbis audio streams, including conversion to standard PCM audio	
Main web site	`http://pecl.php.net/package/oggvorbis`
Main documentation and installation info	`www.php.net/manual/en/book.oggvorbis.php`

Toolbox	PHP MIDI
A class for reading, writing, analyzing, modifying, creating, downloading, and playing standard MIDI files	
Main web site	`http://valentin.dasdeck.com/midi/`
Main documentation and installation info	`http://valentin.dasdeck.com/midi/documentation.htm`

Further Reading

- Stack Overflow topic: On Linux, MPlayer can be controlled in slave mode by PHP writing commands to a named pipe file, to play and manipulate audio/video files.

    - `http://stackoverflow.com/questions/4976276/is-it-possible-to-controlmplayer- from-another-program-easily`

- "Getting Started with Web Audio API" by Boris Smus, an introduction to HTML5 web audio. Useful for HTML5-based GUIs (see Chapter 5).

    - `www.html5rocks.com/en/tutorials/webaudio/intro/`

Databases—No Change Here

This book doesn't cover database access, as by and large the processes for connecting to and querying databases are the same when using the PHP CLI SAPI as when using PHP on the Web. The only notes relating to databases refer to time-outs and disconnections, and are covered in the next chapter as we look at the stability of longer-running PHP processes.

Other Hardware and System Interactions

We've covered a few of the common types of hardware and system interactions that you may come across, but many, many others are out there. If you come across a piece of hardware that you need to control, or a system-level process that you need to interact with, the first step is to check through the PEAR, PECL, and Packagist repositories for relevant PHP libraries and extensions. If that fails, check your operating system's software repository for any helper applications or libraries that may be of use. Finally, try your favorite search engine. Although PHP is most common as a web tool, many thousands of developers are already pushing the boundaries of what PHP can do (and generally blogging about it online!), so nine times out of ten, you will find that someone else has already been there, done that, and solved the problem for you. And if all else fails, try looking at how other developers have accomplished a particular interaction in other languages. PHP has many of the same functions as other languages, including many system-level calls, so you may be able to work out a way to do it from translating their code into PHP.

PHP and the Raspberry Pi

The purpose of this section (aside from being an excuse for me to buy a new toy) are to explore the low-power, credit-card-sized-PC phenomenon that is the Raspberry Pi (RP). You'll learn how to get started using PHP on the RP, how to build basic electronic switch circuits for the general-purpose input/output (GPIO) connector, and how to access GPIO-connected electronics from within PHP. This is only an introduction to the subject, covering the points essential to using PHP on the RP, so I will also point you in the direction of other comprehensive (and usually programming language–agnostic) information covering everything the RP can do. You will be building PHP-controlled robot overlords in no time! The code shown has been tested both on the original Raspberry Pi model B and the latest RP 3. It should run on any Pi model, including the Zero.

At its heart, the RP is simply another Linux computer with a low-power ARM-based CPU. An assortment of operating systems are freely available for the RP, mostly based on either Debian, Fedora, or Arch Linux. A version of RISC OS (the ARM-native OS) also is available, but I'll assume that you are using one of the Linux based distros. The latest version of the Pi supports Windows 10 IoT Core, but don't be fooled—this is not a full Windows distro, and PHP won't run on it.

Any commands given have been tested on only Raspbian (the official OS of the RP), which is a Debian derivative. However, these commands should work in a similar manner (or functionality should be similarly available) on the other Linux-based OSs.

Because we are using "just another" Linux box, PHP installation and configuration is mostly identical to desktop/server boxes, so the information provided in the rest of this book generally applies and I don't cover it again here. There are two notable differences, though. The first is that it will usually be a lot slower to do things such as compiling on the RP, as it has a fairly underpowered processor, and so it may be wise to use a precompiled version of PHP from your OS package repository (for example, `apt-get install php5` on Raspbian) to speed things up. Second, the RP's CPU is an ARM chip, not an x86. This means that some PHP extensions that make particular use of x86 features may not be available. Others may work but may not have been compiled/packaged for ARM yet and so might not be available in the standard OS package repository. In this case, you can compile them yourself in the usual way; see Appendix A for details. However, virtually all of the "usual suspects" are there on Raspbian, so you may not notice any difference.

And again, because it's "just another" Linux box, you can install Apache/Nginx, MySQL, and friends alongside PHP and use it as a small-scale web server. But that's not what this book is about!

Once PHP is installed, you can call and use it in the same way as usual; the `php` command is available from the shell. Once again, the usage of PHP on the RP is mostly the same as on standard desktop machines, so read the rest of this book for more information. What is different from most PCs and servers, however, is the availability of GPIO headers on the board, which allow you to start dabbling in the world of homemade electronics, and this is what you're going to look at next. Many tutorials on the Web introduce GPIO programming by using Python, C, or even shell scripts. However, there's no reason not to do it in PHP, so we will!

Raspberry Pi: The Basics of Tri-State Logic

As programmers, we're all very familiar with binary logic: true or false, yes or no, 1 or 0, on or off. These binary states form the basis of all programming, and even in high-level languages such as PHP they are a staple of keeping program state. Likewise, one of the staples of electronic input is the switch. Whether it's a light switch, a key on a keyboard, a magnetic reed switch, a passive infrared (PIR) motion sensor, or many other input types, it often boils down to (one or more) logical switches that we can measure to see whether they are in one state (open, unpressed, no motion) or the other (closed, pressed, motion detected). Figure 8-1 shows some symbols used in wiring diagrams for basic switches.

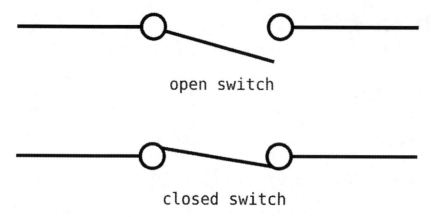

open switch

closed switch

Figure 8-1. *Example switch symbols*

Very binary. The temptation as a programmer with little electronics experience, when presented with an RP and a switch, is to connect one of the GPIO pins to Gnd (ground) via the switch, and poll it to see its state. If you do this, you'll probably notice the state change when you move the switch back and forth. Great. But keep watching. You'll probably start to see the input changing state all on its own, somewhat randomly. What you're seeing is a third flapping, or *floating*, state. Without a direct connection to a positive voltage or ground, the state of the GPIO pin floats or flaps about and can't be relied upon to be correct. It's a bit like a PHP variable with `register_globals` turned on: if you haven't explicitly set it yourself, you can't trust its value.

The RP GPIO pins use *CMOS logic*. This means that a binary 1 (also called *high*) is created by connecting the GPIO pin to +3v3 (positive 3.3 volts, supplied by another pin). The binary 0 (or *low*) is created by instead connecting the GPIO pin to Gnd (the ground pin). To achieve this double switching arrangement by using a single switch of the type pictured previously, you need to use the fact that electrons are as lazy as PHP programmers. Consider the circuit diagram shown in Figure 8-2.

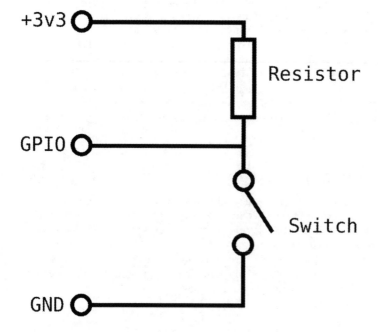

Figure 8-2. *Basic tri-state circuit*

Electrons like to flow through the path of least resistance. With the switch open as shown, the only possible path (circuit) is between the +3v3 pin and the GPIO pin, through the resistor. The resistor makes it hard work, but it's not as hard as jumping across an open switch (impossible at the voltages we are using), so the electrons go the easier route through the resistor. Thus when the switch is open and you poll the GPIO pin from your PHP script, you will get the value 1. When the switch is closed, the electrons are far happier, as most of them can whizz straight down to Gnd across the switch, which will have virtually no resistance, certainly a lot less than the resistor. So with the switch closed, your PHP will get the value 0. You will always get the value and can trust it, as the connection is always either down to ground or being "pulled up" to a positive voltage by the resistor circuit. No flapping about.

One final addition to our circuit is another resistor on the GPIO pin. The RP's GPIO pins can, as the name suggests, act as either an Input or an Output, and they are not *buffered* (that is, they are not protected against misuse). If you accidentally set and use the GPIO pin as an output in this circuit layout, you could damage it. The resistor shown in the final circuit in Figure 8-3 will provide some protection against this, while allowing the electrons to still flow in the manner described previously (as it sits on both possible paths and so doesn't "favor" one over the other).

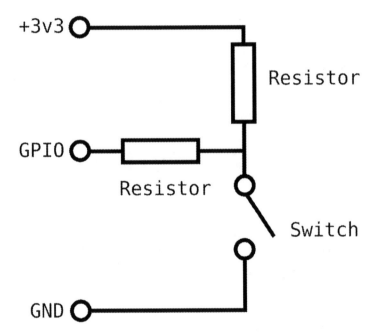

Figure 8-3. *Tri-state circuit with protection*

This should give you some idea about the "logic" of using switched sensors with the RP. Because there are 17 GPIO pins (and even more on the model B+ and above), all of which are individually addressable, you can quickly and easily add many sensors to the RP in this simple fashion.

This section demonstrates that electronics and interfacing aren't quite as straightforward as programming, but like programming, it's all quite logical after you've learned the rules! We won't go any further into the electronics side of the RP, as the circuits (and there are many, many of them available online) are essentially programming-language agnostic. What isn't language agnostic is accessing connected GPIO devices from software, and that's what you'll look at next.

Raspberry Pi: Accessing the GPIO Ports from PHP

Let's say you've built yourself a basic switch circuit like the one described. Perhaps the switch is a doorbell push button, connected to, say, GPIO pin 17, and you want to ring out the chimes via a connected speaker when someone pushes the button. You need to whip up a PHP script that can poll the GPIO pin for its state and detect when the button is pushed. This is really a Hello World type of script, the very basics of what you can do, but it should serve to introduce you to GPIO programming.

Before you look at the PHP code necessary to do this, it is helpful to understand how things work "under the hood." The Linux kernel contains a special interface module for dealing with GPIO pins (not just on the RP, but also on other PCs and embedded boards that have them), and as the interface is implemented using the Unix model of "everything is a file," you can access them with standard shell commands by hand, if necessary.

To access and use a GPIO pin, you follow these basic steps:

1.   Ensure that the Linux kernel has the GPIO module loaded.

2.   Reserve (export) the pin for your process.

3.   Set the pin to be either an input or output.

4.   Manage the pin by either reading from it or writing to it.

5.   Release the pin for others to use.

To temporarily enable the GPIO interface in the Linux kernel, you can issue the following shell command:

```
~: sudo modprobe w1-gpio
```

To permanently enable the module, edit the /etc/modules file, add w1-gpio as a line on its own, and then reboot. To check that the module is loaded, do the following:

```
~: lsmod | grep "w1-gpio"
```

After the module is loaded, a special file path appears at /sys/class/gpio, which is where all the action happens. To reserve (or export) a pin, you write the pin number (in our case, 17) to the pseudo file /sys/class/gpio/export:

```
1 ~: echo 17 > /sys/class/gpio/export
```

If the reservation is successful, you'll find a new pseudo folder at /sys/class/gpio/ gpio17/. This folder allows you to control the pin. First you need to give it a direction (in for input, as in our case, or out for output):

```
~: echo "in" > /sys/class/gpio/gpio17/direction
```

If you were using the pin as an output, you could set the value of the pin by writing either 0 or 1 to /sys/class/gpio/gpio17/value in a similar manner to the preceding commands. However, you're using it as in input, so you need to read the value of the pin instead. To do this, you read it as if it were a file:

```
~: cat /sys/class/gpio/gpio17/value
```

This returns either 0 or 1, followed by a newline (\n) character. You can constantly (or intermittently) read from (or write to) the pin as you need to, for as long as you like. When you are done, for instance when your program is ready to finish, you should release it (or unexport it) for others to use:

```
~: echo 17 > /sys/class/gpio/unexport
```

Given that you likely know the many ways to read from and write to files in PHP, you're probably already thinking of ways to access your doorbell circuit from your script. Stop right there, because Ronan Guilloux has already done the work for us and abstracted the inputs and outputs into a free library called php-gpio, which is what you will use in our script here:

```php
<?php

# First we need to include the library itself, which contains two primary
# files; the first contains the GPIO class and the second contains a class
# representing the RP itself, which is used by the first.

include('php-gpio/src/PhpGpio/Gpio.php');
include('php-gpio/src/PhpGpio/Pi.php');

# Next, create a GPIO object $gpio

$gpio = new PhpGpio\Gpio();

# Reserve pin 17 and set it as an input

$gpio->setup(17, "in");

# Enter a loop and wait for the doorbell to be pressed

while (1) {

  # Read the current state of pin 17

  $currently = $gpio->input(17);

  # If the switch is not pressed, the state will be 1. If the switch
  # IS pressed, the state will be 0. As the state is a "file" designed
  # to be read with a shell command like cat, it will be returned as
  # a string containing the 1 or 0 and \n. Don't just test for 0,
  # e.g. $currently == 0 as the function will return false on certain
  # errors, which would evaluate as 0.

  if ($currently === "0\n") {

    # Ding dong! Someone has pressed our doorbell. Use mplayer to
    # play an appropriate sound file. This requires amplified speakers
    # connected to either the sound jack or HDMI connector on the RP.
```

```
shell_exec('mplayer dingdong.mp3');

# We then continue the loop, awaiting our next visitor.

};

# Give the processor a chance to breathe. Not too long though, or
# we may miss a quick press of the doorbell switch.

usleep(1000);
};
```

Setting the value of output pins is equally as simple. You would just call $gpio->output($pin,$value). Other useful functions provided by the library include the following.

- function getHackablePins(): Returns an array of all of the accessible GPIO pins for your version of the RP

- function setup($pinNo, $direction): Reserves a pin and sets it as either an input or an output pin

- function input($pinNo): Gets the current state of the given pin

- function output($pinNo, $value): Sets the state of the given pin

- function unexport($pinNo): Releases the pin when you are finished with it

- function unexportAll(): Releases all of the pins you have currently reserved

- function isExported($pinNo): Checks whether you have reserved a pin

- function currentDirection($pinNo): Checks whether a pin is an input or output

So there you have it, a basic example of connecting real-world electronics to PHP. One thing to consider when you use an event loop like this is that while you are busy doing something in response to one GPIO event, other events may go unhandled. There are several strategies to work around this:

- Create one PHP script to monitor for GPIO events, which rapidly fires-and-forgets network events in response, and a second PHP script using an event library such as libevent to buffer them and respond as needed (see the "Network Daemons Using libevent" section of Chapter 6).

- Periodically check for further events during your script with timed statements using ticks or POSIX signals (see the "Linux Timed-Event Signals" section earlier in this chapter).

- Fire off additional PHP scripts (or other programs) in the background, in response to the events (see the "Starting External Processes from PHP, or 'Shelling Out'" section of Chapter 7).

Toolbox	php-gpio
A library to simplify GPIO access on the Raspberry Pi	
Main web site	https://github.com/ronanguilloux/php-gpio
Main documentation and installation info	https://github.com/ronanguilloux/php-gpio/#php-gpio

Raspberry Pi: Using the Rest of the Hardware

Much of the RP hardware is standard PC-type hardware; accessing the sound jack, USB ports, or HMDI output is pretty much as you would expect. Beyond those, and the standard GPIO pins we've discussed, there are a couple more specialized pieces of hardware on the RP that you can play with, including I2C and Serial Peripheral Interface (SPI) interfaces.

The RP supports I2C devices via a pair of pins on the board. I2C is a communications bus designed to allow multiple chips to talk to each other, over the same wires. This means that you can connect multiple sensors, devices, chips, expansion boards, and other peripherals easily without running out of connectors. T. Brian Jones has produced a PHP library to control I2C devices, and has written example code for accessing I2C connected accelerometers, magnetometers, and a barometric pressure, temperature, and altitude sensor.

The RP also supports the SPI protocol using five of the pins on the board. SPI is a slightly more advanced communications protocol, and is commonly used by chips such as analog-to-digital converters (ADCs), GPIO expansion chips, and, in particular, peripherals that require higher (full-duplex) communication speeds. Michael Davey has created an SPI extension for PHP to allow you to communicate with SPI devices connected to the RP.

Toolbox	TBJs Raspberry Pi PHP Tools
PHP scripts to access I2C devices on the RP	
Main web site	`https://github.com/tbrianjones/raspberry-pi-i2c-bus`
Main documentation and installation info	`https://github.com/tbrianjones/raspberry-pi-i2c-bus#tbjs-raspberry-pi-php-tools`

Toolbox	php_spi
A PHP extension for accessing SPI devices	
Main web site	`https://github.com/frak/php_spi`
Main documentation and installation info	`https://github.com/frak/php_spi#building`

Raspberry Pi: Further Resources

Many more RP tutorials, articles, books, and kits are available. I've listed some of the more popular online RP resources in this section, and while many of them don't use PHP for the software portion of projects, you should be able to use the preceding PHP libraries to create most of the software you need. Education is one of the drivers behind the RP project, so many tutorials use higher-level languages aimed at programming beginners. This should make it easier to understand them and thus help when "translating" into PHP.

Further Reading

- *The MagPi*, a monthly magazine full of news, articles, and tutorials for the RP, aimed at both beginners and more advanced users. It's free to read online (including the full back-catalog); a printed version is also available to buy.

    - `www.raspberrypi.org/magpi/`

- RP section on the Embedded Linux Wiki. A great resource for hardware specs, software, tutorials, guides, and other information on the RP.

    - `http://elinux.org/RPi_Hub`

- The GPIO section on the Embedded Linux Wiki, in particular, has great reference material about the GPIO capabilities.

    - `http://elinux.org/RPi_Low-level_peripherals#General_Purpose_Input.2FOutput_.28GPIO.29`

- The official RP forums are a great place to get and give help on anything RP related. It's a tolerant and welcoming forum, where "newbie" questions are welcomed and there are very few "personalities."

    - `www.raspberrypi.org/forums/`

- A version of the GUI toolkit wxPHP (see Chapter 5) built for Raspian.

    - `www.wxphp.org/news/raspberry-pi-raspbian-binary-build`

- The Raspberry Pi Stack Exchange Q&A site, currently has over 6,000 questions and 9,000 answers about the RP.

    - `http://raspberrypi.stackexchange.com/`

- The official RP web site. News about the RP and its foundation, educational resources, and associated events and programs.

    - `www.raspberrypi.org/`

▨ ▨ ▨

## CHAPTER 9

Performance and Stability— Profiling and Improving

Or, "Why is PHP sooooo slow?"

PHP *script performance* (a term we use to encompass indicators such as speed of execution and usage of resources) is an issue for both PHP-based web sites as well as other applications written in PHP. This chapter looks at the issues affecting PHP performance in general, specific performance considerations for nonweb applications, and the tools and resources available for solving performance-related problems. We also look at stability of long-running scripts, which is often tied closely to performance issues.

The Background on Performance

PHP is generally considered a *scripting* or *interpreted* language. Rather than compiling or transforming source code into machine-executable instructions and distributing those as a stand-alone program (as is usually the case with languages such as C), PHP programs are distributed as PHP source code. The user of the software requires the PHP interpreter (also known as the *PHP virtual machine*) to run that source code, with the interpreter converting the PHP source code to machine instructions on the fly as the application executes.

This style of execution has pros and cons. The main advantages are ease of code updating and deployment (no compilation steps) and fewer architecture issues (write-once, run-anywhere, and no need to compile for specific platforms). The main disadvantage is the performance hit of the interpretation stage as the application runs. Modern versions of PHP reduce this performance hit by first transforming the code into intermediate *opcodes* that are then executed. Those opcodes don't need to be reinterpreted every time the same code occurs (for example, in a loop). For frequently used scripts, such as web scripts and some applications, these opcodes can even be cached between script runs for faster subsequent execution.

PHP is also a *high-level* language, which means that it uses abstractions to hide much of the lower-level detail of the code the computer needs from the user. Instead of dealing with implementation details such as memory addressing and call stacks, PHP and other higher-level languages present the computer to the programmer with abstract concepts such as variables, arrays, and functions. Much of the appeal of a language such as PHP is the wide range of built-in functions and operators to perform common tasks, which leads to higher developer productivity. Versatile data structures (such as PHP's array type, which is a type of managed, ordered map that can be used as a variety of common data structure types) hide details of memory management, simplify access, and provide a rich variety of related manipulation functions. These abstractions come at a performance cost, however. Behind every function, array operation, or disk access are lower-level algorithms written in C. The implementation of these algorithms must cater to the "general" case and include all possible uses of the algorithm. Thus they will rarely be as optimal as C algorithms

© Rob Aley 2016
R. Aley, *PHP Beyond the Web*, DOI 10.1007/978-1-4842-2481-6_9

written specifically for your particular use case. This level of abstraction again adds overhead to PHP when compared to lower-level languages such as C, although the core PHP developers have invested a lot of time and effort in the last couple of years to optimize, trim, refactor, and otherwise increase the performance of the C back end to great effect, wildly increasing speed and reducing memory consumption in many common cases. And for those common cases, these prebuilt PHP algorithms are often better than those you may be able to write yourself!

The final reason for performance problems is perhaps one of the most prevalent issues but also one of the easiest to fix: the PHP programmer. Many developers aren't aware of how to find and solve performance issues in their own code, often blaming their own failings on PHP itself, even where PHP is just as high performing as other languages. While PHP takes away a lot of the pain and slog from programming, hiding and dealing with numerous tasks for you, it is still a general-purpose programming language and as such it is still perfectly possible to write poorly performing code. Even with an appreciation of the issues, many developers aren't aware of the tools and resources that are available to help improve their programs' performance.

For those who doubt that it is possible to write high-performance systems in PHP, the set of slides in the following "Further Reading" section provides examples from one company that shows that it's not just possible—it happens in the real world. Appendix D also shows some of the things that people are doing with PHP, and performance clearly isn't holding them back.

Further Reading

- "More than Websites: PHP and the Firehose @ Datasift" by Stuart Herbert

  - http://blog.stuartherbert.com/php/2013/04/16/slides-from-brighton-php-more-than-websites-php-and-the-firehose/

Specific Issues for General-Purpose Programming

As I've noted, both web and nonweb PHP scripts can have performance problems. However, you need to take some additional performance-related issues into account when programming longer-running scripts and those without memory restrictions. In the CLI SAPI, as with the traditional web PHP model of programming, PHP manages limits on memory consumption and executes garbage collection on your behalf. This works well on the Web, where the shorter lives and lower resource intensiveness of many scripts mean that limits and management processes are rarely noticed. However, when you program a general-purpose application, you will often want to remove the imposed memory limits to allow your application to consume all the memory it needs on different systems with different amounts of memory. Indeed, the default configuration for the CLI SAPI now sets the memory and execution time limits to 0, unless you specify otherwise. This transfers the burden of managing and limiting memory usage to your script. Likewise, in longer-running, resource-intensive, and response-time-sensitive scripts, garbage collection requires a different approach to avoid unwanted blocking or unnecessary conservancy. This involves the manual management of the garbage-collection process within your scripts.

Inefficient programming and algorithm design on your part as the programmer can also be more noticeable than it is on the Web. The time that an algorithm takes when generating a web page can get lost in the other time overheads of transmitting and displaying a page, but when the exact same algorithm is executed on the command line, a noticeable pause may be visible. Responsiveness to a user is critical on the Web, but also very noticeable to local users as well.

The rest of this chapter looks at how to profile and manage the performance of your scripts and the resources they use, including strategies to target the problems described previously.

Profile, Profile, Profile!

We've all come across slow-running scripts (often our own!), and usually the first response is to start looking up ways to increase PHP's speed. Compiling, caching, refactoring code, accelerators—these are topics that searching on Google for *PHP performance* or *speed issues* will readily turn up. You may have already read about them, and then you want to dive right in to try them out.

My advice (derived from bitter personal experience) is to *stop right now*. Throwing performance trick after performance trick against your code (often that you find online or in good books like this)—even when they appear sensible and you can see the logic—can end up complicating your code or adding dependencies for no good reason. Why? Because when you don't know the root cause of the problem, you don't know whether a particular solution, no matter how good on paper, will address the issue you are having in this particular case. And even if it does appear to work, you don't know if it is the simplest way to fix it, and thus whether you're saddling yourself with extra "technical debt" when you don't have to.

The step we often miss is to ask our script directly, "Why are you running so slowly?" If your script tells you, you can then attempt to fix the issue directly without the use of external tools such as compilers and caching systems. So how do you ask your script the *why* question? By profiling it.

A *profiler* watches a piece of software (usually from the "inside") as it runs and breaks down the time (and sometimes resources) that each part of the program uses. The profile information is often reported down to the level of an individual line of code or function call. This helps you spot exactly where your scripts are slowing down. Is it that complex database query? A badly written loop? A function that's called more times than expected? Disk or network access pausing execution? Whatever the problem, the profiler will tell you. Once you know the exact cause of the slowdown, the solution is usually apparent (or at the very least, you can rule out potential solutions that won't actually fix it). It may just mean rewriting a few lines of code or caching some data instead of repeatedly generating it. The profiler may point out problems external to PHP, such as a slow database server, or laggy network connection or resource. Of course, in some cases you may end up having an intractable problem from a PHP programming point of view that does indeed require the help of an accelerator or external caching system. In any case, you will likely save time and prevent making unnecessary changes to your code or deployment environment by using a profiler to ask the *why* before you start trying the *what*.

With PHP, you have several choices when it comes to profiling. You can manually profile your code by adding profiling/measuring statements directly to your code base, or you can use a tool to automatically profile your code for you. The former is quick and easy to do, with no changes to your development environment, if you know roughly where in your code the problem lies. The latter, while requiring the setup and configuration of the tool, and learning how to use it the first time, provides more-comprehensive profiling. It also doesn't rely on you knowing where your problems may be located, and usually requires minimal or no changes to your code base. You'll look at both options in this section.

Manual Profiling

Manual profiling entails adding code to your source to measure time or resources directly from within the scripts. The following is an example of measuring execution time of different lines of code:

```php
<?php

# Let's fill some variables using loops

$something = $anotherthing = '';

# Let's create a "checkpoint" by recording the current time and memory
# usage
```

```php
$time1 = microtime(true);
$memory1 = memory_get_usage();

# Now let's do a loop 10 times, having a quick usleep and adding just a
# little data to our variable each time

for ($counter = 0; $counter < 10; $counter++) {
    usleep(10);
    $something .= 'a';
};

# Now create a second checkpoint

$memory2 = memory_get_usage();
$time2 = microtime(true);

# Let's do this second loop 1000 times, having a longer sleep and adding
# lots of data to our variable each time

for ($counter = 0; $counter < 1000; $counter++) {
    usleep(100);
    $anotherthing .= str_repeat('abc',1000);
};

# and create a final checkpoint

$memory3 = memory_get_usage();
$time3 = microtime(true);

# Now let's output the time and memory each loop used.

echo ("1st Loop : ".($time2-$time1)." msecs, ".
($memory2-$memory1)." bytes\n");

echo ("2nd Loop : ".($time3-$time2)." msecs, ".
($memory3-$memory2)." bytes\n");

echo ("Peak memory usage : ". memory_get_peak_usage()." bytes\n");
```

Run this script and you should see that the second loop takes a lot longer and consumes a lot more memory. You now know that the problem is the second loop, and you can fix it by removing the usleep statement, and maybe removing the loop altogether and using str_repeat('abc',1000000) to fill your variable. You should also see that the peak memory usage reported on the last line is higher than that of the two loops. This demonstrates that without active management of variables (for example, unset()ting them), memory usage accumulates throughout a script. This is obviously a simple, contrived example, but the principles apply to real-world code as well.

As you can see, manual profiling is quick and simple for a few lines of code. However, profiling larger code bases can quickly become cumbersome, massively increasing the size of the code base if you're not careful. When hunting down a particular problem, you can profile larger sections of code, and when the larger section at fault is found, profile that into smaller chunks, and so on, until the problem code is found (effectively doing a binary search). If you're spending a lot of time doing it this way, the time necessary to implement and learn a profiling tool like those detailed next would probably be time well spent instead.

One other thing to remember is that manual profiling code adds a performance penalty to your scripts—which, although usually small, can add up, especially if you are repeatedly logging profiling information to disk as you go. So it may be worth considering stripping out or disabling profiling code before the code hits production (perhaps as part of your build/deployment process). In some cases, of course, consciously adding profiling code to the production code base can be helpful (for example, when it is necessary/useful to collect profiling information from your end users who aren't likely to have dedicated profiling software installed). Automatic profiling tools also usually add some overhead, although it is often smaller (they are typically written in lower-level languages and often integrate directly with the PHP interpreter), and are usually easier to switch on and off. These automatic tools are often used only in the development environment and not on live production machines, so any overhead is restricted to development work.

Profiling Tools

Several profiling tools are available for PHP. While the Xdebug debugger provides profiling options (and is worth looking at if you already have it installed for debugging), the most common and comprehensive tool is *XHProf*. Originally developed by Facebook, it is available as a PECL extension and so can be simply and easily installed. The data collection side is written in C, and a graphical PHP interface is provided for viewing the collected profile data, including call graphs (visual graphs of which functions call which) if you have Graphviz installed. A related project, *XHGui*, which is a fork of XHProf, provides an expanded visual interface, stores multiple runs in a MySQL database, and provides access for sorting and comparing multiple runs. XHGui requires a little more work to install and configure, and is particularly geared toward web scripts, but provides a lot of flexibility if you are regularly profiling code, or profiling live code on production systems. For basic profiling to find obvious problems in development code, though, XHProf is a good place to start.

Another up-and-coming profiler is *php-profiler*, a profiler written in pure PHP. Less comprehensive than XHProf, it is nevertheless useful and easy to deploy: simply `include()` `profiler.php` in your code. Note that because it is designed with the Web in mind, the output from this profiler is attached to the web page it has profiled by default. If using it with nonweb scripts, you need to use output buffering or something similar to redirect the output to (for example) a separate HTML file on disk for later viewing in a browser.

Further Reading

- "The Need for Speed: Profiling PHP with XHProf and XHGui" by Matt Turland

    - `www.sitepoint.com/the-need-for-speed-profiling-with-xhprof-and-xhgui/`

- "XHProf PHP Profiling" by Adam Culp

    - `www.geekyboy.com/archives/718`

- "Profiling with XHGui" by Paul Reinheimer

    - `http://webadvent.org/2010/profiling-with-xhgui-by-paul-reinheimer`

- "Profiling PHP Applications with XHGui" by Lorna Mitchell

    - `https://inviqa.com/blog/profiling-xhgui`

- "Advanced CodeIgniter Profiling with XHProf" by James Constable

    - `http://net.tutsplus.com/tutorials/php/advanced-codeigniter-profilingwith-xhprof/`

- XHProf in the PHP manual

    - `www.php.net/manual/en/book.xhprof.php`

Toolbox	XHProf
Function-level hierarchical PHP profiler	
Main web site	`https://github.com/phacility/xhprof`
Installation info	`www.php.net/manual/en/xhprof.setup.php`
Main documentation	`www.php.net/xhprof`
Tool for visual function graphs	`http://graphviz.org/`

Toolbox	XHGui
Expanded profiler based on XHProf	
Main web site	`https://github.com/preinheimer/xhprof`
Installation info and main documentation	`https://github.com/preinheimer/xhprof/blob/master/INSTALL`

Toolbox	php-profiler
An embedded PHP profiler library	
Main web site	`https://github.com/jimrubenstein/php-profiler`
Installation info and main documentation	`https://github.com/jimrubenstein/php-profiler#php-profiler`

Toolbox	PHP-Benchmark
A profiling library like php-profiler, with an emphasis on profiling/comparing individual algorithms	
Main web site	`http://victorjonsson.github.io/PHP-Benchmark/`
Installation info and main documentation	`https://github.com/victorjonsson/PHP-Benchmark#benchmarking`

Toolbox	KCachegrind
A tool for profile-data visualization. Use with Xdebug for visual profile information.	
Main web site	`https://kcachegrind.github.io/html/Home.html`
Main documentation	`https://kcachegrind.github.io/html/Documentation.html`

Toolbox	Webgrind
An alternative web-based profiling front end for Xdebug that implements a subset of KCachegrind's features	
Main web site	`https://github.com/jokkedk/webgrind`
Installation info and main documentation	`https://github.com/jokkedk/webgrind#webgrind`

Low-Level Profiling

When you really need to "go deep" into what's happening with your script, you sometimes need to look not at what your code is doing, but at what PHP itself is doing instead. To be clear, most of us will never need to do this to solve performance problems, though it can be quite interesting and instructive to look at how PHP translates your code into calls to the system on which it's running. PHP itself is a C program compiled into a binary executable, which means you can use general-purpose tools such as `strace` (shows system calls and signals), `ltrace` (shows library calls), and `gdb` (a debugger for C programs like PHP itself) to see what's going on under the hood. If this interests you, have a look at the following tutorial from Derick Rethans. As the author of Xdebug, he's somewhat of an expert on the mechanics of PHP.

Further Reading

- "What Is PHP Doing?" by Derick Rethans

  - `http://derickrethans.nl/what-is-php-doing.html`

Profiling—The Likely Results

Profiling can reveal an inordinate number of performance problems. However, the following are some of most common types of problems discovered when profiling PHP, along with strategies for addressing them:

- *Database access*: Calls to databases (and indeed any other external service) can often be a source of slowness. One line in your code may be calling many thousands of code lines in the responding software/service. Database performance is the topic of a whole book or two of its own, but areas to look at for improving database performance include database indexes and normalization, server load, database cache settings, and inappropriate SQL usage. You can sidestep some database issues directly in PHP by thinking about whether you need to call the database at all. Can you, for instance, cache some oft-requested data? Can you batch multiple queries together in one request? Can you request more data in one query rather than over multiple queries? Do you really need the data in the first place?

- *Disk access*: Particularly for large files and files from network drives, disk access can be time-expensive. Possible workarounds include caching data in PHP (or in Memcached or a similar extension), reading in a whole file at once (at the expense of memory) rather than repeatedly opening the same file, using local disks (or caching to them before use) rather than network drives, using better hardware (for example, SSDs), or using memory-based drives (for example, tmpfs). Be aware that modern operating systems are usually quite good at optimizing disk access and perform some memory caching, particularly for disk writes and for reads of often-accessed files, and so some optimizations may not give the expected level of speed improvement. Always profile your proposed solutions!

- *Loops*: Repeated calculations and other operations inside loops can quickly eat up time in what appears to be a low number of lines. If the same calculation (or partial calculation) is repeated in the body or control structure of a loop, move it outside the loop and store the result in a variable to be used in the loop. Look at functions called from within the loop as well to see if anything in the function can be cached, removed, or otherwise sped up. Often functions assume that they will be called only once or twice, and so using things like `static` variables to preserve state between calls can sometimes speed up a repeatedly called function.

- *No clear cause and/or solution*: Occasionally the slowness has no clear, single cause; everything is a bit slow, and it all adds up. Likewise, there may be a clear cause, but no clear solution because your script is doing something that is naturally time-expensive and it is the only way to achieve the outcome you need.

In this last case, it may be time to start looking for some "silver bullets"—generic solutions for increasing the speed of your script.

Further Reading

- An article benchmarking "Fast Line Iteration in PHP" by Stephan Soller. Of particular interest is the comment section at the bottom, detailing why disk caching had a big effect on the author's numbers but not on another commenter's.

    - `http://arkanis.de/weblog/2013-09-27-fast-line-iteration-in-php`

Silver Bullets

Silver bullets are solutions that you can "throw" at your script, which will hopefully speed them up without you having to think too much about the cause of the slowdown. In my first version of this section, I wrote the words *silver bullet* followed by a question mark. I took it out because it cluttered up the place, but the point remains that there are no guaranteed, universal silver bullets for increasing performance in PHP. Each of the oft-called "performance solutions" that follow have downsides, aren't suitable for everyone, and require a reasonable amount of thought to implement. Nevertheless, they can be useful, particularly when you have improved your script as much as you can manually and you are stretching the capabilities of PHP or the available hardware.

Silver Bullet 1—Better Hardware

If funding allows, sending out for a beefier server or desktop can often produce instant performance gratification. In some cases, hardware is cheaper than developer time, so it's a no-brainer. However, downsides exist, particularly for those who are cash challenged:

- You still need to do some profiling to work out exactly what new hardware you need. Is your script processor intensive? Does it guzzle RAM? Is it spending a lot of time hitting the disks? Or do you need all of the above? Is it, in fact, hitting problems with external access such as network or database access? If that's the problem, new hardware likely won't help.

- Costs incurred include both purchase/lease costs, as well as potentially increased power-consumption costs, maintenance costs, and depreciation/replacement costs.

- With many algorithms, increased hardware capacity will eventually hit natural barriers where script performance doesn't scale linearly with increases in hardware performance.

Silver Bullet 2—Newer PHP Versions

Each new version of PHP typically increases performance and reduces resource usage in many areas, so moving up to a new version of PHP can often give your scripts more headroom. For instance, benchmarks between versions 5.3 and 5.4 often show a performance increase of between 7 percent and 31 percent on common scripts, and memory usage improvement of between 17 percent and 50 percent. Going from 5.6 to 7.0 has even better results, with some benchmarks reaching 100 percent speed-up in the new version for some types of script. There are other benefits too, such as bug fixes and new features. There are, of course, some downsides as well:

- Although generally backward compatible, most releases also have a handful of functions that are deprecated or fully removed, and the functionality of others is altered, sometimes subtly. You need to thoroughly test your code when upgrading and may need to make changes to your code base.

- Some extensions (particularly older, less-maintained or more-obscure ones) may not be compatible with the new version. This will require you to alter your code base or that of the extension.

Silver Bullet 3—Opcode Caching

Opcode caches work by caching the executable opcodes created by the PHP binary when a PHP script is run, and (assuming the PHP script remains unchanged) using the same opcodes the next time the script is called rather than regenerating them each time. This provides a performance increase mainly at the startup of a script. Web scripts are short scripts called repeatedly, often many times a second on busy sites. In such cases, opcode caches can provide a slightly faster experience for the individual user and a larger resource saving for the server as a whole. Opcode caches such as the Alternative PHP Cache (APC) are usually easy to install and configure, and so are in most cases a no-brainer for web developers and server administrators, providing the silver bullet of increased performance for not much work.

However, opcode caches aren't always as effective for offline applications. These applications are typically longer lived, so the relative gain in startup performance is often much less than with short-lived web scripts. For this reason, the main cache systems for PHP aren't written to deal with the CLI SAPI, and really run only under the web server model, where many requests are served by the same PHP process. You can enable the APC for use with the CLI SAPI by setting `apc.enable_cli` in `php.ini`. However, this is meant for testing purposes and usually provides no benefit for your script, because the cache is destroyed at the end of each process run. We don't cover opcode caches here, but further resources are offered next if you are running on a web-style model.

Further Reading

- List of opcode caches and related software on Wikipedia
  - `http://en.wikipedia.org/wiki/List_of_PHP_accelerators`
- "Using PHP 5.5's New OPcache Opcode Cache" by Christopher Jones
  - `https://blogs.oracle.com/opal/entry/using_php_5_5_s`

Silver Bullet 4—Compiling

PHP compilers have existed for a while, typically taking PHP source code and transforming it into an intermediate language (such as C++) before using a commonly available compiler for that language to compile it into a machine-executable file. These compiled files typically execute faster, and with a lower resource overhead, than standard interpreted code. Previous incarnations have had limited success, often suffering from a lack of coverage of all PHP syntax and functions, incompatibilities with common PHP extensions, and prohibitive licensing restrictions. The lack of decent compilation tools serves as a hat-tip to the notion that PHP, in fact, performs well for most use cases and so a strong market for these tools does not exist.

One company with an understandable need for higher performance from PHP has started to change the game, however. Facebook, the popular social networking company, has introduced and developed the PHP HipHop compiler project over the past couple of years. The Facebook interface was originally written primarily in PHP, and although various subsystems have since been written in lower-level languages, much of Facebook's legacy (and new) interface code remains coded in PHP. Facing enormous scaling and performance challenges with a user base of over 1 billion (a nice problem to have), but still recognizing the benefits of developing in PHP and with a large existing code base to support, Facebook has invested considerable resources into the HipHop project.

The first fruits of the project, which have been released as open source, were the HipHop for PHP compiler (HPHPc) and HPHPi "developer mode interactive" version of HPHPc. Both are reliable, production-ready tools with great features. As with all programming, specific performance gains will depend on the ins and outs of what your PHP script is trying to do. However, various benchmarks have pegged HipHop-compiled binaries with performance increases of up to 600 percent in real-world usage, compared to the standard PHP 5.x interpreters. HPHPc works in a similar way to other PHP compilers: it first converts your code to C++ and then uses G++ to compile that C++ down to an executable binary.

Whichever compiler you look at using, and several more are listed later, there are downsides to consider:

- *New toolchain and deployment process*: None of the available compilers are drop-in replacements for the standard PHP interpreter, so you need to invest time in learning to use the compiler and updating/changing your build process.

- *Involved compiler deployment*: PHP compilers are typically not included in software repositories such as the standard PHP binaries, so deployment becomes more involved and often requires compiling the compilers themselves on each development/build machine.

- *Compiling code takes time, particularly in large projects*: Each build you make will be slowed down, although some of this is mitigated with the HPHPi tool in the Facebook suite of programs.

- *Lack of function coverage*: All currently available compilers, including the HPHP suite, do not cover all of the core PHP functions, let alone many of the available extensions. Support for dynamically accessing other extensions varies by compiler and is often patchy or nonexistent. Thus, you need to ensure that your code is supported by your chosen compiler, or you may need to rewrite or remove sections of your code/functionality.

- *Your users won't have access to the source code by default*: For proprietary software, this may be a plus. As a consequence, if you use other open source code within your project, you may need to make arrangements to provide the source code to your users or bundle it with the executable (depending on the license requirements). It also may dissuade knowledgeable users from helping you to develop your code and identify existing and potential bugs (and their fixes).

Because of (some of) these downsides, the Facebook project has (since early 2013) deprecated the HipHop compilers in favor of a JIT-based virtual machine, discussed in the next section. Other available compilers are also now either defunct or haven't been updated to support recent PHP versions. However, they may be of some use for certain projects so I have listed the main ones for your reference.

Further Reading

- HPHPc benchmarks for Drupal

    - `http://php.webtutor.pl/en/2011/05/17/drupal-hiphop-for-php-vs-apc-benchmark/`

- An instructive rant by Paul Biggar, the developer of the phc compiler, about PHP compilers

    - `https://medium.com/@paulbiggar/a-rant-about-php-compilers-in-general-and-hiphop-in-particular-65061e972aed#.5ogok3wa4`

Toolbox	phc
An open source compiler for PHP with support for plug-ins. Supports PHPv5.2 and earlier.	
Main web site	`https://github.com/pbiggar/phc`

Toolbox	bcompiler
PECL extension to compile PHP to bytecode and optionally into executables	
Main web site	`http://pecl.php.net/package/bcompiler`
Installation info and main documentation	`www.php.net/bcompiler`

Toolbox	Roadsend PHP
An open source compiler that is no longer actively developed, but the source code is still available	
Main web site	`www.roadsend.com/`
Installation info and main documentation	`https://github.com/weyrick/roadsend-php`

Silver Bullet 5—JIT Compilers and Alternative Virtual Machines

Before we discuss them in detail, I'll define a couple of terms in case you're not familiar with them:

- *Virtual machine*, or *VM*: This is generally used to mean what, in the old days, we would call the interpreter. Specifically, I am talking about what is more formally called a *process virtual machine* (rather than a system virtual machine,' which is typically a virtualized operating system running on something like VirtualBox). When you write PHP code (or code in many other programming languages including Python or Java), rather than being compiled into machine-executable instructions (as C is, for instance), it's first compiled into an intermediate set of instructions that are then executed by a virtual machine or interpreter. The VM is typically written in C and compiled into machine-executable code itself. This means that code written in PHP is effectively platform independent; it doesn't need to know anything about the instruction set usable on a specific platform. The VM worries about that (which is why you will find individual PHP executables for Windows, Linux, Mac, and so on to download, but most PHP scripts themselves don't require different scripts for different platforms).

- *JIT compiler*: JIT stands for *just in time*. Rather than code being compiled completely in advance (like C), or at the start of each script run (like traditional PHP), JIT compilers compile code function by function as the code runs, in real time. The advantages of doing this are twofold: only the code that is actually executed needs to be compiled, and the compiler can use runtime information such as current variable types (which are not defined until they are run in dynamically typed languages such as PHP) to produce more optimized code. In short, they're faster than traditional interpreters.

Further Reading

- "Virtual machine" on Wikipedia

  - http://en.wikipedia.org/wiki/Virtual_machine#Process_virtual_machines

- "Just-in-time compilation" on Wikipedia

  - http://en.wikipedia.org/wiki/Just-in-time_compilation

Numerous alternative VMs are now available for PHP, with the most recent making some waves in the PHP community. *HipHop Virtual Machine* (*HHVM*) is the latest output from the Facebook HipHop project (discussed in the preceding compiler section), and is making waves in part because of its built-in JIT compiler. It's certainly one to watch, as it's more than 50 percent faster than the HPHPc compiler it replaces in some benchmarks, it fits more naturally in most production workflows, and it has greater compatibility with PHP and its extensions.

Other VMs and JITs are available, and these are listed in the following Toolbox entries.. All of them, including HHVM, however, share a few drawbacks:

- *Limited coverage of PHP and extensions*: None of them yet have full coverage of PHP and common extensions. The HHVM team has committed to operating with the top PHP frameworks and applications, and is making great strides toward that. Other VMs, such as QB, explicitly state that they are focused on a particular subset of PHP, and so aren't a general-purpose solution. Thus you need to thoroughly test (and possibly alter) your code when considering using an alternative VM.

- *Not all alternate VMs are faster for all tasks*: The JIT in HHVM, for instance, requires multiple runs of CLI scripts before it learns enough to produce optimized code. As Sara Golemon wrote on the PHP Internals mailing list:

> *As the maintainer of the OSS version of HipHop (HHVM), I'll be the first to admit that the official PHP engine and runtime have a broader range of platform/architecture support, and stronger community, and a larger library of extensions and functionality behind it. Also, because of its lifecycle design, PHP outperforms HHVM on single-run command-line scripts. On the other hand, HHVM does outperform Apache+PHP for web requests quite well. Facebook would need at least 5x as many web servers (and we use a lot as it is) if we were using normal PHP.*
>
> http://marc.info/?l=php-internals&m=135399266632008&w=2

So you need to benchmark each possible VM against your typical use case, to make sure you are really getting the speed improvement you expect.

Toolbox	HHVM
Facebook's HipHop project VM, which includes a JIT compiler and has fairly broad language coverage (with better PHP 7 coverage coming soon)	
Main web site	`http://hhvm.com/`
Installation info and main documentation	`https://docs.hhvm.com/hhvm/`

Further Reading

- Presentation on building HHVM by Keith Adams, a Facebook engineer

  - `www.infoq.com/presentations/PHP-HHVM-Facebook`

- "First steps on HHVM" tutorial by Allan MacGregor

  - `http://coderoncode.com/programming/development/hhvm/vagrant/2013/07/27/first-steps-on-hhvm.html`

- Q&A about HHVM performance in CLI scripts

  - `http://stackoverflow.com/questions/17898783/hhvm-poor-performance`

- "Debugging PHP Applications with HHVM" in debug mode

  - `http://labs.qandidate.com/blog/2013/10/29/debugging-php-applications-with-hhvm/`

Toolbox	Quercus
100 percent Java implementation of PHP that supports a growing range of extensions and common PHP applications, claims a 4× performance boost and an API to allow PHP to access Java libraries	
Main web site	`http://quercus.caucho.com/`
Installation info and main documentation	`http://quercus.caucho.com/quercus-3.1/doc/quercus.xtp`

Toolbox	QB
A VM aimed at using PHP for graphics programming. Achieves impressive performance improvements but implements static typing and has array limitations. Can compile to an executable with G++ or other external compiler.	
Main web site	`https://github.com/chung-leong/qb`
Installation info and main documentation	`https://github.com/chung-leong/qb/wiki`

Toolbox	Roadsend PHP: Raven (rphp)
A rewrite of the Roadsend compiler using the LLVM VM framework and a C++ runtime. Includes a JIT compiler, but it doesn't appear to still be actively developed.	
Main web site	`https://github.com/weyrick/roadsend-php-raven`
Installation info and main documentation	`https://github.com/weyrick/roadsend-php-raven#readme`

Toolbox	Parrot
A polyglot VM designed for optimal and efficient execution of dynamic languages such as PHP, Perl, and Python. The PHP-specific project is PIPP.	
Main web site	`www.parrot.org`
PHP main site	`https://github.com/bschmalhofer/pipp/wiki`
Installation info and main documentation	`http://docs.parrot.org/parrot/latest/html/`

Further Reading

- "HappyJIT—A Tracing JIT Compiler for PHP," an academic paper exploring a tracing JIT engine for PHP

  - `http://dl.acm.org/citation.cfm?id=2047854&dl=ACM&coll=DL`

- "HippyVM," a Facebook-sponsored project looking at how to use the Python PyPy toolchain to produce a PHP VM

  - `http://morepypy.blogspot.co.uk/2012/07/hello-everyone.html`

- A basic, proof-of-concept PHP VM written in JavaScript

  - `http://phpjs.hertzen.com/`

- Presentation on "Building a JIT Compiler for PHP in Two Days" by Nuno Lopes

  - `http://llvm.org/devmtg/2008-08/Lopes_PHP-JIT-InTwoDays.pdf`

The Standard PHP Library

At the beginning of this chapter, we discussed the fact that some of PHP's performance problems arise from the overhead necessary to provide users with easy-to-use and versatile data structures and functions. If this overhead starts limiting your scripts, one port of call is the Standard PHP Library (SPL), a core PHP extension that contains common and esoteric data structures and functions. These are designed to solve common programming problems, albeit with a little more thought required than for PHP's more common structures such as the normal PHP array type.

So, for instance, if large arrays of data are causing your script to hit memory limits, you might want to look at the SplFixedArray class. It has some restrictions (you can use only integers as indexes, and the length of the array is fixed) but provides a faster implementation that uses less memory than a normal array. The PHP documentation is fairly comprehensive. If you're not familiar with some of the data structures (heaps, linked lists, and so forth), most basic introductions to computer science (or programming in more traditional languages) should help.

Further Reading

- PHP SPL documentation

  - `www.php.net/manual/en/book.spl.php`

- Presentation on "Intro to the SPL," a quick overview of the SPL, by Chris Tankersley.

  - `www.slideshare.net/ctankersley/intro-to-the-php-spl`

Garbage Collection

In every programming language, creating variables, arrays, and other resources uses up some of the memory in your PC. While that memory is in use, it isn't available for your software, or indeed any other software, to use. When you have no further use for that memory, it needs to be freed up so that it can be used again. When memory isn't freed up (usually accidentally), we get a *memory leak*: the available memory is gradually (or in some cases, quickly!) filled up by unused data, or *garbage*. In lower-level languages, such as C, programmers are responsible for memory management themselves—for instance, assigning memory for a variable and freeing it again when finished with. In higher-level languages such as PHP, memory is managed for you, and unused memory is returned to the available pile automatically.

In PHP, there are several mechanisms for this. The most basic is that when a program ends, all of the allocated memory is freed. Second, memory for resources that are created within a particular scope is automatically freed when you exit that scope as the resources are unset. For instance, variables declared within a function (rather than the global scope) will disappear when the function ends (unless you use `static` or something similar) and the memory will be freed.

Finally, PHP keeps track of values by *reference counting*. When you create a variable or an array, for instance, PHP creates a container in memory to hold the value of that variable, and starts a counter to keep track of how many things are using that value. When you refer to that variable (for instance, by assigning it to another variable), PHP increments the counter so that it knows who is using it. Once no one is using it, and the counter drops to 0, PHP knows it can safely remove that container and free up the memory.

However, reference counting isn't perfect. In particular, circular references can be created (a child with a reference to its parent, and vice versa, for example), and references may still exist even when the resource is no longer in use. In such cases, they aren't automatically freed and so can create a memory leak. To cope with this, PHP has *automatic garbage collection*, also called *cycle collection*. Once in a while, PHP will go through everything it knows about, looking for unused memory like this that hasn't been freed, and will then free it. The current algorithm for doing this, which is much more effective than previous ones, is available from PHP v5.3 onward. A fuller description of reference counting and cycle collection can be found in the PHP manual.

Further Reading

- "Garbage Collection" section in the PHP manual

- www.php.net/manual/en/features.gc.php

In theory, this is great. Automatic garbage collection prevents memory leaks and prevents the programmer from having to do too much work managing memory. However, in some applications it has a downside. PHP keeps a buffer of the currently created values, and kicks in garbage collection each time the size of this buffer reaches 10,000. If your program is doing something particularly time sensitive at that point, then tough, it has to wait until garbage collection is done. This wasn't usually a problem with short-lived web scripts, but definitely can be with longer-running CLI-based scripts that may frequently and repeatedly hit the 10,000 limit and kick off a collection cycle. That said, for many applications, the slowdown may not be noticeable or a problem, and the advantages of the automatic memory management may outweigh the disadvantages.

PHP will let you manage garbage collection yourself if you need to, turning it on and off as you require. As with any other performance issues, the benefit to your particular script is hard to estimate in advance, so profiling/benchmarking your software (or the higher-performance parts of it) with and without garbage collection disabled is advised.

To turn it off, call the `gc_disable()` function. When you are ready to turn it back on, use the `gc_enable()` function. If you want to manually run a garbage-collection cycle at a time to suit you, use the `gc_collect_cycles()` function, which will initiate a one-off collection of garbage.

▓ **Caution** To enable proper collection when you call `gc_collect_cycles()` or when you re-enable automatic collection with `gc_enable()`, PHP continues to keep and update its buffer of up to 10,000 values in the background. This buffer has a fixed size, so if you leave garbage collection off for too long, older values will get pushed out of the buffer. Some of these values may be the problematic variables that garbage collection is designed to free up, so you may unwittingly introduce a memory leak even if you re-enable garbage collection later. Thus use these functions with caution.

Multithreading and Concurrent Programming in PHP

Multithreading is the use of concurrent programming "threads" within a process, allowing a given program to do multiple things at once. Multithreading is commonly used to increase performance in processes with tasks that are suitable for concurrent processing (that is, when one step of the process doesn't rely on the completion of the other). PHP was not designed with multithreading capabilities, nor facilities to otherwise natively do concurrent processing or take advantage of multiple processors/cores. In the past, this wasn't a particular issue; web development rarely calls for the performance gains associated with multithreading, and a web server can spin up multiple PHP instances to prevent interface blocking in AJAX-type applications. Typical CLI scripts also didn't require it, often being smaller-scale or batch-type applications.

However, as larger and larger applications are developed in PHP, and web server admins are looking to get greater resource utilization from their existing hardware, the lack of multithreading or other methods of parallel processing is beginning to become a more pertinent issue within the PHP community. Indeed, it is already a great "problem" that PHP's detractors often try to latch onto. As Moore's law begins to falter (depending on who you talk to), performance gains are typically coming instead from multicore and multiprocessor architectures, where multithreading and parallel programming will be more and more important.

The topic of multithreading is a contentious one within the PHP community. Some people believe that multithreading is needed for PHP to be taken "seriously" as a general-purpose programming language. Others believe that multithreading is of little use in PHP's core area of web interfaces and that it would add complexity to the language that, as a rule, has tried to stay as simple and straightforward as possible. It is true that even if threading was added to PHP with the simple, easy-to-grasp interfaces that PHP is well liked for, that is only half of the story. Programming with threads, regardless of syntax, is a somewhat advanced discipline that delves deeper into the intricacies of code interdependence and structure than PHP programmers usually have to deal with.

That the best way to take advantage of multiple processors and cores is through multithreading is not a settled argument in any case. The following IBM article outlines some of the thoughts in play around multithreading vs. multiprocess programming, and this particular article comes down on the multiprocess side of the fence.

Further Reading

- "Why Thread-Based Application Parallelism Is Trumped in the Multicore Era" by Vasudevan Thiyagarajan

  - `www.ibm.com/developerworks/java/library/j-nothreads/index.html?ca=drs-`

Each type of concurrency has pros and cons. Threading has less overhead and easier communication, for instance, whereas multiprocess programming has easier and greater isolation of tasks and minimal shared state. Regardless of the arguments, PHP doesn't support threads, and they aren't currently on the roadmap for the 7.*x* series of releases. With the PHP core development community lacking the appetite for such overhauls, these developments are likely several years away at best, if ever. Even then, implementing threading in a successful manner isn't a given. Python programmers often complain about the way threads are implemented and their performance characteristics (or lack thereof) in their own language, causing some to default to multiprocess programming, even though threads are available. So for the moment, if we want to do concurrent or parallel processing, we need to do it without threads. Luckily, there are several ways to work around this in and around PHP, with the best way depending on what you need to achieve.

The most common way is by creating and controlling new PHP processes. With this method, when your PHP script needs to carry out concurrent programming, it can fire up multiple copies of another PHP script as separate processes (or indeed fork itself multiple times as new processes), pass data to the other scripts, and wait for them to finish running. See Chapters 6 and 7 for details on forking and interprocess communication. Multiprocess programming is in some ways easier than multithreaded programming; you usually don't have to worry about shared state (for instance, accidentally overwriting variables/data/ memory in use by other threads). However, you do still need to think about how to handle interactions between the processes, how to deal with failures in another script (for example, if the user, the system, or an error kills one of your worker scripts, what do you do?), and how to manage/monitor system resources.

An alternative to managing process control yourself is to use a task dispatch and management system to manage it for you. Systems such as Gearman (discussed in Chapter 6) take your tasks and allocate them to worker scripts, managing the process from starting the scripts, to passing task information and monitoring scripts and system resources. There can be a few downsides to such systems in some cases though. You need to deploy and support additional software (the Gearman software), and the options for timing, error handling, and resource management might not exactly meet the needs of your scripts. However, for many cases, it removes a lot of the programming overhead that multiprocess software requires and hence helps speed development (as well as avoiding the reinvention of wheels).

If your performance problems come from processing very large amounts of data, a task typically improved by threading or concurrent processing, see the following section for a tool that may be able to help.

Big Data and PHP—MapReduce

In 2004, Google opened a window into their world of *big data* processing by releasing a seminal paper on MapReduce, the programming model used to handle the web-scale data needed for Google's search engine. Although Google has now moved on from MapReduce, it is still considered state of the art for the rest of us. A popular open source implementation called *Hadoop* enables you to run MapReduce jobs with PHP scripts.

Before we continue, let's clarify what we mean by *big* data. Hadoop and other MapReduce algorithms have inherent overhead in the way they work. They start producing benefits (at least performance wise) only as the data set becomes larger. Your mileage will vary depending on the algorithms you want to apply to your data and on the alternatives methods available, but typically your data set needs to be well into the gigabyte range before you start seeing noticeable benefits, and significantly bigger before these may outweigh the engineering effort needed to implement MapReduce on your task.

If your data falls into this particular definition of *big data*, you can harness the power of Hadoop with PHP. Although Hadoop is written in Java, it is language agnostic when writing the map-and-reduce jobs that drive the data processing. It also uses standard streams (STDIN and friends) for data interchange, which you've seen in earlier chapters are easy to handle natively in PHP. There is even a PHP framework to aid in writing those map-and-reduce jobs.

The following links should start you along the road of big data processing in PHP if you think that your data set qualifies as big.

Further Reading

- "MapReduce: Simplified Data Processing on Large Clusters," the original Google paper

    - http://research.google.com/archive/mapreduce.html

- "What is MapReduce?" a simple explanation of MapReduce

    - www-01.ibm.com/software/data/infosphere/hadoop/mapreduce/

- "Using Hadoop and PHP," a beginner's tutorial by Jason Graves

    - http://collaboradev.com/2010/12/10/using-hadoop-and-php/

- HadooPHP, the PHP Hadoop framework

    - https://github.com/dzuelke/HadooPHP

- "Big Data Analytics (with Hadoop and PHP)," a presentation by David Zuelke

    - https://speakerdeck.com/dzuelke/big-data-analytics-with-hadoop-and-php-dpc2013-2013-06-06

Data Caching

At various points in this chapter (and elsewhere), I have mentioned that it is often good practice to cache data where possible. For the uninitiated, this simply means that when you generate data that you may want to use again later (whether it's variables for use in your script, or text, or other program output), then instead of regenerating it each time, you instead store it somewhere until you need it again.

It should be obvious as to how to do this. You are likely familiar with creating variables, writing files to disk or a database, and so on. However, although caching data can speed up your programs, it can also come with its own set of problems, such as when to delete the cached data (cache invalidation), how to deal with cache priorities when disk space or memory runs low, how to share cached data between processes and even machines, and other things you (and I) haven't even thought of.

> *There are only two hard things in computer science: naming things, cache invalidation,*
> *and off-by-one errors.*
>
> —Saying based on a quote by Phil Karlton

Although PHP can't help with the first and last of those, it can help out a little when working with caches. The following information sources give some details of caching in PHP.

Further Reading

- Using Memcached, the generic, high-performance, distributed, memory-object-caching system, with PHP

    - www.php.net/manual/en/book.memcached.php

- MySQL query caching

    - http://php.net/manual/en/mysqlnd-qc.quickstart.caching.php

- Using output buffering for simple caching

    - www.theukwebdesigncompany.com/articles/php-caching.php

- "Virtual Files—tmpfs" section in Chapter 7 of this book for information on accessing memory-based disks

- "More—The File System Is Slow" by Kevin Schroeder, which discusses file-system performance and why OS caching may mean that using memory drives isn't necessarily much better for cache uses

  - www.eschrade.com/page/more-on-the-file-system-is-slow/

Know Thy Functions

When profiling, you may find sections of problematic code, often as little as one or two lines, that are running slowly—but for the life of you, you can't work out how to rewrite them. It's worth knowing that in PHP multiple functions often do the same or similar things, but they are implemented in a different way and so can take (sometimes vastly) different times to achieve the same goal.

This section presents two cheat sheets for this situation. The first is a web page (which you can also download to run on your own machine) that benchmarks groups of functions that perform similar tasks. This can let you see at a glance which alternative functions may be available and how they might perform. Do be aware that the performance of most functions depends on the code surrounding them, so always profile each one in the context of your own application!

The second link is a Q&A that attempts to list Big O times for many PHP functions. Again, this can be used to estimate which function may perform better in your scenario. Big O notation is a way to describe how the time (or resource) taken by an algorithm increases as the data-input size increases. A link to the Wikipedia article on Big O notation is also given.

Further Reading

- PHP benchmarking script, grouped by function performed

  - http://maettig.com/code/php/php-performance-benchmarks.php

- Q&A listing Big O times for various functions

  - http://stackoverflow.com/questions/2473989/list-of-big-o-for-phpfunctions

- "Big O notation" on Wikipedia

  - http://en.wikipedia.org/wiki/Big_O_notation

- An article that shows how using alternative functions in unusual ways can elicit performance gains

  - www.puremango.co.uk/2010/06/fast-php-array_unique-for-removing-duplicates/

- An alternative benchmarking web page

  - www.phpbench.com

Outsourcing Code to Other Languages

When you really hit the limits of PHP performance, and more hardware is not an option, one strategy is to move resource-heavy code out into better performing languages. There are two ways to do this, either by creating stand-alone programs that you shell out to (see Chapter 5) or by creating PHP extensions (which are generally faster to access than separate processes). If you're going to do this, you need to learn or leverage another language, so it's a topic mostly beyond the scope of this book. The following links should give you a good idea of where to start.

Further Reading

- "PHP at the Core: A Hackers Guide" on the official PHP documentation. Covers PHP internals with reference to writing extensions.

    - www.php.net/manual/en/internals2.php

- "Extension Writing" on Zend Developer Zone, a good introduction to writing extensions

    - https://devzone.zend.com/303/extension-writing-part-i-introduction-to-php-and-zend/

- "Writing Extensions" in Hacking with PHP

    - www.hackingwithphp.com/20/0/0

- Extsample, examples of basic code for creating extensions by Mikko Koppanen

    - https://github.com/mkoppanen/php-extsample

- *PHP Internals Book*, a free book written by several PHP core contributors

    - www.phpinternalsbook.com

- php4delphi, creating extensions using Delphi/Pascal

    - http://code.google.com/p/php4delphi/

- Embed the V8 JavaScript engine in PHP to run JavaScript code directly from your scripts

    - www.php.net/manual/en/book.v8js.php

- Embed PHP into C/C++ (effectively the opposite way around to extensions) by using SWIG

    - www.swig.org

Other Performance Tips and Tricks

A wealth of information about PHP performance and optimization is out there. Much of it revolves around web-based scripts, but a lot of it is still relevant to CLI scripts. The following are some good reads in this area, and a quick search on Google will bring you even more. Just to repeat myself once again, optimizations are often dependent on the code they are applied to, so always profile solutions on your own code to see if they make a difference. Also, make sure you read the following section on avoiding premature optimization.

Further Reading

- "Website Performance: PHP" by Warren Gaebel

    - http://blog.monitor.us/2012/03/website-performance-php/

- "Common Optimization Mistakes" by Ilia Alshanetsjy

    - http://ilia.ws/files/Dutch_PHP_Conference_2010_OPM.pdf

- "Fast PHP—Effective Optimisation and Bottleneck Detection" by Howard Yeend

  - www.puremango.co.uk/2010/04/fast-php/

- "A HOWTO on Optimizing PHP" by phpLens

  - http://phplens.com/lens/php-book/optimizing-debugging-php.php

Stability and Performance of Long-Running Processes

It's not just performance that can be affected by the issues raised in this chapter. Stability of your scripts is also affected by the poor management of resources and nonoptimal algorithms. By stability, I mean, essentially, crashes. PHP was initially "designed to die." It was designed for shorter-running scripts with little prospect of still being running many minutes later , let alone many hours or days later. That said, if you program carefully, there is no reason you can't create scripts (usually daemons) that can run pretty much indefinitely.

The key areas to think about when designing a stable program are as follows:

- *Resource time-outs*: Open resources, such as database connections and network sockets, can "go away." This can be for a variety of reasons, such as "lack of activity" time limits on the service you are connected to, network glitches, password/ credential changes, session time/resource limits, and so on. You may be used to opening a database connection at the start of your script and simply using the resource handle whenever you need to run an SQL query. This typically works fine on the Web; if you can connect to the database OK in the first place, the chances of anything happening during your script run are minuscule. However, when your script runs for hours or days, the odds mount for something bad occurring. There are several strategies for dealing with this:

  - Open connections only when needed, and close them immediately afterward. This is OK for occasional connections, but less OK if the overhead of connecting will cause responsiveness issues for scripts with time-sensitive responses.

  - Keep the connection open by occasionally interacting with the service (for example, via ticks). This may be unacceptable to the operator of the service that you are connecting to, and you also still need to check for disconnections for other reasons (for example, network glitches), although this can be done at the same time as these periodic connections to reduce the chance of a reconnection being needing during "real" interactions.

  - Periodically close and reopen connections. This has similar pros and cons to the preceding strategy.

  - Check the connection state at each attempt to access the resource. This is usually the safest way, reconnecting immediately if needed, although it usually requires the most effort from you, the programmer. It can also be combined with the two preceding strategies to reduce the chance that the resource will have "gone away," which is important in scripts with time-sensitive responses.

- *Overconsumption of memory, and memory leaks*: If your script uses too much memory, or uses functions or extensions that leak memory, eventually your script will hit a limit. That will be either a limit imposed in the PHP configuration (for example, in php.ini) or the natural limit of the amount of memory available on the machine itself. In either case, this will result in a fatal error causing your script to stop running. Even if you don't reach those limits, overconsumption that causes your system to, for instance, start swapping memory to disk can lead to systemwide slowness and instability (and eventually a Ctrl+Alt+Delete three-finger-salute from the user, perhaps). Small, persistent uses of memory, such as the repeated creation (without subsequent unsetting) of new variables in the global scope or new static variables in functions, may not be noticeable when profiling your application over even a few hours. However, over days or weeks or months, these small additions to the memory footprint may add up to something that causes unexpected crashes. It's important, where possible, to profile over longer periods of time, and to review the use of memory (for example, dynamic creation of variables and functions) in persistent scopes.

- *Fatal error handling*: PHP has a range of functions to deal with handling errors, but a couple of error types can't be handled within PHP. Fatal runtime errors (specifically, E_ERROR, E_CORE_ERROR, E_COMPILE_ERROR, and E_USER_ERROR) are nonrecoverable and will always cause your script to exit. These errors can be caused by many things, such as memory allocation problems (low memory), missing named functions, and so on. On the Web, unexpected transient E_ERRORs such as a system temporarily out of memory aren't always a problem; the web user hits Reload in the browser, and the next run may be successful. However, if your daemon hits an unexpected E_ERROR, then it's game over because your daemon will stop running completely. Strategies for dealing with this include the following:

  - Better testing (for example, full-coverage unit testing) to try to ensure that the errors don't occur.

  - Better resource handling, such as keeping on top of memory management. See the rest of this chapter for information on this!

  - Running under external supervision. Use a system such as supervisord to monitor and restart your daemon where necessary. This is good as a backup, but is no substitution for stopping the fatals from occurring in the first place.

Internal memory leaks and resource persistence issues with PHP itself are sometimes harder to work around, but these days they are quite rare, so upgrading to a modern version is really worthwhile where possible. The better resource usage and higher performance of modern versions also have the benefit of minimizing the impact of inefficiencies in your own code.

Avoid Micro and Premature Optimizations

Now that I've convinced you of the need to consider performance and instructed you on the finer arts of speed and resource management in PHP, I'm going to try to convince you to put it to the back of your mind, at least for now. It is easy to get caught up with performance and optimization and let it affect your workflow and productivity. Although it is generally positive to follow good practices and consider the performance of your code at all stages of development, premature optimization is often just that—premature—and micro-optimizations are not usually worth the paper they are written on.

As your author, I have an embarrassing confession to make. Having started programming in PHP many years ago, when the performance difference between using single and double quotes around a string was measurable in some contexts (or at least it was "common knowledge" that it was), I still find myself automatically considering what type of quote to use each time I type out a string, not for syntactical reasons but for performance reasons. That's despite the fact that the performance difference between the two nowadays is definitely extremely negligible. Old habits die hard, though, and many of the micro-optimizations that you will find on the Web fall into a similar category. Profile your code, and you will likely find that a single verbose database call will make the time saved by calling isset() dozens of times to check variables instead of falling back on @ to simply suppress warnings look incredibly small (that's not to say that there aren't other good reasons to do that, though!). Developer time spent in writing and thinking about micro-optimizations is typically much more expensive than the extra processor cycles used to execute unoptimized code.

Premature optimization typically occurs when developers start thinking about how to scale their code, before they have any of the code working and deployed. There is no point working out how to scale code that may never see the light of day because the project runs out of time or money and isn't delivered. Unless you are sure of the volume of customers/users/data that you will be processing, it's usually a better idea to get something up and running, as a proof of concept if nothing else, and then scale it when you know that it will be needed. Indeed, scaling methods vary considerably, depending on exactly what your code needs to do, and often this is not finalized until you have something up and running. So even if you deliver on time, your scaling efforts may all be in the wrong direction compared to how your project ends up functioning.

"But, but, but…" you cry, your project is different. It may well be. You might be lucky enough to work on a large-scale, well-funded project that has a known high-performance requirement, or be developing a tool that is specifically geared toward high-performance uses. Congratulations—you can ignore this section (if you're even at the level where reading this book is useful!). For the rest of us, and this is the majority of PHP projects, concentrate on getting it working and deployed first. Keep performance in mind during development, but don't let it interfere with your workflow too much. Most projects fail for reasons other than poor performance.

CHAPTER 10

■ ■ ■

Distribution and Deployment Issues

Now that you've written your perfect piece of software, your audience eagerly awaits its delivery and installation onto their precious machines. Distributing and deploying software comes with its own set of headaches above and beyond those you encountered just writing the similar thing. This chapter covers some of the issues that you may come across when thinking about deployment and distribution of your software. These issues may vary from those that arise from the common situation of pushing code to your own web server for a PHP-driven web site. In particular, this chapter focuses on scenarios of distributing your software in a way that it is no longer under your direct control and not on your own systems.

Error Handling and Logging

You need to think about how you handle and log errors (and other information) in your scripts when you run your code with the CLI SAPI. You can use the standard PHP error-handling functions and allow PHP to log errors to the file specified in error_log in php.ini. You should bear in mind that you may not be able to control which user your software is run under, so you need to log to an appropriate location where you can be sure your user has appropriate write permissions.

One alternative to the standard "log to a file" method in PHP is to instead send errors and other log information to the system's *syslog*. In Linux systems, this is the syslog(3) system (man syslog gives more information).I In Windows, this is the system event log. Using syslog has several advantages:

- Virtually all users have permission to log to syslog (usually).

- You don't need to manage log rotation or truncation, concurrent accesses/file locking, or other routine tasks.

- There is a wide ecosystem of tools for exploring and interacting with syslog.

- For system daemons and other critical software, system administrators often expect to find (at least important) logging/error information in the syslog.

- On systems designed to be scalable, syslog is often redirected to a central logging server/system. Writing your logs to syslog means that your software can scale to centrally managed log servers without any changes to your code.

© Rob Aley 2016
R. Aley, *PHP Beyond the Web*, DOI 10.1007/978-1-4842-2481-6_10

To send your errors automatically to syslog, you simply need to set `error_log` in `php.ini` to the special string syslog rather than a file name. You can also set this from within your script by using `ini_set('error_log', 'syslog')`. To log information other than PHP's own errors, or if you've chosen to handle PHP errors internally and need to subsequently log them manually, you can use the `syslog()` function. `syslog()` takes two parameters: a priority level, and the message to be logged. The priority levels range from `LOG_DEBUG` for debugging messages at the lowest level, up to `LOG_EMERG` to describe errors that render the system unusable. The second parameter is a string with the message to log. Before you can call `syslog()`, you need to use `openlog()` to open a connection to the syslog first. The following is a brief example:

```php
<?php

# Openlog takes an "ident" e.g. ('mysoftware') that appears in the logs to
# help you quickly filter for your own software, a set of OR'd options (we
# use LOG_PERROR to also print the logs to STDERR and LOG_PID
# to include the Process ID in the logs), and a "facility" to specify what
# type of software is logging (only LOG_USER is valid in Windows, in Linux
# you can have LOG_DAEMON, LOG_AUTH, and so on).

openlog('mysoftware', LOG_PERROR | LOG_PID, LOG_USER);

# We'll log a "notice," a routine notable message

syslog(LOG_NOTICE, 'Script started. All running smoothly.');

# Then when all hell breaks loose, we'll up the anti with an alert level
# message.

syslog(LOG_ALERT, 'BACON ALERT! Script has run out of bacon!. OMG.');

# Finally, we can close the log as we have no more messages to log. If we've
# specified syslog in php.ini as the location for error messages, those
# will continue to be logged, only our route for logging custom messages
# is closed here.

closelog();
```

If you run this script in a terminal, you will see the messages being printed to STDERR (usually back to the command line). If you then look at your syslog (on Linux this can often be done with the command `tail /var/log/syslog`), you should see two entries similar to these:

```
Oct 4 19:44:46 dev-machine mysoftware[6205]: Script started. All running smoothly.
3 Oct 4 19:44:46 dev-machine mysoftware[6205]: BACON ALERT! Script has run out of bacon!.
OMG.
```

In Windows, you can use the Event Viewer tool to view the logs, usually found under Start ä Control Panel ä System and Maintenance ä Administrative Tools ä Event Viewer.

Some other logging tools and further reading in this area are listed next.

Toolbox	Alternative PHP Monitor
Collects error events and stores them in a localSQLite database	
Main web site	https://pecl.php.net/package/apm
Main documentation and installation info	https://github.com/patrickallaert/php-apm#apm-alternative-php-monitor

Further Reading

- Article on using a logging server (Graylog2) for PHP logging

  - http://jeremycook.ca/2012/10/02/turbocharging-your-logs/

Installers and Bundling Files

In Chapter 3, you looked at different ways to run PHP, but before you can run your PHP scripts, you need to get them (and any related assets) onto your target machine. Generic software installer systems are widely available, and many platforms have their own software repositories and bundling systems that are well documented, so I don't cover those in any detail here (although I mention a few good open source ones at the end). Instead, let's look at a couple of PHP-specific options for bundling files and resources ready for distribution and installation.

Embedded Data Files at the End of a PHP Script

If you need to include just a chunk of data with a PHP script, you can use a language construct introduced in PHP 5.1, the __halt_compiler() instruction. Simply put this at the end of your PHP script, and you can then put anything you want (text strings, binary data, another PHP script, and so forth) after it in the same script file.

When PHP execution hits the __halt_compiler() line, it stops as if it had hit the end of the file itself. Whatever follows isn't executed and won't throw any syntax or similar errors.

Your script can access the data that follows it by opening a file handle to itself and seeking to the __COMPILER_HALT_OFFSET__ constant that is created when a __halt_compiler() instruction is present. The following example shows the "unbundling" of a text file from a PHP file:

```php
<?php

# Open a pointer to this file using the magic constant __FILE__

$thisfile = fopen(__FILE__, 'r');

# Seek down to the 1st byte after the __halt_compiler(); instruction. This
# is contained in the automatically created __COMPILER_HALT_OFFSET__
# constant.

fseek($thisfile, __COMPILER_HALT_OFFSET__);

# Let's grab everything that follows that ...
```

```
$ourtext = stream_get_contents($thisfile);

# and write it out to a new file.

file_put_contents('textfile.txt', $ourtext);

# Our script stops here.

__halt_compiler();The additional content starts here.

This is the text file.
It would normally cause a PHP fatal syntax error if
this text was simply dumped into a PHP file.
```

If you run this script and then look at the created `textfile.txt` file, you will see that it contains the rest of our script, starting with the `The additional content starts here` line. Although this example uses plain text (because it's easier to show in a book), there is nothing to stop you from adding binary files, PHP files, or even tar/zip archives containing multiple files that your script can save and expand. If you are intent on including multiple files or large amounts of data, you might want to consider the Phar format option instead, discussed next.

Phar Executable Bundles

Phar bundles are a native PHP way of pulling together lots of files, both PHP code and ancillary data files, into a single file for distribution. Phar bundles are, at their core, either a zip file, tar file, or custom Phar format file. You can access the individual files in the bundle by using the Phar stream wrapper as you would a normal file, without having to unbundle the files before use. For example, if you have a bundle called `mybundle.phar` in /home/rob/, you can do the following:

```php
<?php

# include() a php file from the bundle

include('phar://home/rob/mybundle.phar/sample.php');

# or load some csv data from the bundle into a variable

$data = file_get_contents('phar://home/rob/mybundle.phar/data.csv');

# or stream an image from the bundle out to the browser

$resource = 'phar://home/rob/mybundle.phar/images/cat.jpg';

$fp = fopen($resouce, 'rb');

header("Content-Type: image/jpeg");

header("Content-Length: " . filesize($resource));

fpassthru($fp);
```

Note that there is a small overhead for accessing files in a Phar bundle compared to stand-alone files, though it is too small to notice in most applications. Phar files used in this way are good for easily deploying support files, and can be opened and managed with existing zip/tar-aware programs as well as PHP. However, this method still requires you to deploy at least one PHP script to access the Phar file and control the whole show, and the Phar PHP extension must be installed to access them.

Phar bundles that have the custom Phar format rather than the zip or rar format have a couple of tricks up their sleeve, which remove these requirements. With the custom Phar format, you can specify PHP stub code. This *stub code* allows you to directly execute the Phar file, as if it were just a standard PHP file. This means that at the command line you can use commands like these to run your application, as if the Phar file was just a standard PHP file:

```
~$ php mybundle.phar
```

Or

```
~$ php mybundle.phar - x something -l something-else
```

This format also allows PHP to automatically recognize the file as if it were a standard PHP file, negating the need for the phar extension to be installed. With the right file associations set, you can even set a Phar file to be self-executing (see Chapter 2) in the same way as a standard PHP script. The stub code simply acts as an entry point for PHP, telling it where to begin, and is often just a require() statement for the main PHP script in the bundle. Even with stub code, the Phar file can still be accessed with the phar:// stream wrapper from external (and internal) scripts, so can act both as an executable bundle and a simple collection of files at the same time. The only real downside to the custom Phar format is that it can be created only with PHP itself (specifically, with a copy of PHP that has the phar extension installed). The zip and tar varieties can be created using most third-party archive tools.

Further Reading

- "Phar: PHP Libraries Included with a Single File" tutorial by Giorgio Sironi

  - http://css.dzone.com/articles/phar-php-libraries-single-file

- Phar documentation in the PHP manual

  - www.php.net/manual/en/intro.phar.php

Generic Installers

The following are two of the leading open source generic software installers. These can be used to install PHP itself and other software along with your PHP application, and can of course be used to deploy and run Phar bundles (see the previous section).

Toolbox	WiX Toolset
Comprehensive set of tools for creating .msi and .exe installers for Windows	
Main web site	http://wixtoolset.org/
Main documentation and installation info	http://wixtoolset.org/documentation/manual/

Toolbox	fpm
Easy-to-use tool to create .deb, .rpm, Solaris and Puppet packages/modules	
Main web site	`https://github.com/jordansissel/fpm`
Main documentation	`https://github.com/jordansissel/fpm/wiki`

Toolbox	IzPack
Create installers for macOS and other platforms (requires Java Runtime)	
Main web site	`http://izpack.org/`
Main documentation	`https://izpack.atlassian.net/wiki/display/IZPACK/IzPack+Home`

Controlling the (PHP) Environment

When you deploy scripts on your own servers or PCs, you can control the environment in which they are deployed. However, if you are distributing your software more widely, you will suddenly find that environmental factors on external machines can make your PHP scripts misbehave or even stop working completely. Some of the PHP-specific environmental factors you need to consider include the following:

- *Installed PHP version*: Check the current version (using `phpversion()` from within your script) to ensure that you script is compatible. Consider deploying PHP itself with your installer. If you do, it may be worth installing it in a nonstandard location, with a nonstandard name, and without setting the PHP environment variable, to avoid confusion with any existing versions.

- *Installed extension version*: As with the main PHP installation, you can check versions of critical extensions by using `phpversion('extension_name')` and act accordingly.

- `php.ini` *settings*: These are likely to be different from those on your machine. Ideally, you will supply your own custom `php.ini` file and use that (for example, call `php --php-ini my-php.ini myfile.php`; see Chapter 2 for details) to ensure that everything is set as you require. You can alternatively set important settings from within your script by using `ini_set()`. However, be aware that the ability to use `ini_set()` can be disabled from within the existing `php.ini` file.

- *Location of common paths*: The system temporary directory on Linux is often `/tmp`. But not always. Where possible, use functions such as `sys_get_temp_dir()` and `get_env('PATH')` to find relevant folders on the system, or at least allow users to specify them in a configuration file.

You also need to check any other non-PHP dependencies you may have, assess whether appropriate levels of hardware resources (memory, disk space) are available, and check for any network/Internet connectivity required.

Toolbox	3v4l.org
Web service that allows you to test chunks of code in 150+ versions of PHP (including HHVM) with the click of one button. Helpful in determining which versions of PHP your code can support.	
Main web site	`http://3v4l.org/`

Extending Your Application with Plug-ins

When working on your own web site or software, if you need additional functionality, you typically add it directly into your software. When you distribute software, it's often useful to allow users to provide their own additional functionality, particularly functions that are relevant to only their particular needs. The usual way to do this is via a plug-in/extension/add-on system. There are a thousand and one ways to implement plug-ins, and the following article by Anthony Ferrara outlines some of the common plug-in design patterns and examples of implementing them in PHP. You can also implement an application programming interface (API) much as you would with a web site, using one of the methods outlined earlier in the book (network daemon, shared memory, message queues, and so forth) to communicate with plug-in processes.

Further Reading

- "Handling Plugins in PHP" by Anthony Ferrara

    - http://blog.ircmaxell.com/2012/03/handling-plugins-in-php.html

- "Build APIs You Won't Hate" by Phil Sturgeon

    - https://leanpub.com/build-apis-you-wont-hate

Documentation

Ideally, your application will be so easy to use that your users won't require any documentation, right? (When you've finished laughing, we'll continue.) You may be familiar with providing end-user documentation and support information on web projects, but a typical software project requires even more. You need installation and upgrade docs, information for system administrators, licensing documentation, and so on. If you allow or encourage users to tinker with the code, you may even need to include code documentation and architecture/design documentation.

You should aim to provide all the documentation in two locations: online and included with the software. The copy with the software allows users access when they may not have an Internet connection, or when your web site is down (or your company has gone bust...). The online documentation provides an easy-to-update source for corrections or additional information, and it also allows prospective users and customers to assess the software without having to download or purchase it.

Finally, when distributing your software widely, fully comprehensive and high-quality documentation can reduce the number of requests for technical/user support that you get. This will usually save you much more time than it takes to write the documentation.

Further Reading

- "Software documentation" on Wikipedia

    - http://en.wikipedia.org/wiki/Software_documentation

Licensing and Legal Issues

▨ **Caution** All the legal information presented in this section and elsewhere in this book may be incorrect and will depend on your jurisdiction, though it is believed to be somewhat correct by the non-legally-trained author at the time of writing. The information is provided to give you an overview of the topics that you may wish to consider in terms of your particular project. Always consult a qualified legal professional for legal advice. And never drink coffee just before bed.

If you're coming from a web development environment to, for instance, desktop software development, it is worth taking a moment to think about the consequences and differences in licensing and legal liabilities in your new mode of programming, particularly when programming commercially.

With the Web, your product is usually your web site content, not the PHP script itself. Selling software reverses the situation, with your carefully honed PHP code being the saleable commodity and the output belonging to the end users. Any negative effects of your PHP web script are usually confined to your own server, but when your desktop PHP script decides to wipe the hard drive it is on, someone else will be experiencing the loss (and picking up the phone to their lawyers).

The law generally applies equally to scripts written in PHP as it does to compiled binaries written in other languages, so I don't cover general legal issues in this book.

However, there is one legal issue specific to scripted software such as PHP, and that is the distribution of the interpreter itself. Every PHP script requires the PHP (or HHVM, and so forth) binaries to run, and most systems don't come with PHP installed by default. Luckily, PHP itself is licensed under a permissive Open Source Initiative (OSI) certified license, imaginatively called the PHP License. With very few restrictions, you are free to distribute the PHP code base and compiled binaries with your application. If you choose to modify or alter them, then it's worth checking the license (an easy-to-read 68 lines, in plain English) to make sure you're still OK. If you're not changing them in any way, go right ahead! Commercial distribution is also fine; there are no limits on charging or including with paid-for software.

Another important point is that the license covers only PHP itself, and not any of your scripts written in PHP, so you can release those under any license you deem appropriate.

You should also bear in mind that PHP is supplied *as is*, so on a warranty basis, you will have very little (or most likely, no) comeback should a bug in PHP cause you or your customers problems. Likewise, you will not be covered by the PHP team against patent violations (in countries where Byzantine laws still allow software patents) that may result when you deploy PHP as part of your product. These downsides, however, are common among most programming languages, commercial and open source alike.

If you want to sidestep the issue of distributing PHP yourself, remember that most modern operating systems with software repositories have PHP installable via a couple of clicks or one line of code. If you're distributing your software as a .deb or .rpm package on Linux, you can simply include PHP as a required dependency and let the user's package manager deal with it for you.

As with all software, you (unfortunately) need to consider all relevant laws, including but not limited to copyright, patents, trademarks, data protection, trading standards, consumer protection, database rights, equality legislation, and any regulatory requirements in your field of endeavor. I'll leave that as an exercise for you (or, ideally, your legal representative!).

Further Reading

- *career.fork()* by Steve Jalim contains a chapter on contracts, NDAs, IP, and other legal issues that are relevant to freelance developers in particular.

  - `https://leanpub.com/freelancedeveloperbook`

Deploying Frameworks

If you are using a coding framework, you will likely need to deploy its components alongside your script. You should carefully check the license for the framework to ensure that it is legally compatible with your project, including any subcomponents that the framework may have used or licensed from other projects. You should ensure that any necessary files are included in your deployment, and remember that any configuration the framework may require may also need to be updated to reflect the environment on the machine that the software is deployed on. There are more details on code frameworks at the end of Chapter 2.

Compiling and Installing PHP, Extensions, and Libs

There are a dozen ways to get PHP, including downloading and compiling it yourself, downloading precompiled binaries, using package managers and software repositories, and finding it preinstalled by a forward-thinking administrator. On most Linux distributions, PHP can be installed with a one-line command such as sudo apt-get install php5 or through graphical package managers such as the Synaptic Package Manager or the Ubuntu Software Center. Many common PHP extensions and add-ons are likewise available as prebuilt packages or alternatively through the PECL and PEAR systems. However, sometimes it becomes necessary to do a little more work to install PHP; for instance, in the following situations:

- Your project has requirements for a specific version of PHP that is different from the one shipped with your OS.

- You need extensions not available as packages.

- You want to compile a customized version of PHP specific to your needs.

Like anything involved in computers and software development, compiling PHP can take you down a rabbit hole of options, customizations, compatibility issues, libraries, and dependencies. A whole book could be written about the possibilities (and possible headaches) involved. Luckily for us, in most use cases, the basics of compiling a standard version are quite straightforward. And like most things in life, it gets easier after you have done it once. The following section outlines the steps necessary for getting, compiling, and installing PHP and its core extensions. PHP is written in C, and because you might not be familiar with the process of compiling C programs, I have explained each step to give you an idea of what is happening. This makes the process seem a little more verbose, but in reality it is straightforward. Go ahead and try it if you don't believe me! The next sections are also worth a read; they cover installing extras such as libraries and extensions from the PECL, PEAR, and Packagist repositories.

Compiling and Installing PHP

The process for compiling and installing PHP itself varies depending on the operating system you are deploying to. This section covers the main OSs that PHP is available on.

© Rob Aley 2016
R. Aley, *PHP Beyond the Web*, DOI 10.1007/978-1-4842-2481-6

Windows

The steps outlined in the following sections are for Linux/Unix-type systems and use free compiler tools almost always included with the OS. For Windows, the proprietary Visual Studio compiler is required, and the steps are somewhat different (and more complicated) and thus beyond the scope of this book. You can find Windows source code, prebuilt binaries, and instructions for compiling at `http://windows.php.net/download/`, with older versions in the archive at `http://windows.php.net/downloads/releases/archives/`. New unreleased versions can often be found at `http://windows.php.net/qa/`.

macOS

One of the easiest ways to get different versions of PHP on your Mac is by using the MacPorts software repository. It has more than 700 PHP *portfiles* covering various versions of PHP, extensions, applications, and related tools.

Toolbox	MacPorts
An easy-to-use system for compiling, installing, and upgrading open source software on macOS	
Main web site	`www.macports.org`
Installation information and documentation	`www.macports.org/install.php`
Directory of software available (click "php" for relevant software)	`www.macports.org/ports.php`

PHP also comes installed by default with recent macOS versions, although it's not always up-to-date.

If you need to compile from scratch, you can follow these steps for Linux/Unix systems. You may run into some issues, depending on the version of macOS you are using and the version of PHP you are trying to compile. The following are the two main issues that may trip you up:

- *File/dependency locations*: These are sometimes different on macOS and may vary between versions. Where possible, always try to explicitly specify the full location path for dependencies and installation.

- *Dependency versions*: The default versions of libraries that come with macOS that core PHP and various extensions require aren't always in step with those that various versions of PHP require. Check any error messages produced during compilation (usually the first error message) for any hints as to version requirements, or check the documentation for PHP or the extension in question. Then check the documentation for the dependency to see whether it can be safely upgraded/downgraded or whether you need to install a different version in parallel.

Linux/Unix

Many *nix-based operating systems have package repositories containing not just the current version of PHP but often older versions (albeit usually just the major versions). Third-party repositories can also sometimes offer an easier route to getting particular versions or configurations. So, check these out before starting to compile things yourself.

When you need to compile PHP, the first step is to download the source code from the PHP web site at `www.php.net/downloads.php`. This page lists the current stable release and the previous supported stable release. Newer versions that are still under development are available at `http://windows.php.net/downloads/snaps/`, and older end-of-life versions are available at `http://museum.php.net/`. Git users can also pull the source code down from the official mirror at `https://github.com/php`. When you have identified which version you want, make a note of the URL of the `.tar.gz` source code file that you will use later.

```
~$ mkdir php5.4
~$ cd php5.4
~$ wget http://uk3.php.net/get/php-7.0.11.tar.gz/from/uk.php.net/mirror -o
php-7.0.11.tar.gz
~$ tar zxvf php-7.0.11.tar.gz
~$ cd php-7.0.11
```

The first two lines create a directory for your work and step into it. The directory holds the source code and intermediate files and can be deleted after PHP is installed if you want. However, it is often a good idea to keep this directory in case you need/want to reinstall or check which version of the file you downloaded later. The third line downloads a copy of the source code file into your directory. Change the URL in the third line to that of the `.tar.gz` file you want to use, and change the `-o` option to the name of the file (otherwise, in the previous example, `wget` will simply call your file mirror). The fifth line unpacks the archive into a directory containing the individual source code files and changes the name of the file to the one you used on line 3. Finally, the last line steps you into the source code directory. Now you start the compilation process:

```
~$ ./configure
```

The `configure` command creates the setup for compilation. You use it to provide the settings and arguments you want for your compilation session. For instance, you can specify which core extensions you want to include in your build. If you don't specify any arguments as earlier, the defaults provided by the PHP dev team are used. This is a good choice if you don't have any particular needs and want a version that is fairly similar to or compatible with the versions included with most distributions. You can also install extensions at a later date either individually or by recompiling PHP from scratch, which I discuss in the next section. If you want to include an extension at this stage that's not included in the default settings, this is the place to do it. For example, if you want to include the LDAP extension, then you would change the previous command to `./ configure --with-ldap[=DIR]`, where `[=DIR]` is the base installation directory of LDAP on your system. You can find the exact option to use and any necessary dependencies in the PHP manual, under the "Installing/Configuring" section for the extension in question. For example, you can find details for the LDAP extension at `www.php.net/manual/en/ldap.setup.php`. You can find a (slightly out-of-date) list of options that you can pass to the `configure` command at `www.php.net/manual/en/configure.about.php`; for a full list of those supported on your system in the current version you are trying to compile, you can issue the command `autoconf` followed by `./configure --help`. You can find more information about the `configure` command at `www.airs.com/ian/configure/`. Now you will compile PHP:

```
~$ make clean
~$ make
~$ sudo make install
```

You compile the binary PHP files by using the `make` tool. The first line removes any previously created files and resets you to the start of the `make` process. This is not strictly necessary on your first run at compiling, but it can help if your attempt fails for some reason (such as missing dependencies, incorrect settings, unintended interruptions to the process, and so on), so including it by default is often a good choice. The second line does the actual building and compiling of the files. The third line then takes those files and installs them on the system. By default, PHP will usually be installed in the /usr/bin directory on Linux. However, you can choose where to install it by specifying a prefix directory at the ./configure stage. Simply add the switch --prefix=/path/to/dir, where /path/to/dir is the directory where you want PHP to be installed. This is often useful if you want to install multiple versions on the same machine (although be aware that there are other considerations when doing so). Note that the make install line must be run with higher permissions (sudo) to allow it to copy files into "privileged" locations. If all goes well, congratulations! You have installed PHP. To check that the correct version is installed and available, use php -v at the command line, and PHP will display the current version number. If you have installed PHP in a location outside your search path, you will need to specify the full path name; for example, /path/to/dir/php -v. To check which extensions and other options were installed, use php -i at the command line to run the phpinfo() function. In addition to extension information (and a lot more besides), this returns a list of the options used with the ./configure command. This can be useful when reinstalling PHP or when trying to clone an installation on another machine (where the same binaries cannot just be reused).

If all doesn't go well, take a close look at the errors produced. The most common type of errors happen when your system doesn't have the relevant dependencies installed for a particular extension. Often the error message will say this explicitly, but even if it just gives you an obscure error message mentioning the name of an extension, the best advice is to double-check the installation section for that extension in the PHP manual to find out exactly what dependencies are required. Missing dependencies can often be installed by using your systems package manager rather than having to manually compile them. You should also check that you have provided the location of any dependencies at the configure stage if required.

If all else fails, copy and paste the exact error message into your favorite Internet search engine, probably starting with the first error message shown if multiple errors appear. Many people have compiled PHP, and most errors have been encountered and documented online. Don't let all this talk of errors put you off trying to compile PHP. Errors are more likely to occur the more complicated you make your configuration, and if you're careful about dependencies, you can often avoid them altogether. So, first try a straightforward compilation with the default options to get the hang of things and then take it from there!

You can find more information on installations, with a general focus on web servers but otherwise useful, in the PHP manual at www.php.net/manual/en/install.php.

Compiling and Installing (Extra) Core Extensions

As you saw in the previous section, the most common way to install core extensions is to enable the relevant flags at the configure stage during compilation of the main PHP installation (note, by default, many extensions are automatically enabled). However, it's not uncommon to come across the need to install an additional extension later, for instance, as the requirements for your program change from its initial design. There are two ways to approach this. The first, which you'll find recommended a lot online, is to redo the compilation/installation of PHP from scratch, adding the newly required modules at the configure stage (after issuing php -i to remember what configure options you used the first time). Although this works perfectly well, compiling the full PHP binaries is a bit of a slog, which can take older PCs in particular a long time to complete. There is a shortcut, however.

Each of the core extensions is a separate .so binary that can be compiled independently. To do this, follow the first steps in the previous section to download and unpack the PHP source code and step into the directory. If you haven't deleted it from when you compiled PHP, it should be ready to go. Within the source code is a directory called ext, inside of which are separate directories for each of the extensions.

```
~$ cd ext
~$ ls
```

This shows you all the core extensions available. For instance, if you want to add the pcntl extension (used in this book for daemon software), you can enter the pcntl directory and compile/install just that extension in a similar manner to how you compiled the whole PHP package in the previous section:

```
~$ cd pcntl
~$ phpize
~$ ./configure
~$ make clean
~$ make
~$ sudo make install
```

The additional command, phpize, is used to prepare the build environment for the extension. This is not necessary when building the full PHP binaries, but it is when building individual extensions. If you don't have phpize on your system, it is often available through your system's package manager in the php-dev package (for example, on Ubuntu, it is available as phpize5 in the php5-dev package for version 5 installations). You can find more details about phpize and getting it at http://us.php.net/manual/en/install.pecl.phpize.php.

After you have run the previous commands, you should find that a .so file (pcntl.so in this example) has been compiled and placed in PHP's extension directory. The final step is to tell PHP about it by adding the following line somewhere in your php.ini file:

```
extension=pcntl.so
```

If you're not sure where your php.ini file is, you can run php -i | grep "Loaded Configuration File" on the command line to find out. You can also use php -i to check that your extension is now correctly installed and available for use.

Installing Multiple Versions of PHP

Sometimes (particularly on development machines) you may want to install multiple versions of PHP at the same time—for instance, if you are deploying to end users with PHP already installed but who may have different versions. One straightforward way to achieve this is to create a set of virtual machines (I use VirtualBox for this) with a different version of PHP installed in each. In this scenario, you can always be sure which version you are running and that the installation and configuration of one version isn't interfering with that of another. The downside is that it can be slow to start up and shut down different VMs (or a hit on resources to run them all at once), and if you are using proprietary OSs like Windows, you can incur additional licensing costs.

It is possible to have multiple versions installed and running directly on the same machine; however, if you are not careful, it can become a nightmare trying to keep the versions and their dependencies separate and making sure you know which version you are using at all times. As such, I don't delve into it in this book. However, the following are two articles from respected PHP community members who have done just that, which may give you some pointers on what to do and the pitfalls involved. I suggest that before you try this, you become intimately familiar with compiling and installing PHP, the file and directory structures and locations that PHP uses, and how to check which versions of PHP and extensions are running.

There are also a couple of relevant tools listed here. The first is php-build, which automatically builds multiple versions of PHP from source, although you still need to exercise care installing and using them simultaneously. The second is 3v4l.org, a web service that allows you to test chunks of code in more than 100 versions of PHP at the same time. This may avoid the need for installing multiple versions at all.

Further Reading

- Installing multiple versions, using SVN

  - `http://derickrethans.nl/multiple-php-version-setup.html`

- Installing multiple versions, using GIT

  - `http://mark-story.com/posts/view/installing-multiple-versions-of-php-from-source`

Toolbox	php-build

Automatically builds multiple PHP versions from source that can be used in parallel

Main web site   `https://php-build.github.io/`

Toolbox	3v4l.org

Web service that allows you test chunks of code in 90+ versions of PHP with the click of one button

Main web site   `http://3v4l.org`

Using PEAR and PECL

The *PHP Extension and Application Repository* (*PEAR*) is a library of code and extensions written in PHP, with an easy-to-use packaging and distribution system. *PHP Extension Community Library* (*PECL*) is essentially the same but is for extensions written in C.

Both PECL and PEAR work in a similar way to package managers such as Debian's `apt-get`. For example, to install the Cairo graphics extension from PECL, simply use `sudo pecl install cairo` at the command line. This will download, compile, and install Cairo for you, and you can then start using it from within your PHP scripts. Similarly, to install the RDF extension from PEAR, use `pear install rdf`. The `pear` and `pecl` commands are included as standard with PHP; however, some package managers put them in the optional php-dev or php-pear package. On Ubuntu, for instance, use `sudo apt-get install php-pear` to install both PEAR and PECL. You can find more information on both tools as well as the hundreds of extensions and libraries available, at `http://pear.php.net` and `http://pecl.php.net`, respectively.

Using Composer

Composer is a dependency manager. Although it deals with packages, it is not a package manager like PEAR. Rather than installing packages centrally, it deals with them per project, ensuring that the appropriate versions of the relevant packages, and their dependencies, are installed automatically for that project.

The basic Composer workflow happens as follows:

1. You install Composer.

2. In the base directory of your project, you create a JSON-formatted file called `composer.json` that specifies which packages (and versions) your project needs.

3. In that directory, you run Composer. It will fetch and install all of the specified packages and will automatically also install any of the other packages that those you have specified depend on (and so on, until all dependencies are satisfied).

4. In your PHP code, add the function `require 'vendor/ autoload.php';` and your libraries will be automatically available when you use them.

Fully comprehensive documentation, aimed at beginners as well as advanced users, is available on the Composer web site. Composer itself doesn't host any packages; that is the job of package repositories. *Packagist* is the main, and currently the only, comprehensive public repository, and it is the default used by Composer. You can browse the thousands of available packages on the Packagist web site. You can, of course, specify a different repository and indeed create and use your own packages privately if needed.

Toolbox	Composer dependency manager
The easy way to keep libraries consistent and up-to-date on a per project basis	
Main web site	`http://getcomposer.org`
Package repository	`https://packagist.org`
Tutorial *"Easy Package Management with Composer"*	`http://code.tutsplus.com/tutorials/easy-packagemanagement-with-composer--net-25530`

Using Symfony2 Bundles

If you're using the Symfony2 framework, you can choose from and download thousands of useful code bundles from KnpBundles. These can be installed manually or often by using the Composer dependency system (see the previous section). Visit `http://knpbundles.com/` for more information and to browse the available code.

■ ■ ■

File and Data Format Libraries for PHP

When you're writing longer-running, general-purpose scripts, you'll have much more latitude to expend time and resources processing external data files. These data files come in thousands of formats, many typically not used in web-based scripts, and PHP can handle most of them.

This chapter lists extensions, libraries, and API bindings, broken down by category, that can be used to work with various file and data formats in PHP. Within each category you will find the name of the library, followed by a list of file types (specified by their common file extension for brevity) that it supports, and the main web site for that library. If there isn't a common file extension (for example, streaming data formats), the name of the format is used instead.

The following lists are not exhaustive, and not all libraries allow you to both read and write the given formats, or support all features of the format. Check the relevant documentation for the library and try it out before selecting it for your project. If you haven't found a library to help you with the file format you're looking for, try using your favorite search engine to find one, or consider "shelling out" to non-PHP helper applications.

Office Documents

OpenDocument

Formats	odt
Web site	http://pear.php.net/manual/en/package.fileformats.opendocument.php

PHPExcel

Formats	ods, gnm, gnumeric, xlsx, xls (biff), xls (SpreadsheetML), htm, html, sky, slk, sylk, csv, pdf
Web site	https://github.com/PHPOffice/PHPExcel

php-excel-reader

Formats	xls (biff)
Web site	http://code.google.com/p/php-excel-reader/

© Rob Aley 2016
R. Aley, *PHP Beyond the Web*, DOI 10.1007/978-1-4842-2481-6

Excel Writer (XML) for PHP

Formats	xls (SpreadsheetML)
Web site	http://sourceforge.net/projects/excelwriterxml/

php-export-data

Formats	xls (SpreadsheetML), csv, tsv
Web site	https://github.com/elidickinson/php-export-data

Spreadsheet_Excel_Writer

Formats	xls (biff)
Web site	http://pear.php.net/manual/en/package.fileformats.spreadsheet-excel-writer.php

SimpleExcel

Formats	xlsx, htm, html, csv, tsv, json
Web site	http://faisalman.github.com/simple-excel-php/

PHPPowerPoint

Formats	pptx
Web site	http://phppowerpoint.codeplex.com/

PHPWord

Formats	docx
Web site	http://phpword.codeplex.com/

Cairo extension

Formats	pdf, ps, svg
Web site	www.php.net/manual/en/book.cairo.php

TCPDF

Formats	pdf
Web site	www.tcpdf.org/

Dompdf

Formats	pdf
Web site	https://github.com/dompdf/dompdf

mPDF

Formats	pdf
Web site	www.mpdf1.com/mpdf/index.php

Haru PDF extension

Formats	pdf
Web site	www.php.net/manual/en/book.haru.php

PDF extension (PDFlib)

Formats	pdf
Web site	www.php.net/manual/en/book.pdf.php

Forms Data Format extension

Formats	fdf
Web site	www.php.net/manual/en/book.fdf.php

Document Object Model extension

Formats	htm, html
Web site	www.php.net/manual/en/book.dom.php

Contact_Vcard

Formats	vcf, vcard
Web site	http://pear.php.net/manual/en/package.fileformats.contact-vcard.php

File_MARC

Formats	mrc, marc
Web site	http://pear.php.net/manual/en/package.fileformats.file-marc.php

Compression, Archiving, and Encryption

File_Archive

Formats	tar, gz, gzip, bz2, tgz, tar.gz, tbz, tar.bz2, zip, ar, deb
Web site	http://pear.php.net/manual/en/package.fileformats.file-archive.php

Zlib extension

Formats	gz, gzip
Web site	www.php.net/manual/en/intro.zlib.php

Bzip2 extension

Formats	bz2
Web site	www.php.net/manual/en/book.bzip2.php

Rar extension

Formats	rar
Web site	www.php.net/manual/en/book.rar.php

Zip extension

Formats	zip
Web site	www.php.net/manual/en/book.zip.php

RPM Reader extension

Formats	rpm
Web site	www.php.net/manual/en/book.rpmreader.php

LZF compression

Formats	lzf
Web site	www.php.net/manual/en/book.lzf.php

File_Cabinet

Formats	cab
Web site	http://pear.php.net/manual/en/package.fileformats.file-cabinet.php

Phar extension

Formats	phar, tar, zip
Web site	www.php.net/manual/en/book.phar.php

GNU Privacy Guard extension

Formats	gpg, pgp
Web site	www.php.net/manual/en/book.gnupg.php

Graphics

Gmagick extension

Formats	art, avi, avs, bmp, cals, cin, cgm, cmyk, cur, cut, dcm, dcx, dib, dpx, emf, epdf, epi, eps, eps2, eps3, epsf, epsi, ept, fax, fig, fits, fpx, gif, gplt, gray, hpgl, html, ico, jbig, jng, jp2, jpc, jpeg, man, mat, miff, mono, mng, mpeg, m2v, mpc, msl, mtv, mvg, otb, p7, palm, pam, pbm, pcd, pcds, pcl, pcx, pdb, pdf, pfa, pfb, pgm, picon, pict, pix, png, pnm, ppm, ps, ps2, ps3, psd, ptif, pwp, ras, rad, rgb, rgba, rla, rle, sct, sfw, sgi, shtml, sun, svg, tga, tiff, tim, ttf, txt, uil, uyvy, vicar, viff, wbmp, wmf, wpg, xbm, xcf, xpm, xwd, yuv
Web site	www.php.net/manual/en/book.gmagick.php

ImageMagick extension

Formats	aai, art, arw, avi, avs, bmp,bmp2,bmp3, cals, cgm, cin, cmyk, cmyka, cr2, crw, cur, cut, dcm, dcr, dcx, dds, dib, djvu, dng, dot, dpx, emf, epdf, epi, eps, eps2, eps3, epsf, epsi, ept, exr, fax, fig, fits, fpx, gif, gplt, gray, hdr, hpgl, hrz, html, ico, info, inline, jbig, jng, jp2, jpc, jpeg, jxr, man, mat, miff, mono, mng, m2v, mpeg, mpc, mpr, mrw, msl, mtv, mvg, nef, orf, otb, p7, palm, pam, clipboard, pbm, pcd, pcds, pcl, pcx, pdb, pdf, pef, pfa, pfb, pfm, pgm, picon, pict, pix, png, png8, png00, png24, png32, png48, png64, pnm, ppm, ps, ps2, ps3, psb, psd, ptif, pwp, rad, raf, rgb, rgba, rfg, rla, rle, sct, sfw, sgi, shtml, sid,mrsid, sparse-color, sun, svg, tga, tiff, tim, ttf, txt, uil, uyvy, vicar, viff, wbmp, wdp, webp, wmf, wpg, x, xbm, xcf, xpm, xwd, x3f, ycbcr, ycbcra, yuv
Web site	www.php.net/manual/en/book.imagick.php

File_DICOM

Formats	dcm
Web site	http://pear.php.net/manual/en/package.fileformats.file-dicom.php

Ming extension

Formats	swf, flash
Web site	www.php.net/manual/en/book.ming.php

Cairo extension

Formats	pdf, svg, ps
Web site	www.php.net/manual/en/book.cairo.php

Exif extension

Formats	exif
Web site	www.php.net/manual/en/book.exif.php

Audio

MP3_Id

Formats	mp3
Web site	http://pear.php.net/manual/en/package.fileformats.mp3-id.php

OGG/Vorbis extension

Formats	ogg, oga, ogv, spx
Web site	www.php.net/manual/en/book.oggvorbis.php

php-reader

Formats	mp3, asf, wma, wmv flac, 3gp, 3gpp, avc, dcf, m21, m4a, m4b, m4p, m4v, maf, mj2, mjp, mov, mp4, odf, sdv,qt, abs, mp1, mp2, mpg, mpeg, vob, evo, ogg, oga, ogv, spx
Web site	http://code.google.com/p/php-reader/

ID3 extension

Formats	mp3
Web site	www.php.net/manual/en/book.id3.php

KTaglib extension

Formats	mp3
Web site	www.php.net/manual/en/book.ktaglib.php

Multimedia and Video

PHP-FFmpeg

Formats	4xm, 8088flex tmv, act voice, adobe filmstrip, audio iff (aiff), american laser games mm, 3gpp amr, amazing studio packed animation file, apple http live streaming, artworx data format, adp, afc, asf, ast, avi, avisynth, avr, avs, beam software siff, bethesda softworks vid, binary text, bink, bitmap brothers jv, brute force & ignorance, brstm, bwf, cri adx, discworld ii bmv, interplay c93, delphine software international cin, cd+g, commodore cdxl, core audio format, crc testing format, creative voice, cryo apc, d-cinema audio, deluxe paint animation, dfa, dv video, dxa, electronic arts cdata, electronic arts multimedia, ensoniq paris audio file, ffm (ffserver live feed), flash (swf), flash 9 (avm2), fli/flc/flx animation, flash video (flv), framecrc testing format, funcom iss, g.723.1, g.729 bit, g.729 raw, gif animation, gxf, icedraw file, ico, id quake ii cin video, id roq, iec61937 encapsulation, iff, ilbc, interplay mve, iv8, ivf (on2), ircam, latm, lmlm4, loas, lvf, lxf, matroska, matroska audio, ffmpeg metadata, maxis xa, md studio, metal gear solid: the twin snakes, megalux frame, mobotix .mxg, monkeys audio, motion pixels mvi, mov/quicktime/mp4, mp2, mp3, mpeg-1 system, mpeg-ps (program stream), mpeg-ts (transport stream), mpeg-4, mime multipart jpeg, msn tcp webcam, mtv, musepack, musepack sv8, material exchange format (mxf), material exchange format (mxf), d10 mapping, nc camera feed, nist speech header resources, ntt twinvq (vqf), nullsoft streaming video, nuppelvideo, nut, ogg, playstation portable pmp, portable voice format, technotrend pva, qcp, raw adts (aac), raw ac-3, raw chinese avs video, raw criadx, raw dirac, raw dnxhd, raw dts, raw dts-hd, raw e-ac-3, raw flac, raw gsm, raw h.261, raw h.263, raw h.264, raw ingenient mjpeg, raw mjpeg, raw mlp, raw mpeg, raw mpeg-1, raw mpeg-2, raw mpeg-4, raw null, raw video, raw id roq, raw shorten, raw tak, raw truehd, raw vc-1, raw pcm, rdt, redcode r3d, realmedia, redirector, redspark, renderware texture dictionary, rl2, rpl/armovie, lego mindstorms rso, rsd, rtmp, rtp, rtsp, sap, sbg, sdp, sega film/cpk, silicon graphics movie, sierra sol, sierra vmd, smacker, smjpeg, smush, sony openmg (oma), sony playstation str, sony wave64 (w64), sox native format, sun au format, text files, thp, tiertex limited seq, true audio, vc-1 test bitstream, vivo, wav, wavpack, webm, windows televison (wtv), wing commander iii movie, westwood studios audio, westwood studios vqa, xmv, xwma, extended binary text (xbin), yuv4mpeg pipe, psygnosis yop
Web site	`https://github.com/alchemy-fr/PHP-FFmpeg`

Programming, Technical, and Data Interchange

File_Fstab

Formats	fstab
Web site	`http://pear.php.net/manual/en/package.fileformats.file-fstab.php`

File_Passwd

Formats	passwd
Web site	`http://pear.php.net/manual/en/package.fileformats.file-passwd.php`

YAML extension

Formats	yaml
Web site	www.php.net/manual/en/book.yaml.php

Assorted extensions

Formats	xml
Web site	www.php.net/manual/en/refs.xml.php

XSL extension

Formats	xsl, xslt
Web site	www.php.net/manual/en/intro.xsl.php

JSON extension

Formats	json
Web site	www.php.net/manual/en/book.json.php

Native file and string functions

Formats	txt
Web site	http://www.php.net/manual/en/refs.basic.text.php

Miscellaneous

File_Fortune

Formats	fortune
Web site	http://pear.php.net/manual/en/package.fileformats.file-fortune.php

APPENDIX C

■ ■ ■

Sources of Help

Even with excellent books like this on the market, you will sometimes need a little additional help when you come across a tricky problem with PHP. The following are some potential sources of help.

The PHP Manual

You can find the official PHP manual online at http://php.net/docs.php. The manual provides fairly comprehensive documentation, in the main, on PHP installation, syntax, functions, and many extensions. Of particular note are the user comments at the bottom of each page. These are generally helpful and offer real-world advice related to the function or topic of the page. Occasionally some duff advice is given in the comments; however, this is usually corrected or mentioned in a subsequent comment, so reading through all the comments on a given page is worthwhile.

A handy function of the online manual is that you can do a quick lookup of a function or topic by typing it as the first part of a URL. For instance, if you can't remember what the parameters of strripos() are, you can type http://php.net/strripos into your browser and you will be sent straight to the relevant page. Likewise, if you want a quick refresher on how PHP handles arrays, visit http://php.net/array and you'll go straight to the array page in the language/types section of the manual. It also searches for nonexact matches, so http://php.net/csv will get you a handy list of CSV-related functions.

If you don't always have an Internet connection, you can download a copy of the manual from www.php.net/download-docs.php. It is available as HTML, as Unix-style man pages, and in Microsoft Compiled HTML Help (CHM) format.

Official Mailing Lists

Several official mailing lists covering a wide variety of topics are available at http://php.net/mailing-lists.php. Of note for getting help are the General User List for general queries and the Windows PHP Users List for Windows-specific questions. Beware when subscribing that some of the lists are quite busy, and you will get many e-mails each day. The archives are available online if you just want to browse them or get a feel for the volume generated on each list.

Stack Overflow

Stack Overflow (http://stackoverflow.com) is a prolific question-and-answer site aimed at programmers. Unlike some Q&A sites, you don't need to join or pay to view the answers to questions, and ads are limited. Millions of answered questions are on the site, including a good chunk of PHP-related questions.

© Rob Aley 2016
R. Aley, *PHP Beyond the Web*, DOI 10.1007/978-1-4842-2481-6

All questions and answers are tagged with their topics so that you can find the ones relevant to you. To browse questions tagged with *PHP*, visit http://stackoverflow.com/questions/tagged/php. You can also use the site's search facility; to narrow your search to only PHP-related answers, add *[tag]* to your search. For example, if you want to search for questions about the date function, which is a common word in English and a common function name in many programming languages, search for *[php] date* to get only PHP-specific information.

At the time of writing, there were 984,139 questions tagged with *php*, 1,126 tagged with *php* and *command line*, and 1,172 tagged with *php* and *cli*. The moderators are usually quick at shutting down duplicate questions, so you can see from these numbers that a lot of relevant information is available.

Other Books

Although you may think that this is the only book on PHP you will ever need, I have been told that other PHP books may be available. I can't recommend any specifically (other than those I have already noted in the relevant chapters), but if you browse any big-name bookseller, you will find a plethora of PHP-related titles. And of course you can browse the more than 100 PHP-related books by my esteemed publisher at www.apress.com/programming/php.

Newsgroups

PHP has a set of official newsgroups listed and archived at http://news.php.net/ that cover a wide range of PHP topic areas. These may be worth a browse and sometimes can elicit a response to queries (although some of the internal lists are definitely not for the faint-hearted).

PHP Subreddit

The PHP subreddit on Reddit at www.reddit.com/r/PHP/ is a mixture of PHP news, opinions, useful links, and requests for help. Although usually genuinely interesting with helpful responses to questions, an occasional assortment of trolls and unhelpful/rude people can be found here as well. A more tolerant subreddit for getting help is PHPhelp at www.reddit.com/r/phphelp, which was specifically set up to answer questions (even from beginners).

PHP on GitHub

Sometimes the best way to solve a problem is to look at similar code other people have written. GitHub, the popular source repository web site, has tons of the stuff to plow through. You can search all the code repositories at https://github.com/search, and you can use the modifier *language:php* in your search terms to narrow your results to projects using your favorite language. If you just want to keep an eye on what PHP projects are popular these days, you can check out the PHP trending list at https://github.com/trending?l=php.

PHP News Sites

Although not usually good for direct help, PHP news sites and mailing lists can keep you up-to-date with essentials such as security alerts, useful and interesting articles, and announcements of new projects, libraries, and tutorials that you may not even know you needed yet! Some of the more popular ones are listed here:

- *PHPDeveloper*: `http://phpdeveloper.org/`

- *Planet PHP*: `www.planet-php.net`

- *PHP Weekly News*: `www.phpweekly.com`

- *PHPBuilder*: `www.phpbuilder.com`

APPENDIX D

Interesting Libraries, Tools, Articles, and Projects

Throughout this book, you've seen links to numerous libraries and tools related to the topic at hand. This appendix lists many more PHP-related projects that don't fit neatly into other sections of the book but are nevertheless interesting. Many show off the potential of PHP beyond just web sites, and others provide libraries for tasks that are often performed with desktop, server, or other longer-running software. Some are just cool!

Alternative Programming Styles

Toolbox	Pharen
Lisp-like language for PHP	
Web site	www.pharen.org

Toolbox	pEigthP
Basic Lisp implementation embedded in PHP	
Web site	https://github.com/cninja/pEigthP#readme

Toolbox	Syngr
OO standard interface library to PHP core functions	
Web site	https://github.com/hassankhan/Syngr

Toolbox	Functional Programming in PHP
Tutorial by Patkos Csaba	
Web site	http://net.tutsplus.com/tutorials/php/functional-programming-in-php/

© Rob Aley 2016
R. Aley, *PHP Beyond the Web*, DOI 10.1007/978-1-4842-2481-6

Toolbox	phpQuery
Like jQuery, but for PHP	
Web site	http://code.google.com/p/phpquery/

Toolbox	PHPLinq
Mimics C# LINQ extension methods	
Web site	http://phplinq.codeplex.com/

Toolbox	phinq
Another C# LINQ emulation library	
Web site	https://github.com/tmont/phinq

Toolbox	PHPz
Functional programming library	
Web site	http://blog.clement.delafargue.name/posts/2013-04-01-delicious-burritos-in-php-with-phpz.html

Toolbox	XHP
Facebook's brand of PHP, which brings XML directly into the syntax and is now part of Hack, Facebook's PHP on steroids	
Web site	https://github.com/facebook/xhp

Machine Learning, Artificial Intelligence, and Data Analysis

Toolbox	Running Monte Carlo Simulations in PHP
Article by J Armando Jeronymo	
Web site	www.sitepoint.com/running-monte-carlo-simulations-in-php/

Toolbox	PHP Clarke and Wright Algorithm
Class to solve truck-routing problems	
Web site	www.phpclasses.org/package/8135-PHP-Solve-a-truck-routing-problem-with-Clarke-Wright.html

Toolbox	PHP/ir
Web site full of algorithms related to machine learning and information retrieval in PHP	
Web site	http://phpir.com/

Toolbox	cPerceptron
A Simple Perceptron neural network in PHP	
Web site	https://github.com/gzanitti/cperceptron#readme

Toolbox	neural-network
Advanced multilayer neural network	
Web site	https://github.com/infostreams/neural-network

Toolbox	Learning Library for PHP
Assorted ML and AI algorithms	
Web site	https://github.com/gburtini/Learning-Library-for-PHP

Toolbox	Finite-State Machine Library
Does what it says on the tin	
Web site	https://github.com/chriswoodford/techne

Toolbox	SVM Extension
Support Vector Machine problem solver	
Web site	www.php.net/manual/en/book.svm.php

Toolbox	PredictionIO PHP SDK
PHP SDK for the open source machine-learning server	
Web site	https://github.com/apache/incubator-predictionio-sdk-php

Databases

Toolbox	Gladius DB
SQL database written in PHP	
Web site	http://gladius.sourceforge.net/index.php

Toolbox	UnQLite Extension
SQLite-like NoSQL database	
Web site	https://github.com/kjdev/php-ext-unqlite

Toolbox	The Underground PHP and Oracle Manual
Official, free book from Oracle	
Web site	www.oracle.com/technetwork/topics/php/underground-php-oracle-manual-098250.html

Toolbox	Introduction to Document Databases with MongoDB
Tutorial by Derick Rethans	
Web site	http://derickrethans.nl/introduction-to-document-databases.html

Toolbox	Handling Hierarchical Data in MySQL and PHP
Tutorial by Voja Janjic	
Web site	www.phpbuilder.com/articles/databases/mysql/handling-hierarchical-data-in-mysql-and-php.html

Natural Language

Toolbox	Article Readability Stats with PHP
Discussion of, and code for, readability algorithms	
Web site	www.maratz.com/blog/archives/2012/07/26/article-readability-stats-with-php/

Toolbox	Counting Syllables and Detecting Rhyme in PHP
Tutorial by Cameron McKay	
Web site	http://cdmckay.org/blog/2012/08/15/counting-syllables-and-detecting-rhyme-in-php/

Toolbox	nlptools
Natural language analysis library	
Web site	http://nlptools.atrilla.net/web/

Toolbox	Talking Machine
Learns a language idiom and generates idiomatic text	
Web site	www.phpclasses.org/package/3848-PHP-Learn-an-idiom-and-generate-wordsin-that-idiom.html

Graphics and Imaging

Toolbox	Instafilter
Instagram-like filters for PHP	
Web site	https://github.com/fbf/instafilter#readme

Toolbox	OpenCV for PHP
Bindings for the OpenCV image recognition/processing library	
Web site	https://github.com/mgdm/OpenCV-for-PHP#readme

Toolbox	phpColors
Color-manipulation methods	
Web site	http://mexitek.github.io/phpColors/

Toolbox	Libpuzzle
Image-comparison library	
Web site	www.pureftpd.org/project/libpuzzle/php

Unicode

Toolbox	Bringing Unicode to PHP with Portable UTF-8
Tutorial by Hamid Sarfraz	
Web site	www.sitepoint.com/bringing-unicode-to-php-with-portable-utf8/

Audio

Toolbox	Create PHP Voice Recognition Apps on the Cheap
Tutorial by W. Jason Gilmore	
Web site	www.phpbuilder.com/columns/Voice_Recognition/PHP_Voice_Recognition_1-12-2012.php3

Event-Driven PHP

Toolbox	React PHP
Node.js-type framework for PHP	
Web site	http://reactphp.org/

Toolbox	Phastlight
Another Node.js-like framework	
Web site	https://github.com/phastlight/phastlight/

Toolbox	Database connection pooling with PHP and React
Tutorial by Gonzalo Ayuso	
Web site	https://gonzalo123.com/2012/05/21/database-connection-pooling-with-php-and-react-node-php/

Toolbox	XPSPL
Signal- and event-processing library	
Web site	https://github.com/prggmr/XPSPL/

PHP Internals

Toolbox	PHP's Source Code for PHP Developers

Article by Anthony Ferrara

Web site   `http://blog.ircmaxell.com/2012/03/phps-source-code-for-php-developers.html`

Toolbox	PHP Parser

A full PHP parser written in PHP

Web site   `https://github.com/nikic/PHP-Parser#php-parser`

Toolbox	PHP Manipulator

Library for analyzing and modifying PHP code

Web site   `https://github.com/schmittjoh/PHP-Manipulator`

Toolbox	How to Add New (Syntactic) Features to PHP

Article by Nikita Popov

Web site   `http://nikic.github.io/2012/07/27/How-to-add-new-syntactic-features-to-PHP.html`

Toolbox	Introspection and Reflection in PHP

Article by Octavia Anghel

Web site   `http://phpmaster.com/introspection-and-reflection-in-php/`

Web Site/Service APIs

Toolbox	Stack Exchange API

Stack.PHP library (unofficial)

Web site   `http://stackphp.quickmediasolutions.com/`

Toolbox	Access Dropbox Using PHP

Tutorial by Vito Tardia

Web site   `www.sitepoint.com/access-dropbox-using-php/`

Toolbox	Goutte
A web-scraping library, ideal for sites without APIs	
Web site	https://github.com/fabpot/Goutte#readme

Security Related

Toolbox	PHP Secure Communications Library
Pure PHP implementations of many security/encryption algorithms	
Web site	http://phpseclib.sourceforge.net/documentation

JavaScript

Toolbox	Phype
Experimental JavaScript-based VM for PHP	
Web site	http://code.google.com/p/phype/

Toolbox	php.js VM
Another JavaScript-based PHP VM	
Web site	http://phpjs.hertzen.com/

Toolbox	Locutus
Formerly php.js, Locutus is a Library for using PHP-like functions in JavaScript	
Web site	http://locutus.io/php/

Servers

Toolbox	Pancake
Accelerated PHP HTTP server written in PHP	
Web site	https://github.com/pp3345/Pancake

Toolbox	Nanoweb
Another HTTP server written in PHP	
Web site	http://nanoweb.si.kz/

Programming

Toolbox	PHPCPD

Copy/paste detector for PHP code

Web site   https://github.com/sebastianbergmann/phpcpd/#readme

Toolbox	Binary Parsing with PHP

Article by Igor Wesome

Web site   https://igor.io/2012/09/24/binary-parsing.html

Toolbox	Collections

PHP library implementing .NET/C++ STL-style collection types

Web site   https://github.com/IcecaveStudios/collections

Financial

Toolbox	Trader

Technical analysis for traders

Web site   www.php.net/manual/en/book.trader.php

Hardware

Toolbox	Building a Sensor Phalanx with PHP

Tutorial by Thomas Weinert

Web site   www.a-bsl-of-papayas.net/2013/11/building-sensor-phalanx-with-php.html

Toolbox	Controlling an LED with PHP

Tutorial by Thomas Weinert

Web site   www.a-basketful-of-papayas.net/2013/11/carica-chip-101-controlling-led-with-php.html

Toolbox	Control a Drone with PHP

Library to control Parrot drones

Web site   https://github.com/jolicode/php-ar-drone

APPENDIX E

■ ■ ■

Integrated Development Environments for PHP

The following is a list of integrated development environments (IDEs) aimed at the PHP market. The purpose is to help you explore the options available. None of these IDEs is specifically recommended for, or dedicated to, CLI/nonweb programming. The list is broken into two parts: first the open source options and then the commercial offerings.

Open Source Options

Toolbox	Eclipse PDT
Eclipse PHP Development Tools	
Web site	http://projects.eclipse.org/projects/tools.pdt

Toolbox	NetBeans PHP
Multilanguage IDE with heavy PHP support	
Web site	https://netbeans.org/features/php/

Toolbox	Aptana Studio
Modern IDE with heavy PHP support	
Web site	www.aptana.org/products/studio3

Toolbox	GitHub Atom
A (very good) text editor rather than an IDE, with many PHP plug-ins that bring IDE-like capabilities	
Web site	https://atom.io/
PHP plug-ins	https://atom.io/packages/search?q=php

Commercial Options

Toolbox	Zend Studio
The original PHP IDE	
Web site	/www.zend.com/products/studio/

Toolbox	PhpStorm
Very flexible PHP IDE	
Web site	www.jetbrains.com/phpstorm/

Toolbox	PhpEd
Integrates well with other PHP tools	
Web site	www.nusphere.com/products/phped.htm

Toolbox	phpDesigner
A fast PHP IDE	
Web site	www.mpsoftware.dk/phpdesigner.php

Toolbox	Komodo IDE
A multilanguage IDE with PHP tooling	
Web site	www.activestate.com/komodo-ide

Toolbox	CodeLobster
A PHP IDE with plug-in integration for many popular code frameworks	
Web site	www.codelobster.com

Toolbox	Rapid PHP
A lightweight PHP editor	
Web site	www.rapidphpeditor.com

Toolbox	Kodiak for iPad
A PHP IDE that runs on the iPad	
Web site	www.becomekodiak.com

Toolbox	Visual Studio add-ons

Two add-ons to enable better support for PHP in Visual Studio

Web site	VS.Php
	www.vsphp.com
	PHP Tools for Visual Studio
	www.devsense.com/products/php-tools

Toolbox	SublimeText

A (very good) text editor rather than an IDE, but the following article shows how to enable IDE-like facilities using extensions

Web site	www.sublimetext.com/

Article

"Setting Up Sublime Text 2 for PHP Development"	http://blog.stuartherbert.com/php/2012/02/28/setting-up-sublime-text-2-for-php-development/

■ ■ ■

Where Now?

If you've read this far, thank you. I sincerely hope that this book has held your interest and has, at the least, informed or inspired new directions in your future PHP programming. If it has, I encourage you to start coding right now based on one or more topics in this book while they are still fresh in your mind. People far smarter than I have shown that the sooner relevant activity occurs after learning, the easier it is to retain information and techniques over the longer term. If you use any of the techniques presented in the book in real life, I would be interested to know! Finally, if you haven't already headed for the keyboard, don't forget to glance through the appendixes that follow. There may be something interesting or useful in there for you (either to use now or to be aware of for the future).

Giving Feedback and Getting Help and Support

E-mail: author@active-net.co.uk

Your feedback on this book, good or bad, fundamental or trivial, is solicited and welcomed. Tell me what you think about the book, overall or regarding a particular section. Let me know if any areas aren't covered in enough depth (or in too much detail), if any topics you were expecting aren't present, or if any information isn't clear. Likewise, if you have any problems getting the sample code to run or any issues implementing the techniques discussed, please drop me a line and I'll see if there is any way I can help.

© Rob Aley 2016
R. Aley, *PHP Beyond the Web*, DOI 10.1007/978-1-4842-2481-6

Index

A

Adobe AIR, 73
Advanced Command-Line Input, 53–56
Alternative PHP Cache (APC), 106, 141
Alternative programming styles, 187–188
Analog-to-digital converters (ADCs), 131
Apache Subversion (SVN), 44
APC Cached Variables, 106
Application programming interface (API), 19,
    44–46, 61, 63, 73, 75, 96, 100, 105, 114, 124,
    145, 163, 175, 193, 194
Artificial intelligence, 188–189
Audio, 123–124, 180, 181, 192

B

Big data, 149, 150
Build systems
    performance, 33
    Phing, 33
    tasks, 33

C

Continuous integration (CI), 34–36, 41
CGI/Fast GGI or server module, 7
CI. See Continuous integration (CI)
CLI. See Command-line interface (CLI)
CLI SAPI
    command-line programs, 14–16, 18–19
    execution, 23–26
    installation, 14
    php-win.exe, 23
    source code file, 20
    STDIN, 21
    string, 20
    Unix/Linux, 21
    Windows, 23
CMOS logic, 126
Code editors, 45

Code repositories, 44
Command-Line Interface, 50–53
Command-line interface (CLI)
    coding frameworks, 11
    features and compatibility, 5
    helper libraries, 58
    security, 5
    speed, 5
Compiling and installing PHP
    Linux/Unix, 168–170
    macOS, 168
    Windows, 168
Composer, 33, 35, 47, 109, 172–173
Concurrent programming, 148–149
Concurrent Version Systems (CVS), 44
Core extensions, compiling and installing, 170–171
Cross-platform and remote file systems, 113
CVS. See Concurrent Version Systems (CVS)
Cycle collection, 147

D

Daemons
    characterization, 75
    creation
        extension, 76
        process, 76
        script, 77, 79
        Unix/Linux-type systems, 76
    database connection, 79
    file conversion, 85
    file monitoring, inotify
        file and directory events, 85
        inotifywait command, 89
        limits, 90
        PECL extension, 86–88
    file sync, 85
    network (see Network daemons, libevent)
Data analysis, 39, 188–189
Databases, 124, 190
Data caching, 150–151

© Rob Aley 2016
R. Aley, *PHP Beyond the Web*, DOI 10.1007/978-1-4842-2481-6

Data files and formats, 109
Debuggers, 15, 29, 36–37, 45, 137, 139
Deploying frameworks, 165
Direct bindings, 63, 68, 69, 73
Documentation, 163
Documentation generators, 45–46
Documentors. *See* Documentation generators

■ E

Electron, 74
Embedded data files, 159–160
Error handling and logging, 157–158
Event-based programming, 63
Event-driven PHP, 193
Event Viewer tool, 158

■ F

File and data format libraries
    audio, 181
    compression, archiving, and encryption, 178
    graphics, 179–180
    miscellaneous, 175
    multimedia and video, 181
    office documents, 175–177
    programming, technical,
        and data interchange, 182
file() and file_get_contents(), 110
File conversion daemons, 85
File search services, 85
File status cache, 112
File sync daemons, 85
File-system interactions, 109, 112
Financial, 195

■ G

Garbage collection, 147
Gearman, 90–91
General-purpose input/output
    (GPIO) connector, 125
Generic installers, 161–162
Gnome-based systems, 60
Graphical user interfaces (GUIs), 63
    Adobe AIR, 73
    electron, 74
    event-based programming, 63
    local web server and browser, 70
    NW.js, 73
    PHP-GTK, 68–69
    PHP-Qt, 74
    PHP's built-in web server, 70–71
    PHP/TK, 74
    SiteFusion, 72–73

    toolkits, 63
    websocket and browser, 71
    WinBinder, 73
    wxPHP, 64–68
Graphics and imaging, 191

■ H

Hardware, 195
Hardware and system interactions, 124
Help sources
    GitHub, 184
    newsgroups, 184
    official mailing lists, 183
    PHP manual, 183
    PHP news sites and mailing lists, 185
    PHP subreddit, 184
    stack overflow, 183
HipHop Virtual Machine (HHVM), 144
Hoa Console, 58
HTTP server, 7, 8, 11, 13, 70, 71, 80, 81, 83, 194

■ I

IDEs. *See* Integrated Development
        environments (IDEs)
Inotify
    inotifywait command, 89
    limits, 90
    PECL extension, 85–88
Integrated development environments (IDEs), 45
    commercial options, 198
    open source options, 197
Interactive shell, 29

■ J, K

JavaScript, 63, 72, 73, 74, 146, 152, 194

■ L

LAMP-type stacks, 71
Libevent, 80–85, 130
Licensing and legal issues, 164
Linux signals, 116–119
Linux timed-event signals, 119–121
Long-running processes, 153–154
Low-level profiling, 139

■ M

Machine learning, 188–189
Manual profiling, 135–136
MapReduce, 149
Message queues

display2.php, 100–101
generator2.php, 100
msg_qbytes, 104
msg_queue_exists(), 104
msg_receive() parameters, 102–103
msg_send() function, parameters, 102
msg_stat_queue(), 104
random-number generator scripts, 100
sending process, 100
sysvmsg message queue, 100
Micro and premature optimizations, 154–155
Multiple versions installation, 171
Multithreading, 148–149

▓ N

Natural language, 191
Network daemons, libevent
advantage, 80
event tools and frameworks, 84
file descriptors, 80
pecl-event, 80–83
pecl-libevent, 80
NW.js, 73–74

▓ O

Object-oriented programming (OOP)
techniques, 63
Opcode caches, 141
Open Source Initiative (OSI), 164
Output buffering, 61

▓ P, Q

Partial GUI elements (dialog boxes)
shell dialog commands
kdialog, 60
notify-send pops up, 59
zenity, 60
Windows dialog boxes, 61
Passive infrared (PIR) motion, 125
PCNTL extension, 76
Personal Home Page (PHP)
environmental factors
installed extension version, 162
installed PHP version, 162
location, common paths, 162
php.ini settings, 162
high-performance requirements, 9
internals, 193
performance, 152, 133–134
PHP-GTK, 68–69

php-profiler, 137
PHP-Qt, 74
PHP/TK, 74
rapid application development (RAD)
environment, 65
source code, 9
versions, 8
Phar bundles, 160
Phar executable bundles, 160–161
PHP. See Personal Home Page (PHP)
PHP 5, 7
language features, 1
types of software, 2
PHP Extension and Application
Repository (PEAR), 172
PHP Extension Community Library (PECL), 172
PHP-GTK, 68–69
PHP-Qt, 74
PHP/TK, 74
Plug-ins, 163
Printing, 121–123
Profile, 135, 155. See also Profiling
Profilers, 36, 46, 135
Profiling
database access, 139
disk access, 139
loops, 139
low-level, 139
manual, 135–137
no clear cause, 140
tools, 137
Program flow control, 53
Programming, 195
Programming purpose, 134

▓ R

Raspberry Pi
ARM-based CPU, 125
GPIO connector, 125
GPIO ports, PHP, 128–130
hardware reset, 131
PHP, 125
resources, 131
RP GPIO pins, 126
switch symbols, 126
tri-state logic, 125–127
Read-eval-print loop (REPLs)
Bash shell, 30
features, 32
initialise.php, 31
interactive shell, 29
WSL, 30

■ S

SAPI. *See* Server Application
Programming Interface (SAPI)
Security, 10–11
Semaphores, 94–95
Serial Peripheral Interface (SPI) interfaces, 131
Server Application Programming Interface (SAPI), 8
Servers, 195
Shared memory, 96
extensions, 96
ftok(), 98
generator.php, 97
JSON, 100
memory leak, 99
shmop_delete() and shmop_close(), 99
shmop_open(), 98–99
shmop_read(), 99
shmop_write(), 99
standard Unix-type permissions, 96
Shelling out, 89, 93, 94, 175
Silver bullets
better hardware, 140
compiling, 141–142
JIT compiler, 144
opcode caches, 141
PHP versions, 140
virtual machine, 143–145
SiteFusion, 72–73
Software interaction
message queues, 100–104
semaphores, 94–95
shared memory, 96–100
third-party message queues, 104–105
Source-control systems, 44
SplFixedArray class, 146
Stability
fatal error handling, 154
overconsumption, memory
and memory leaks, 154
resource time-outs, 153
Stack overflow, 183–184
Standard PHP Library (SPL), 146
Standard streams (STDIN, STDOUT, STDERR), 107
Static code analysis
description, 39
lint, 40
SonarQube, 42
Static HTML output, 61–62

STDIN, STOUT, and STDERR, 56–58, 107
Symfony2 Bundles, 173
Symfony Console, 58
System software
daemons (*see* Daemons)
Gearman, 90, 92
sysvsem extension, 94

■ T

Task dispatch and management systems, 90
Task dispatch systems, 92
Testing and unit testing. *See* Unit testing
Text-based interface, 49, 50
Third-party message queues, 104–105
Thy functions, 151

■ U

Unicode, 192
Unit testing, 37–39

■ V

V sysvshm extension, 96
Version-control systems, 44
Virtual files
tmpfs, 106–107
Windows RAM disks, 107
Virtual machines, 42–43

■ W

Webmozart console toolkit, 58
Web site/service APIs, 193–194
WebSocket and Browser, 71
Widget toolkits, 63
Win32 API, 61
WinBinder, 73
Windows Registry, 114–116
Windows Subsystem for Linux (WSL), 3, 30, 53
WSL. *See* Windows Subsystem for Linux (WSL)
wxPHP, 64–68

■ X, Y, Z

XHProf, 137, 138
XML User Interface Language (XUL), 63
XULRunner, 72

Get the eBook for only $4.99!

Why limit yourself?

Now you can take the weightless companion with you wherever you go and access your content on your PC, phone, tablet, or reader.

Since you've purchased this print book, we are happy to offer you the eBook for just $4.99.

Convenient and fully searchable, the PDF version enables you to easily find and copy code—or perform examples by quickly toggling between instructions and applications.

To learn more, go to http://www.apress.com/us/shop/companion or contact support@apress.com.

Printed in the United States
By Bookmasters